Mr. Chittenden. Gov.

Thomas Chittenden

Thomas Chittenden

VERMONT'S FIRST STATESMAN

Frank Smallwood

THE NEW ENGLAND PRESS, INC.
SHELBURNE, VERMONT

Manufactured in the United States of America
First Edition
Design by Andrea Gray
Frontispiece portrait courtesy of The University of Vermont

For additional copies of this book or a catalog of our other titles,
please write:

The New England Press
P.O. Box 575
Shelburne, VT 05482
or e-mail us at nep@together.net
The New England Press is on-line at www.nepress.com

Smallwood, Frank.
    Thomas Chittenden : Vermont's first statesman / Frank Smallwood. -
- 1st ed.
       p. cm.
    Includes bibliographical references and index.
    ISBN 1-881535-28-2. -- ISBN 1-881535-27-4 (pbk.)
    1. Chittenden, Thomas, 1730-1797. 2. Governors--Vermont-
-Biography. 3. Vermont--Politics and government--To 1791.
I. Title.
F52.C5S63 1997
974.3'03'092--dc21
    [B]   97-49984
                                                                         CIP

But what is government itself but the greatest of all reflections on human nature? If men were angels, no government would be necessary. . . . In framing a government which is to be administered by men over men, the great difficulty lies in this: You must first enable the government to control the governed; and in the next place oblige it to control itself.

—JAMES MADISON
FEDERALIST PAPER #51

Contents

＊＊＊

Foreword

*T*homas Chittenden: Vermont's First Statesman is the first full-length biography of Vermont's first and longest-serving governor. For many years academics have speculated about why only short sketches of Thomas Chittenden have existed. The standard explanations include the fact that many public papers issued over his name were written by others. The lack of personal papers was assumed to be a consequence of his not writing very well. Equally significant, he was depicted as a secondary member of the younger, more colorful, and more articulate Allen family faction. This view has persisted despite the fact that Chittenden continued to exercise power long after both Ethan and Ira Allen had relinquished their hold on state affairs, and its persistence merits further comment.

The Allens' enduring tyranny over Vermont's history resulted from early works by Zadock Thompson and the Green Mountain Boy narratives of Daniel P. Thompson. In contrast to the more adventurous Allens, Thomas Chittenden was depicted as being a simple farmer who was skilled in human nature and agriculture, which enabled him to serve as a steadfast patriot with good sense and firmness of character. It was character, not intellect, that earned Chittenden his fame. That being said, there was nothing significant to add to his story.

Until Smallwood's book arrived, contemporary readers seeking a Chittenden biography were most likely to encounter Daniel Chipman's short 1846 *Memoir of Thomas Chittenden,* as condensed and republished in Volume XVII of the Vermont State Papers, *The Public Papers of Thomas Chittenden.* Daniel Chipman's uncritical acceptance of the prevailing view of Chittenden as being sensible and steadfast may at first seem to be incongruous. Daniel was the admiring younger brother of Nathaniel Chipman who, along with Isaac Tichenor, led the Federalist opposition to Chittenden, often by means of ridicule and expressions of contempt. Daniel Chipman's *Memoir* avoided a detailed analysis of the rise of political factions that took place in Vermont after the Revolutionary War, however, so he was able to omit references to the contentious struggles between Thomas Chittenden and the emerging Federalists that Professor Smallwood refers to as "the new lawyer reformers."

In this book, Frank Smallwood, the Dartmouth College Nelson A. Rockefeller Professor of Government Emeritus, expands the Chittenden legacy to embrace Chittenden's complexities as well as his extraordinary leadership abilities, which contributed so much to Vermont's early survival. A highly respected political scientist and a seasoned veteran of the state's political wars, Smallwood has written the fullest biography of Chittenden ever attempted and treats us to heretofore unpublished material on the governor's English forebears as well as a detailed analysis of the usually slighted post-independence years. Professor Smallwood argues that during the quest for Vermont's independence, Chittenden provided "the essential survival skills" required for success. In addition, he concludes that, while Chittenden's second decade in office was "less demanding and dramatic" than the first, his later contributions have been undervalued. Although Smallwood does not explicitly pose the question, his analysis suggests that the Federalist lawyer reformers would not have been able to maintain the state's relatively peaceful post-war authority if they had displaced Chittenden and assumed control of the executive branch earlier than they did.

Governor Chittenden's political opponents were likely to attribute his opposition to Federalist policies to a lack of education. Smallwood suggests otherwise. His assessment is that Chittenden was an extremely intelligent politician. Possibly encumbered in childhood by a learning disorder he never fully overcame, he went on to become not only Vermont's most powerful political personality but also one of its wealthiest citizens. He was hardly a simple farmer. He farmed commercially while engaging in land speculation, personal banking, and a variety of other activities. He was a "shrewd leader who was capable of protecting the authority of the state while, at the same time, enhancing his own interests."

And enhance his own interests he did. Never to a point, however, where he overreached as did so many of his contemporaries who courted the confines of debtors' prison. Instead, he managed to provide handsomely for himself, his wife, and his progeny. After analyzing Chittenden's estate inventory, Smallwood calculates that, at the time of his death in 1797, he was one of the richest men in the state.

This wealth brings us to a most fascinating aspect of Governor Chittenden's political behavior. As a creditor who loaned many individuals money, he recognized it was in his own personal financial interest to maintain the anti-inflationary policies advocated by the Federalists. Yet, throughout his career, he opposed the Federalists, and he identified with the poorer settlers who were burdened with debt. He never betrayed their cause.

Readers will almost certainly conclude the author has made good his claim that Thomas Chittenden's legacy has been undervalued. At the same time Smallwood maintains an impartiality that enables him to keep from overstating his subject's virtues. Chittenden's dramatic and momentous early years in office provided an ideal test for his innate leadership skills. By the end of his career, the times called for a more professional brand of public service than he could provide, although he was able to draw upon his personal political popularity to promote stability in Vermont's government until he died in August 1797.

Thomas Chittenden was a complex individual who utilized his simple farmer image to perpetuate an extraordinarily successful political and business career. Now, on the occasion of the bicentennial of his death, we are indebted to Frank Smallwood for providing a comprehensive analysis that clarifies the many different roles he played in shaping the early history of Vermont.

Samuel B. Hand
Professor of History Emeritus
University of Vermont

Preface

⤜✠⤛

W hen I first began to conduct research on Thomas Chittenden's ancestors during a trip to England in May 1995, I knew he was an important political leader in early Vermont. He served as the state's first governor, and he was reelected to this office nineteen times between 1778 and 1797. Surprisingly, however, his contributions seemed underrated, even overlooked, in the historical literature of the state. Indeed, only one individual, Daniel Chipman, had ever attempted to write a biography of Thomas Chittenden, which he published as a memoir almost 150 years ago.[1]

A few other writers, such as David Read, have prepared brief biographical sketches of Chittenden.[2] Most other authors, however, have referred to Governor Chittenden only in the context of the "Allen-Chittenden faction." As historian Marshall True points out, "Chittenden remains perhaps as the most elusive member of Vermont's founding generation."[3]

A significant factor in Governor Chittenden's relative obscurity is what historian Kevin Graffagnino has labeled "the remarkable tyranny of the Allens over Vermont historiography."

Both Ethan and Ira Allen were gifted writers and propagandists, and they passed along many of their observations to Vermont's earliest historian, Reverend Samuel Williams. As Graffagnino observes, "as the only early Vermont leaders who published voluminous accounts of their own accomplishments, the Allens dictated to succeeding generations the context in which they and their exploits would be judged for the next two hundred years. . . . Every Vermont historian accepted the interpretations of Samuel Williams and Ira and Ethan Allen." [4]

Thus, most of the early books on Vermont—written by authors such as Nathan Hoskins, Zadock Thompson, Hosea Beckley, Governor Hiland Hall, and Roland Robinson—were based on the Allens' interpretations and descriptions of Vermont's early politics. The myth of the Allens was further reinforced by Daniel Pierce Thompson's hugely popular 1839 saga, *The Green Mountain Boys*, which was published in more than fifty editions.

During the twentieth century, researchers have reached out to cover a more diverse range of the early Vermont social, economic, and political topics, but very few have concentrated on the role of Thomas Chittenden. Actually, the only major recent work that focuses exclusively on Chittenden is *The Public Papers of Thomas Chittenden,* edited by John A. Williams in 1969. [5] A more recent book that provides some interesting observations of Thomas Chittenden is Robert E. Shalhope's study of early Bennington. Other books have continued to focus on Ethan and Ira Allen, the most informative being works by Charles A. Jellison, Kevin Graffagnino, and Michael Bellesiles. [6]

Ethan and Ira Allen were both powerful writers, and a lot of their written material survived for historians to scrutinize. Thomas Chittenden, on the other hand, was a very poor speller and writer who left virtually no private papers or personal correspondence. According to one line of speculation, Chittenden's private correspondence may have ended up being sold as scrap paper. [7]

The fact that there appears to be very little in the way of private written records about Chittenden leads to both an observation and a personal admission. Historical biographies often rely very heavily on archival research into private papers and correspondence. Since such private papers simply do not exist in Thomas Chittenden's case, it is impossible to do this type of conventional research. Hence, the following study is based on research into public records at the Chittenden County Courthouse, as well as town records in Williston and Arlington, Vermont, plus Guilford and Salisbury, Connecticut. These records, however, were not the primary sources for this book. Instead, the primary sources are Chittenden's public papers in Williams Volume XVII and other official state documents, such as the four volumes of Governor and Council records, plus the Assembly Journals, which were compiled during Chittenden's tenure as governor. These sources were supplemented by additional state papers on land grants, petitions, and other related matters. In addition, I used materials from every major book I could find on Vermont's early history that helped to clarify different aspects of Chittenden's career. Numerous stimulating discussions with Joseph Morel, my research assistant, also provided invaluable insights into the political climate of early Vermont.

I must admit, however, that I have never received any formal training as a professional historian. I am, instead, a political scientist with experience in both academic and legislative environments. In light of my own background, I have written this book as a political portrait of Thomas Chittenden. My focus has been to describe, analyze, and evaluate his performance as a political and governmental leader, based primarily on his long service as the first governor of Vermont. My conclusion is that Governor Chittenden was an almost ideal frontier leader, who was uniquely qualified to preside over Vermont's tumultuous formative years. Lacking a finished formal education, he relied on his own extensive experience, maturity, and native common sense to make critical policy decisions. He pursued his own interests during his years as governor, but his primary concern was the survival and well-being of the new state of Vermont.

Thomas Chittenden's performance during the first decade of Vermont's existence from 1777 to 1786 was incredibly strong. He was certainly one of the critically important individuals who worked for Vermont's survival, and I do not think the state could have existed without his leadership.

Chittenden's second decade in office was less dramatic. As is the case with many new governmental institutions, Vermont went through a two-stage process during its formative years. Thomas Chittenden possessed the perfect set of attributes to lead Vermont through the first of these stages. He was a tough, durable, persistent, shrewd leader who enabled the new state to meet an extraordinarily difficult series of external challenges from all sides during the wartime years. Once Vermont had survived these initial challenges, however, a new group of younger, more professional reformers moved into the state and set about the task of refining its governmental structure and procedures. Chittenden experienced difficulties dealing with this group, although he did provide a continuity that helped the older settlers adjust to the changes taking place.

I have based these conclusions on my evaluation of the actions he took to further the interests of Vermont. In other words, a great deal of my analysis is inferential. I attempted to determine the challenges Vermont faced at various stages during Chittenden's tenure as governor, and to determine whether the actions the state took under his leadership provided an appropriate and effective response to the issues at hand.

My objective in writing this book is to make Thomas Chittenden more accessible to current and future generations of Vermonters. The year 1997 marks the bicentennial of Governor Chittenden's death. Hopefully, he will come alive again in the following pages.

Frank Smallwood
Burlington, Vermont

Acknowledgments

A great many people provided a great deal of help to me while I was working on this book. First and foremost, I want to thank my research assistant, Joseph Morel. I met Joseph during the summer of 1995, just after he had graduated from Dartmouth College, where he wrote a History Honors Thesis on "Governing a Republic: Vermont State Government 1777-1791." When I advised Dartmouth History Professor Jere R. Daniell that I was writing a biography of Thomas Chittenden, he strongly urged me to contact Joseph, who agreed to provide background research on Governor Chittenden. As our work progressed, Joseph became an inexhaustible source of insights and ideas. He wrote the initial drafts of both chapters IV and V, which deal with Vermont's first attempts to form a government. We worked together very closely for a year, and, quite frankly, I could not have written this book without his invaluable help. Joseph is now engaged in graduate study in history at Brown University, and I am pleased and honored to dedicate the book to him.

I received very useful comments from the many knowledgeable people who were kind enough to read various chapters on the Vermont aspects of Thomas Chittenden's career, including Samuel Hand, Kevin Graffagnino, Paul Gillies, Jeffrey Potash, Scott Stevens, and Bill Doyle. I am especially grateful to Professor Hand for his foreword and to Kevin Graffagnino, who suggested I should write a book about Chittenden. Readers who provided insights into the early history of the Chittenden family in England and Connecticut included Joel Helander, the town historian of Guilford, Connecticut, Lillian Baker Carlisle of Burlington, Vermont, and Thomas Chittenden of South Burlington, Vermont. In addition Marshall True offered helpful advice on Chittenden's performance in Vermont's government.

The background research for this book involved a number of trips, the first being a journey to the early home of the Chittenden family in the town of Cranbrook, Kent, England. I am indebted to Lee and Joyce Bridges for the hospitality they provided during a visit to Dulwich, England, and to Betty Carman at the Cranbrook Museum.

I was fortunate to receive a grant from the Chittenden County Historical Society, which covered the expense of research trips to Guilford, Madison, and Salisbury, Connecticut, as well as to Arlington and other towns in southwestern Vermont. Many people provided hospitality and assistance on these trips. I am especially grateful to Marion and Natalie Chard of the Madison Historical Society; Ted and Rene Ayres of Guilford; David Batchelor of Salisbury; Virginia Moskowitz, the Salisbury Town Historian; the staff of the Scoville Library in Salisbury; the staff of the Russell Historical Collection at the Canfield Library in Arlington; and Linda P. Crosby from the Arlington town clerk's office.

Closer to home I carried out a great deal of library research. I appreciate the help I received from all the members of the Special Collections staff at the University of Vermont's Bailey-Howe Library—Connie Gallagher, Karen Campbell, Jeff Marshall, David Blow, Ingrid Bower, Elizabeth Dow, and Sylvia Knight. I also was the beneficiary of assistance provided by

Gregory Sanford, the Vermont State Archivist, and his assistant Christie Carter; Michael Sherman, Paul Carnahan, and Barney Bloom at the Vermont Historical Society; Marge Zunder at the Vermont State Library; Robert Jaccaud at the Dartmouth College Library; Rickie Emerson, the Williston Library Director; and Penny Pillsbury, the Director of the Brownell Library in Essex Junction with its excellent Vermont Collection. Individuals who were especially helpful in searching for local records were Victor Fremeau and Debby Brunell at the Chittenden County Courthouse in Burlington and both Kathy Boyden and Kathy Smardon at the town clerk's office in Williston.

Last but certainly not least are the many people who provided all sorts of unique special help. In Williston, Mary Tuthill served as an enthusiastic guide to the town and its historic sites, while Patrice and Wright Clark, whose family has lived on the Thomas Chittenden homestead since 1835, provided photographs and background information. Danielle Petter of Williston shared an interesting essay with me about Thomas Chittenden. Don Maynard at UVM's Dairy Research Center also provided very useful advice about Thomas Chittenden's estate inventory by determining the nature of his farming practices two hundred years ago.

Another source of special assistance was Arthur Woolf, Professor of Economics at the University of Vermont, who translated Governor Chittenden's 1790 finances into modern currency equivalents. Also, Bradley Rink prepared a number of maps for the book, and Kristin Peterson-Ishaq of UVM's Center for Research on Vermont sent out a very important early call for research assistance that led to my recruitment of Joseph Morel.

Certainly one of the most unique contributions to this endeavor was made by Blanche Podhajski and Sarah Gray at the Stern Center for Language and Learning in Williston, who read and analyzed samples of Thomas Chittenden's handwriting for me and provided perspectives on his literacy.

As always, I owe a special debt of gratitude to my wife, Ann. She provided constant encouragement and assembled the maps and pictures for the book. In addition, she was a very helpful copy editor who read and reread every draft chapter and provided insightful comments while also correcting numerous distracting typos.

Finally, many thanks to my editor, Mark Wanner. He was willing to take on this project despite his very heavy work schedule, and he always kept me on target by reminding me to focus on Thomas Chittenden and ignore the superfluous.

In the end, none of the above individuals are responsible for the final content of the book, since I bear the burden of any mistakes and misinterpretations. Let me close with a final word of thanks to all of those noted above, however, because it simply would not have been possible for me to complete this project without their help and encouragement.

CHAPTER I

The Early Chittendens

(1594-1749)

Thomas Chittenden, Vermont's first governor, descended from a family of pioneers who participated in the "Great Migration" from England to New England during the decade of the 1630s. Although this movement was referred to as a great migration, it was actually relatively small. A recent study reports that it is now generally estimated that during the seventeenth century "between 100,000 to 150,000 people crossed the Atlantic to the Chesapeake . . . compared to only 21,000 emigrants to New England." [1] An even bigger English group, estimated to be as large as 250,000, ventured out to colonize the Caribbean.

In addition to being relatively small, the "Great Migration" was very brief. English migration to the Chesapeake continued for more than a century, but the movement to New England lasted scarcely a decade. Of most significance, the New England migration differed dramatically in terms of the motivation of the settlers. The migrations to the Caribbean and Chesa-

1

peake areas involved individuals who were primarily interested in seeking their fortunes. The New England migration, on the other hand, involved families, very often mature couples in their thirties who were already in the process of raising children. Many of these families were quite well off economically. Instead of seeking their fortunes, most of them "were prompted by religious sentiment. . . . [This] is the key to their willingness to undertake a risky, economically disadvantageous move to the wilderness. . . . Puritanism played an essential part in convincing otherwise ordinary English men and women to take the extraordinary step of separating themselves from their society and embarking for New England." [2]

Puritanism also provided the rationale for naming this movement the "Great Migration." As historian Virginia Anderson has noted, "those who christened the movement never intended to commemorate its size. The name was invented not by the founders of New England, but by their descendants, who wished to celebrate the religious mission of their forefathers. . . . Though small in size, this migration was great in purpose." [3]

Cranbrook, Kent

William and Joanna (Sheafe) Chittenden and their two children, three-year-old Thomas and an infant daughter, Elizabeth, constituted one of the English families who participated in this "Great Migration." The Chittendens arrived in New England on July 10, 1639, as members of a Puritan party led by the Reverend Henry Whitfield, leaving a country where their forebears had prospered for many centuries.

Both William and Joanna Chittenden had grown up as members of established families in Cranbrook, a town in Kent, England's most southeastern county, which juts out into the channel near the coast of France. Cranbrook is located in the Weald ("wooded country"), which was earlier covered by a vast forest. Initially, this forest was divided into small clearings (or

"dens") used as swine pastures, and Cranbrook began as a trading post for local swineherds.

It was not until the 1330s that the town began to flourish.
Its sudden growth came as a result of an action taken by King
Edward III, who initiated a radical policy designed to trans-
form the economic life of England. In an effort to develop a
domestic wool manufacturing industry, he issued an edict in
May 1331 forbidding the import of finished cloth from the
continent as well as the export of raw wool abroad except under license. At this same time he granted special passports and
letters of protection to Flemish weavers in an effort to encourage them to migrate to designated towns thoughout England.
Cranbrook was chosen as one of the most suitable towns in
Kent for the production of broadcloth because of its abundant
supply of water from local springs and streams, as well as its
relative proximity to the port of London and the southeastern
coast of England.[4]

During the next two centuries, the prosperity of Cranbrook
was based on woolen broadcloth. Sophisticated and urbane
Flemish weavers migrated from Ghent and other cities in the
Netherlands to set up residence in the town. In 1310 England
had exported 35,500 sacks of raw wool and only 5,000 bales of
finished cloth to Europe. By the mid-1500s, wool exports had
dropped below 4,000 sacks, but the bales of finished cloth
shipped abroad had risen to more than 100,000. As a result,
Cranbrook's population grew to more than 4,000 residents. [5]

Two of the families benefiting from this prosperity were the
Chittendens and the Sheafes. There are early records of many
different Chittenden families who lived in Kentish wealden
towns. The origins of the name Chittenden are obscure. Some
claim it was Welsh, but it is difficult to find specific evidence
to support this view. A more plausible explanation in Elsdon
Smith's *Dictionary of Names* indicates it meant "one who came
from an opening [den] in Citta's valley in Kent." The original
Britonic name for "forest" was ceto, and the Old English word

for "clearing" was dene. The name Chittenden first appeared in the English charter rolls in 1241.[6]

Whatever the roots of the name, there is no question that many Chittendens settled in the Cranbrook area. Some were farmers while others were weavers and still others became involved with the water mills that played an important role in the growing broadcloth industry. One account from the year 1499 refers to the site of "an old mill pond and mill, associated for many years with the name of Chittenden . . . containing twelve acres in the Den of Beaghenden."[7]

The Chittendens who earned their living as millers played a critical role in the broadcloth manufacturing process known as fulling. Fulling is the means by which the threads of woven woolen fabrics are closed together and made into a smoother surface by pressing and kneading them with the assistance of water, soap, and acid. Fulling was done very effectively by using water power to drive a wheel that raised a heavy oak hammer to pound the cloth when it came from the loom. Fulling mills were used extensively in Cranbrook, which is surrounded by many small streams running in narrow valleys. Mill dams were built thoughout the town, and the Chittendens who ran them became quite affluent.

Members of the Sheafe family, like the Chittendens, were engaged in the broadcloth industry. Early records indicate they originally came from Norwich in Norfolk County in the early fourteenth century. Some of them became clothiers, which was an even more lucrative occupation than operating the mills.

Clothiers provided capital and managerial skills. As the production of broadcloth expanded in Cranbrook, it became necessary to finance and build warehouses, cover shipping costs, and organize the many craftspeople involved in home cottage work. "These functions were fulfilled by the clothier, who was a capitalist, employer, and merchant combined. The clothiers sprang into prominence during the 15th century. . . . Much of the work continued to be done in the cottages, but other processes, notably fulling, dyeing, and finishing, were now performed by workers directly employed in the mills and dyehouses owned by the clothiers. With increasing prosperity, the clothiers built dyehouses with large storerooms in which to keep the finished broadcloth awaiting shipment." [8]

The mid-1500s marked the height of Cranbrook's prosperity, and the Sheafes were one of the prominent families of clothiers who basked in this glory. The oldest brass in St. Dunstan's Church, Cranbrook, is on the memorial stone of Thomas Sheafe, who died in 1520. It depicts a wool merchant in his robes and an infant child with the initials T. S. and his cloth mark in the center. When Thomas Sheafe died, he left his sons much property in Cranbrook, including parcels located at Shepherds, Bakers Cross, and Hancocks. In 1555 his oldest son, Thomas Sheafe, built a large Tudor mansion and a new dyehouse.

As a result of Cranbrook's prosperity, the future appeared to be extremely promising when a young boy named William Chittenden, son of Robert Chittenden, was baptized in the Parish of Marden, just north of Cranbrook in March 1594. [9] More than a decade later, around 1610, a girl named Joanna Sheafe was born in Cranbrook, the daughter of Edmund Sheafe and Joanna Jordan. [10]

The Cranbrook Parish registers and genealogical records indicate that William Chittenden married Joanna Sheafe in 1630. Their first child, Thomas, was born in Cranbrook in 1637, and their second child, Elizabeth, was also born there about 1639. During this period the growing religious dissent that first appeared in England in the mid-fifteenth century was beginning to have a major impact on towns such as Cranbrook. After King Henry VIII broke away from Roman Catholicism and established Anglicanism—the Church of England—as the officially recognized state religion, opposition developed. The dissenters believed in the right of individual Christians to interpret the scriptures—God's convenants as expressed in the

Bible—by means of their own conscience. In addition, these dissenters objected to the institution of the episcopacy, which implied that bishops exercised supreme authority within an Anglican church hierarchy. William Chittenden and Joanna Sheafe became heavily involved with these non-conformist religious groups, and this led directly to their decision to leave England. It was Joanna Sheafe's family that provided the most direct linkage with the Puritan religious dissenters of the time. Specifically, Joanna's cousin, Dorothy Sheafe, was married to the Reverend Henry Whitfield of Ockley, Surrey.

After being educated at New College, Oxford, and the Inns of the Court, Whitfield entered the ministry of the Church of England. For twenty years he served as the rector at Ockley in the county of Surrey. He was an uneasy conformist within the established church, however, and his house provided a safe haven for many Puritan dissenters who later left for America, including Reverend John Cotton of the Massachusetts Bay Colony, Reverend Thomas Hooker, the founder of the Connecticut colony in Hartford, and Reverend John Davenport, who left England in 1637 and helped to found a new plantation in Quinnipiack (New Haven).

Whitfield incurred the wrath of William Laud, the Archbishop of Canterbury and primate of the Church of England, who was disciplining Puritan dissenters in the name of King Charles I. Whitfield was brought before the Anglican High Commission Court for not fully conforming to the ceremonies required in the liturgy service. As a result he resigned his position in Ockley in 1639 and decided to assemble a company to leave for New England.

Whitfield was interested in joining his friend Reverend John Davenport in New Haven, but the man who had the most influence in determining his destination was a distinguished barrister he had met at Gray's Inn named George Fenwick. Fenwick was one of the most prominent members of the Puritan party in England. He was assembling land in Connecticut for a group of Puritan lords under the Warwick patent, a new settlement at Saybrook Point on what is now known as the Long Island Sound, and he encouraged Whitfield and his company to settle in this area to the east of Davenport's New Haven plantation.[11]

Whitfield, a dignified man described as being of "marvelous majesty and sanctity," was a charismatic leader. Within a short period of time he assembled a company of twenty-five families in the southern counties of Kent, Surrey, and Sussex to join him in leaving England to seek a new home across the Atlantic. Many members of the Sheafe family joined this company. In addition to Dorothy Sheafe, Whitfield's wife, they included Joanna Sheafe, William Chittenden's wife, and Margaret Sheafe, who was married to Robert Kitchel. All three of these women were granddaughters of Thomas Sheafe, the Cranbrook clothier. They were joined by Joanna's younger brother, Jacob Sheafe, and by her widowed mother, Joanna Sheafe.

The company sailed from England in May 1639 on the *St. John,* a ship of 350 tons. Their first recorded act as a separate community was to sign the following covenant on shipboard:

> We, whose names are here underwritten, intending by God's gracious permission to plant ourselves in New England, and if it may be, in the southerly part about Quinnipiack, do faithfully promise each, for ourselves and our families, and those that belong to us, that we will, the Lord assisting us, sit down and join ourselves together in one entire plantation and be helpful to each other in any common work, according to every man's ability and as need shall require; and we promise not to desert or leave each other or the plantation but with the consent of the rest, or the greater part of the company who have entered into this engagement.
>
> As to our gathering together in a church way, and the choice of our officers and members to be joined together in that way, we do refer ourselves, until such time as it shall please God to settle us in our plantation. In witness whereof we subscribe our names, this first of June, 1639.[12]

The document was signed on the first day of June 1639 by twenty-five men, including Henry Whitfield, William Chittenden, and Robert Kitchel. These individuals had exercised their religious conviction that "men could form a new relationship . . . as a result of compact, covenant, and condition." [13] Like the pilgrims who had sailed before them on the *Mayflower*, they had created what historians later came to call their own "plantation covenant."

After a passage of seven weeks, Whitfield's party was the first group of English settlers to land directly in present-day Connecticut rather than in the Massachusetts Bay Colony. They arrived at Davenport's plantation in New Haven on July 10, 1639. On this date William and Joanna Chittenden—the great-great-grandparents of Thomas Chittenden—and their two young children began their life in New England as pioneers in the "Great Migration," which, although relatively small in size, was destined to produce some of the most distinguished leaders in early colonial America.

New England

After the pilgrims founded the Plymouth Colony in 1620, almost two decades passed before an English settlement was established on the southern coast of New England. The first European who had explored this area, which later became known as Connecticut, was a Dutchman named Adriaen Block. In 1614 he had sailed north from the Dutch colony in New York until he reached the "Quinatucquet" (the native name for "the Long Tidal River," later Anglicized to Connecticut). He went up this river to the area of present-day Hartford before he returned to the coast and continued east to Narragansett Bay, where he located and named Block Island.

Almost two decades passed before the Dutch returned. In 1633 they erected a fort near Hartford, which they called the House of Good Hope. This same year, however, the Plymouth colony in Massachusetts also sent an English party under William Holmes to found a trading post in Windsor, just north of Hartford. In 1635 William Gardner, a military engineer, erected the first English fort at the mouth of the Connecticut River in Saybrook, and in 1636 Reverend Thomas Hooker led a party from Cambridge to establish the first permanent English colony in Hartford.[14]

When the English settlers began to move inland they encountered the Pequots, the most powerful tribe in the region. The Pequots, a fierce and feared people, were originally united with the Mohicans of the Upper Hudson River. They had only recently migrated into southeastern New England, where they quickly established their primacy.[15] Following a series of incidents that eventually resulted in the death of a trader named John Oldham, the English settlers characterized the Pequots as allies of Satan. Once they had located the devil within the Pequot camp, the English forces felt justified in proceeding without restraint.

Their action took the form of a "pre-dawn surprise attack on the Pequot's Mystic River village while most of the men were away, leaving it in the hands of between 300 to 700 women, children and old men. . . . Despite the sleeping villagers' inability to mount an effective resistance, Captain John Mason ordered the wigwams burned, while the English and their allies surrounded the village so as to cut down those trying to flee. In less than an hour, all but seven escapees were dead. The Pequots [who were] not present scattered and panicked, and most were captured or killed during the next several months. Many of the men were executed; the rest, along with the women and children, were enslaved. . . . Under the terms of the English-dictated Treaty of Hartford, the Pequot nation was declared dissolved in 1638."[16]

This brutal massacre, later known as the "Pequot War," opened up the floodgates for English settlement. In 1638 a Puritan party led by Reverend John Davenport and Theophilus

Eaton left Massachusetts Bay to establish the first major English colony on the southern coast of New England, which they named New Haven. Eaton was a wealthy London merchant, and Davenport had been his pastor at St. Stephens Church in London. They had been boyhood friends who later developed very strong Puritan leanings. In 1637 they organized a party in London and sailed to the Massachusetts Bay Colony, where Eaton was an original proprietor. They became dissatisfied with the Bay Colony, however, and decided to form a new community on New England's southern coast to pursue their religious beliefs while also expanding their own trading interests. Thus, they founded New Haven in response to a mix of religious and commercial motivations. They chose its site because they believed it to be the finest harbor between Boston and New York.

When Whitfield's party arrived in New Haven one year later, they began to search for an appropriate locale for their own plantation. Since neither New Haven nor Connecticut enjoyed any formal legal recognition from England, and since the Dutch no longer played any significant role in the area, the prevailing practice of new settlers was to buy land from the local natives. Six members of the Whitfield group, including William Chittenden, were selected to travel eastward along the coast in an effort to locate a native site they could purchase.

Guilford, Connecticut

According to Benjamin Trumbull's history, "as they were from Surrey and Kent, they took much pains to find a tract of land resembling that from which they had removed. . . . They [eventually] made their principal settlement on low, moist, rich land liberal indeed to the husbandman. . . . The great plain to the south had been already cleared and enriched by the natives. . . . There were also nearby adjoining, several necks or points of land, near the sea, clear, rich and fertile, and prepared for immediate improvement." [17]

Once they located this tract, Whitfield and his colleagues arranged to buy it and hold it in trust for the entire plantation. Five men, including William Chittenden and his brother-in-law Robert Kitchel, accompanied Whitfield on this mission. On September 29, 1639, the Whitfield party purchased all of the land lying between the East River and Stony Creek from Shaumpishuh, the sachem squaw of Menunkatuck.[18]

Although additional lands to the east and north of this tract were later bought from other natives, the purchase from Shaumpishuh constituted most of the territory that was to constitute the town of Guilford. Following the purchase, the land was divided and allocated to the new settlers in Whitfield's party. An important principle established in New England from the beginning was that land should be held by individuals in free tenure, as personal property, without the obligation of continuing payments to a landlord.[19]

As Isabel Calder explains in her study of the New Haven Colony, "all the heads of families who took part in the settlement of a town became shareholders, although not necessarily equal shareholders. . . . The result was that the towns became mosaics of small properties. Each family possessed a home lot near the meeting house, one or more pieces of upland, one or more pieces of meadow, and a share in the undivided lands. In New Haven and Guilford, the size of the home lots varied with the wealth of the planter and the size of his family." [20]

Under the prevailing formula, William Chittenden received a large home lot in town of three and one-quarter acres. In addition, "adjoining said home lot, he hath sixteen acres of upland and seven and one-half acres of meadowland, more or less. . . . Other [scattered] lots are described in a similar manner, and the amount of the whole is about 100 acres." [21] It is obvious Chittenden had sufficient personal funds to command a sizable allotment of land in Guilford.

It also appears he gained ownership of some of the most attractive land. According to one account, "his home site overlooking the silvery Menunkatuck river was the most charming of all the Guilford sites." A second account is even more effusive. "The spot selected by William Chittenden . . . for his new home is a remarkably fine location. It overlooks the Menunkatuck river, which winds its way like a ribbon of silver, through a wide expanse of meadow gained from the sea and level as a floor, clothed in summer with herbage of the richest green, but converted when the tide is high into a smooth lake, half a mile in width which, as if by magic, in six hours vanishes away with the receding tide, leaving only a gently flowing stream." [22]

Despite these idyllic descriptions, it would be a mistake to assume that life in Guilford was easy. The settlers faced a difficult and demanding challenge. Their first task was to prepare for the coming winter. Log houses were erected to provide shelter. By late autumn 1639 the settlers began to move into the plantation. By this time, William Chittenden had taken on a major role as a civic leader in the community. After the land was purchased from Shaumpishuh, the plantation was governed as an independent entity until 1643, when Guilford joined the New Haven colony. As it turned out, "Guilford was the last settlement made in Connecticut independent of an outside authority. All of the future plantations received their right to exist either from the New Haven jurisdiction or from that of Connecticut." [23]

During this period Guilford was ruled by four men, who were designated to serve as a provisional committee for the entire plantation, exercising all civil power required to administer justice and preserve the peace. In effect, these four men acted as a de facto government for the community. They were William Chittenden, Robert Kitchel, William Leete, and John Bishop. Thus, Chittenden and his kinsman Kitchel constituted half of the original town government of Guilford.

Chittenden's civic duties were not confined to the provisional committee. "Military order and discipline were soon established . . . that no enemy might surprise them. The leader in charge of this effort was Chittenden who served as the principal military man in the plantation with the rank of lieutenant." [24] In addition, he later served as an artillery officer for the New Haven colony. He was also a magistrate in Guilford and one of the two town deputies who served as a delegate to the New Haven General Court from 1646 until 1660.[25]

While William was busy with town affairs, his wife, Joanna, was raising a large family. Following the births of Thomas and Elizabeth in England, the Chittendens had eight more children after they arrived in Guilford, three of whom died in infancy. Like most of his associates in Guilford, William engaged in farming. "To some extent all planters engaged in agriculture, raising peas, beans, wheat, Indian corn, hops, and fruit. . . . A variety of livestock—horses, mares, working oxen, cows, sheep, goats, and hogs—was raised, and to the agricultural products of the colony must be added beef, pork, and dairy products." [26]

Over time, life in Guilford became more comfortable as the necessary tradesmen were secured and a grain mill was built.[27] The inhabitants lived in a setting that imposed rigorous constraints growing out of a rigid Puritan religious code, however. As one author has observed, "it is hard nowadays to realize how theocratic early Connecticut was. The original settlers were religious exiles who had crossed the ocean to practice their faith— Calvinistic Protestantism. They did this through the Congregational church which was official in Connecticut and was supported by the state's political organs including the various towns." [28]

When Reverend Davenport moved to New Haven in 1637, he was generally regarded as one of New England's three leading Puritan ministers. The other two were Thomas Hooker, who founded the settlement in Hartford, and John Cotton, who dominated the Massachusetts Bay Colony in concert with Governor John Winthrop. All three ministers were theocrats who drew heavily on the Old Testament for their inspiration.

Under Davenport and his colleagues, New Haven developed into a Bible State in which church membership controlled the political franchise. The most immediate result was a heavy emphasis on conformity that "held high barriers against those of other faiths or ill reputation." [29] In addition, very heavy emphasis was placed on negative prohibitions and constraints in which the "Thou Shalt Nots" of the Old Testament became the prevailing codes of conduct.[30]

The town of Guilford, like New Haven, was also extremely strict and often quite intolerant. In June 1643 its residents instituted their own church following the example of New Haven. In so doing, however, they adopted the narrowest political franchise in New England. Unlike New Haven, they confined political privileges not just to members of the Congregational Church, but more specifically to members of their own new church in Guilford.[31] Once this church was established, the town disbanded its four-member provisional committee and appointed "seven pillars" from their new church to manage town affairs. Neither William Chittenden nor Robert Kitchel served as church "pillars."

In the fall of 1643 New Haven and its four closest towns— Guilford, Milford, Stamford, and Southold, Long Island—decided it would be prudent to create their own association. On October 27, 1643, the constitution of the New Haven Colony was adopted when the four towns joined the New Haven jurisdiction. Within a short period of time, the nearby town of Branford also joined the New Haven Colony.

By the 1650s major changes were taking place. The most significant development in Guilford was Henry Whitfield's decision to return to England. When Whitfield had brought the original settlers to New England, he was generous with his wealth, building the "old stone house" (still standing today) that served as Guilford's first religious meeting place until the town church was established in 1643. Whitfield had retained major estates in England, however, and since he never completely separated from the Anglican Church, he was able to return in 1650 and resume his duties as a minister in the Church of England.

A decade later, in February 1660, William Chittenden died. Like Whitfield, he had been a key founder of Guilford. In addition to his military and political service, Chittenden was a prosperous farmer. His widow Joanna testified at the inventory of his estate, which amounted to 677 pounds, 16 shillings, and 7 pence.[32] This serves as clear evidence of Chittenden's financial success, since estates of 500 pounds or more were classified as "substantial" at that time.[33] Five years after her husband's death, Joanna married Abraham Cruttenden, another surviving member of the original Whitfield party that left England in 1639.

In 1662 King Charles II of Great Britain granted the Connecticut colony its own legal charter. After this charter was in place, New Haven attempted to retain its independent status as a colony, but this proved to be futile. In 1665 New Haven and all of its satellite towns were absorbed into the new colony of Connecticut.

William Chittenden's success enabled the next two generations of his family to remain in Guilford. He left his home lot and the adjoining land to his oldest son, Thomas, who was the great-grandfather of Governor Thomas Chittenden of Vermont. In 1663 Thomas married Joanna Jordan, the daughter of John and Anna Jordan.[34] John Jordan had been one of the signers of the 1639 Guilford covenant during the sea journey from England. When Thomas Chittenden married Joanna Jordan he was 26 years old, and Joanna, who had been born in Guilford in 1642, was 21 years old.

Although little is known about the details of Thomas Chittenden's life, family records reveal he and Joanna had a family of seven children, with four boys and three girls. Their second son, William, born on October 5, 1666, was Governor Thomas Chittenden's grandfather. It turned out that only two of Thomas and Joanna Chittenden's sons got married. William wed a woman named Hannah (her last name is unrecorded), and the youngest son, Josiah, married Hannah Sherman. The marriages of these two boys turned out to be important, because when their father died in 1683, he divided his land in Guilford into two equal parts, which he left to his married sons. Each of them received a home lot of one and three-quarter acres on Broad Street and a portion of the adjoining upland, as well as a portion of marsh land bounded on the west by the river.[35]

Thus, William Chittenden, the grandfather of Governor Thomas Chittenden, remained in Guilford. In 1698 William and Hannah Chittenden were married. Their first child, Ebenezer, who was born in Guilford on August 31, 1699, was the father of Governor Thomas Chittenden. After Ebenezer was born, William and Hannah had a daughter in January 1703, but Hannah died in childbirth. William later remarried and had four more children, two of whom died in a plague in 1712.[36]

East Guilford, Connecticut

Ebenezer Chittenden and his family were faced with a significant problem. They were running out of farm land in Guilford. Although the "Great Migration" to New England had been small in numbers, the families involved had sustained the highest reproduction rate of any group in colonial America. By the end of the seventeenth century, Connecticut's population was increasing rapidly, and there was growing pressure on available land.

After his forebears had lived for three generations in Guilford, Ebenezer Chittenden decided to follow in the steps of his great-grandparents and move to a new location. Instead of voyaging across an ocean, however, he traveled across the East River and located his new home in East Guilford, a town that was later renamed Madison in honor of President James Madison. His home lot was located in the southwestern corner of East Guilford in an area known as the Neck because it lay adjacent to the Neck River, a small tributary of the East River.

On March 21, 1723, Ebenezer Chittenden married Mary Johnson. She had been born in Guilford on March 8, 1699, the daughter of Mary Sage and Deacon Samuel Johnson. Mary's father was a "pillar" of the First Congregational Church in Guilford, and her brother was the Reverend Dr. Samuel Johnson of Stratford.[37] After Ebenezer and Mary moved to East Guilford, they began their own family. In all, they had ten children—five boys and five girls. Two of their daughters and one son died in infancy, while the other seven children survived into old age. Their children were:

Elizabeth (b. Feb. 7, 1725; died Feb. 14, 1725)
Ebenezer (b. Sept. 11, 1726; died May 11, 1812)
Elisheba (b. Jan. 16, 1728; mar. Sylvanus Evarts)
THOMAS (B. JAN. 6, 1730; DIED AUG. 25, 1797)
Timothy (b. Nov. 15, 1732; died Feb. 16, 1816)
Bethuel (b. Dec. 10, 1736; died July 15, 1737)
Mary (b. July 4, 1738; died Sept. 8, 1738)
Bethuel (b. Nov. 4, 1739; died Nov. 5, 1809)
Mary (b. May 25, 1742; mar. Abel Buell)
Abigail (b. Sept. 4, 1743; mar. Nathaniel Dudley)[38]

No structure remains today on the home lot of Ebenezer and Mary Chittenden. In the summer of 1995, however, it was still possible to see a clearly delineated old cellar hole, as well as some rotting beams. According to a letter from the Madison Historical Society, plans are being considered to have some type of memorial on this site to honor Governor Chittenden.[39]

Thomas Chittenden grew up in the Neck River area of East Guilford. Although there is little documentation to shed light on his early childhood, two issues have arisen that deserve further consideration. The first involves a story concerning young Thomas that appears in a number of biographical sketches of early Vermont leaders. According to one version of this story:

As a lad, Thomas labored on the paternal farm until he was eighteen years old, when he went to sea as a common sailor. England and France were then at war, and his vessel was captured by a French cruiser. When he regained his liberty he found himself friendless in a West Indian port. He made his way home in great discomfort, determined upon a rural life from which he was destined to be called by the exigencies of the stirring times which soon followed.[40]

While this story about Chittenden's boyhood adventures at sea appears quite frequently, the details vary slightly. In the above account, he found himself friendless in an unidentified West Indian port. In other accounts he ends up on an unidentified West Indian island, and in some accounts he loses an eye as a result of his encounter with the French and acquires the nickname of "one-eye Tom."

Since the language describing this event is rather ambiguous, the story may be just a heroic myth that grew up around an early Vermont statesman. Research on the early history of the Guilford/ Madison area reveals some interesting information, however, that indicates young Thomas Chittenden may have had the opportunity to embark on such an unusual adventure.

Specifically, Guilford was a shipbuilding community. Since it had so many streams and rivers, as well as an extensive shoreline, much of the local travel during its earliest days was by means of small boats that the residents built for themselves. Although its harbor was not deep enough to moor large vessels, according to one source, "in 1680, Guilford had 'a pretty good tide harbor' . . . where 'vessels of about 30 or 40 tonne may come in.'"[41]

In 1703 Guilford was designated by the Connecticut General Assembly as one of the eight ports of entry to the colony with its own naval officer. In 1730, the year Thomas Chittenden was born, the Connecticut colony sent a report to the board of trade in England that "enumerated forty-two vessels actively engaged in trade. These vessels varied in size from twelve to sixty tons and were distributed among seventeen Connecticut towns. New London and New Haven led with five vessels each. Guilford, Hartford, and Norwich had four each, and Saybrook and Stratford had three each. The remaining fourteen were scattered among ten other settlements." [42]

According to a report published by the Madison Historical Society, the four ships in Guilford in 1730 were the sloops *Mary* (12 tons), *Tyral* (20 tons), *Swan* (25 tons), and *Rubie* (30 tons). [43] These early sloops were single-masted, with a mainsail, topsail, and at least one jib. [44] They usually engaged in the coastal trade with New York, but a few of the shipping routes extended beyond. According to the 1730 report to the English board of trade, Connecticut was involved in "a small trade with the West Indies exporting horses and lumber in return for sugar, salt, molasses, and rum." An even more specific comment indicates "before 1775, Sachem's Head harbor was used by vessels in trade with the West Indies. Many cargoes of cattle and other stock were shipped, and lumber was also shipped to some extent." [45]

Hence, documentation indicates that shipping was taking place between Connecticut and the West Indies. Even if Chittenden did not sail from Guilford, he may have departed from New London. An account written by David Read in Abby Hemenway's *Gazetteer* states this is precisely what happened by asserting that Chittenden "found a merchant vessel about to sail from New London to the West Indies, on which he enlisted as a common sailor . . . but before they reached their port of destination a French man-of-war picked them up, and destroyed their vessel." [46] Esther Swift, on the other hand, states that "young Tom Chittenden shipped out from New Haven." [47] As noted earlier, the evidence regarding young Tom Chittenden's adventure at sea is inconsistent and inconclusive.

In addition to his possible West Indian adventure, a second very controversial question relating to Chittenden's youthful years deserves serious consideration. The question is whether or not Thomas Chittenden was uneducated and illiterate.

Most of Governor Chittenden's public papers were written by his personal secretaries or close associates and then signed by him. In addition, he appears to have left no personal papers or private correspondence of his own. The few examples of his own writing that have been found, such as one of the notes he sent to President George Washington in 1792, reveal serious spelling and grammatical errors.[48]

It is difficult to believe that the man who later served as Vermont's first governor was illiterate, but this possibility has been considered by scholars for many years. One line of conjecture suggests that Chittenden may have left some private papers, but his correspondence was so sloppily managed that these papers were sold as scrap paper.[49] No specific proof has ever been found to support this speculation, however, and nagging questions remain regarding Chittenden's literacy.

Some attribute the idea that Chittenden was illiterate to a comment made by Ethan Allen that Chittenden was "a man without words." There are other sources, however, that flatly claim that Chittenden was indeed illiterate. In 1810, for example, an individual named Ignatius Thomson asserted:

> Destitute of learning, Governor Chittenden's attention was principally directed to agriculture, and he labored personally in the field . . . Governor Chittenden, though an illiterate man, possessed great talents; his discernment was keen. . . .[50]

It turns out, however, that Thomson had inaccurately cribbed these words from Chittenden's obituary, which had appeared more than a decade earlier in *The Vermont Gazette*:

> Destitute of a finished education, without a learned profession, Chittenden applied himself to the study of agriculture and labored personally in the field. . . . Governor Chittenden was possest of great talents and a keen discernment in affairs relative to men. . . .[51]

The obvious discrepancies between the two accounts indicate that the issue of illiteracy was subject to different interpretations. Thomson makes the claim that Chittenden was "destitute of learning," while *The Vermont Gazette* indicates he lacked a "finished education" and a "learned profession." In addition, Thomson describes Chittenden as being illiterate, although the obituary in the *Gazette* makes no reference to illiteracy.

There are a few eyewitness accounts of Chittenden, but they also present a confusing picture. One of the most intriguing was written by John Lincklaen, a Dutch agent for the Holland Land Company of western New York, who visited Chittenden at his farm in Williston during the fall of 1792. After his visit, Lincklaen wrote:

> Governor Thomas Chittenden received us without ceremony, in the country fashion. A man of about 60, destitute of all education . . . [he] . . . was not ashamed to say that when he placed himself at the head of those who wished a separation from New York, he scarcely knew how to write.[52]

Once again, however, Lincklaen's assessment turns out to be mixed. On the one hand, he describes Chittenden as "destitute of all education" and mentions Chittenden's concern that "he scarcely knew how to write," but he also goes on to state that Chittenden "possesses good sense & sound judgment. . . . It is chiefly to him that the disputed territory of Vermont owes her present government. . . . He still retains [an] inquisitive character & overwhelms one with questions to which one can scarcely reply. He is one of the largest & best farmers in the state. . . ."[53]

Even the famous Ethan Allen quote that Chittenden was "a man without words" is confusing. When the full quotation is cited, Allen appears to have described Chittenden as: "the only man he ever knew who was sure to be right in all, even the most difficult and complex cases, and yet could not tell or seem to know why it was so. . . . He was a man without words who formed accurate judgments, but was unable to tell how he arrived at them." [54]

In dealing with the question of Chittenden's literacy, it is very important to define what the term "illiterate" actually meant during his lifetime. In the mid-1700s some people felt that individuals were illiterate if they had failed to complete a classical education that included the mastery of Greek and Latin. This appears to be the case in the *Gazette* obituary, which states that Chittenden lacked a "finished education."

Instead, like most of the frontier settlers who lived in early Vermont, Chittenden had only received a common school education. This was the case with Ethan Allen and with other members of Allen's family, and it was also the case with Thomas Chittenden. The documentation on this is very clear. Records reveal that in 1715 the farmers in "Guilford Este End" sent a petition to the town fathers stating that "being by Divine Goodness blessed with a considerable number of children, the signers ask for a school of their own." In 1716 such a school was established in the Neck area of town, not far from where the Ebenezer Chittenden family lived. [55]

A question remains as to what children were taught in these early Connecticut common schools. Once again, the documentation is very specific. "Protestant Christianity place[d] so much emphasis on individual accountability to God that consistency required a community to provide that every person shall be able to read, in order that he may read the Scriptures." [56] Following this philosophy, the Connecticut General Assembly adopted an "ould deluder Satan" law in 1650, which held that:

It being the chief project of that ould deluder Satan to keep men from knowledge of the Scriptures. . . . It is hereby ordered that every township in this jurisdiction, after the Lord hath increased it to fifty householders, shall then forthwith appoint one within their town, to teach all such children, as shall resort to him, to write and read. . . . [57]

Thus, Thomas Chittenden and his siblings had access to the nearby common school in the Neck district of East Guilford, and the educational focus of this school was to teach children to write and read. All three of Chittenden's brothers attended the same school and later pursued professional careers. His oldest brother, Ebenezer, became a noted silversmith who established his own business in New Haven, where he served as a Warden of Trinity Church. His younger brother, Timothy, became a clockmaker in Salisbury, Connecticut, where he served as a captain in the town militia and a member of the town government. His youngest brother, Bethuel, moved to Vermont, where he became one of the leaders of the early Protestant Episcopal Church.[58]

Hence, it appears that Thomas Chittenden's brothers were literate. There is no reason to suspect that Thomas Chittenden was any different. He had an extensive record of public service in Connecticut and Vermont—while still in Connecticut, he served in many different local offices and represented Salisbury for six terms in the colonial assembly. He was also a colonel in the militia and justice of the peace, and both positions required "a colonywide reputation in addition to proven ability."[59]

While the available evidence indicates that Thomas Chittenden was neither uneducated nor illiterate, he may have experienced difficulty with his writing. In the words of his great-grandson, the Honorable Lucius E. Chittenden, "his orthography was very inaccurate."[60] This is precisely the conclusion UVM historian Marshall True reaches when he observes:

> While I would not go so far as to call Chittenden illiterate, even a cursory examination of the Chittenden papers at the University of Vermont reveals a man uncomfortable with spelling, grammar, and syntax.[61]

If Chittenden did indeed struggle with his writing, he was not alone. This certainly was the case with many of the other notable leaders in early Vermont. One of the problems they faced resulted from the fact that spelling was done in regional dialects due to the absence of standardized guidebooks. Samuel Johnson did not publish his landmark *Dictionary of the English Language*, the first comprehensive lexicographical work in England, until 1755. In the New Hampshire Grants region, it was not until 1779 that Curtis Abel wrote *A Compend of English Grammar*, which was published by Dresden (Dartmouth College) and printed by J. P. & A. Spooner.[62]

The following account indicates the potential extent of illiteracy in one of the northern regions of the New Hampshire Grants:

> The first settlers of Newbury were illiterate, if we consider illiteracy to consist in poor spelling. Of all the men who were in Newbury before the revolution, counting out certain Scotchmen, there were, probably not three, besides the minister, who could write a short letter without making mistakes in orthography. General Bayley could not, nor Colonel Johnson, nor Colonel Kent. It is easy to laugh at their letters, but the men who carried Coos County safely through the revolutionary war, had found little time for the niceties of spelling, but they did know the whole subject of the controversy with Great Britain to the last particular.[63]

In retrospect, it is important to note that individuals like Ethan and Ira Allen, who did write well, were exceptions to the rule. Since Chittenden was probably not a good writer, most of his public papers were written by the secretaries to the Governor and Council—Joseph Fay, Thomas Tolman, and Truman Squire—and by Chittenden's close political associates, Ethan and Ira Allen. There is nothing to indicate that any difficulties he may have experienced with his writing impaired his judgment or infringed on any of his other leadership qualities. To the contrary, his record of leadership supports Professor Marshall True's observation that the circumstantial evidence requires future biographers "to give Chittenden the benefit of the doubt on the question of authorship and acknowledge—as Charles Miner Thompson suggests—that 'we need not think that any letter he signed did not meet the test of his accurate intuitive judgment.'" [64]

Charles Miner Thompson's suggestion is part of a larger comment in his book, *Independent Vermont*, where he observes that many of Governor Chittenden's "state papers and political correspondence were written by Ethan Allen, Ira Allen, and his secretary, the Reverend Thomas Tolman. . . . The idea that he was the pliant tool of cleverer, stronger men can be dismissed. . . . He was an experienced and successful man; a man of substance and standing; moreover he lasted longer in Vermont politics than any other member of the group. We need not think that any letter he signed did not meet the test of his accurate intuitive judgment." [65]

Instead of receiving a "finished education" at one of America's new young universities, Governor Chittenden obtained his own practical political education through his extensive participation in the arena of public affairs. His practical education began shortly after October 4, 1749, when, at age nineteen, he married Elizabeth Meigs, the seventeen-year-old daughter of John and Elizabeth (Dudley) Meigs of East Guilford. Like his great-great-grandparents, who had journeyed from Cranbrook, Kent, to New England more than a century earlier, Thomas Chittenden and his young wife Elizabeth were pioneers who were about to leave East Guilford and travel to the frontier. This time their destination was the town of Salisbury in the northwest wilderness territory of the Connecticut colony. Once again, the Chittenden family was on the move.

CHAPTER II

The Education of Thomas Chittenden

(1749–1774)

Thomas and Elizabeth Chittenden moved to Salisbury, Connecticut, in 1749 because there was not enough land in the Neck district of East Guilford to enable them to make their living as a farm family.

The challenge the young Chittendens faced was not unique. As historian Richard Hofstadter has noted, "in the decades following the Peace of Utrecht in 1713, the New England colonies underwent a period of phenomenal growth. By mid-century there were signs of a new and critical phase in the economic development of older New England, which was now reaching the limits of its internal land supply." [1] The problem resulted from rapid increases in population. During the two decades from 1730, the year Chittenden was born, until 1749, the year he left East Guilford, the population estimates for Connecticut jumped from 38,000 to 71,000.[2] As a result, "town lands were ample for the first generation, and remained sufficient to accommodate the second, but by the third a pinch was felt, and emigration began to be necessary." [3]

The area where Thomas and Elizabeth Chittenden relocated was the northwestern frontier of the colony. This area, now known as Litchfield County, was originally a "virgin wilderness and heavily forested. A number of predators, wolves and snakes . . . posed a danger to the early settlers, and bounties were offered for many years." [4]

As early as 1714 Dutch surveying parties from the Hudson River Valley began moving into this forest. In the 1720s a small number of Dutch families from Livingston Manor, New York, bought land from the natives at Weatogue (later Salisbury), where they hacked out many small clearings in the dark wooded hills that obscured the streams, lakes, and nearby Onsatunnack (Housatonic) River. [5]

At the time there was a controversy over whether this region—the so-called "Western lands"—fell under the jurisdiction of Connecticut. In 1686, twenty-five years after King Charles II had granted the colony of Connecticut its charter, the Connecticut General Assembly staked its claim by ceding all the vacant lands west to the Housatonic to the "plantations of Hartford and Windsor . . . to make a plantation or villages there." [6]

As soon as more Dutch settlers began to move into the region, the towns of Hartford and Windsor acted quickly to conduct their own surveys. In 1732 the assembly ordered a special committee to lay out lots for two new towns—Sharon and Salisbury—in the northwest corner of the colony. In May 1738, after prior claims were settled with the Dutch and the natives, the assembly ordered twenty-five equal shares of land in Salisbury to be sold at auction in Hartford.

Not all of the original proprietors who bought land at this auction settled in Salisbury. Many of them were aggressive speculators. In 1731 iron ore had been discovered in the region. The following year Thomas Lamb, the first English settler, built a crude iron forge. At the 1738 land auction, Lamb purchased six of the twenty-five proprietary town rights. Within three years he ended up owning large amounts of land, as well as extensive ore holdings and a water power site. After Salisbury was officially chartered as a town in 1741, he sold his lands and amassed a fortune of 12,700 pounds.[7]

Thomas Lamb was not unique. From the very beginning Salisbury was a hotbed of land speculators. The early town reports are replete with their names. Thomas Newcombe, for example, purchased three proprietary rights in 1739–40. He later sold more than 3,700 acres of land for 12,500 pounds, ten times their recorded cost. John Smith, an early settler who had paid Thomas Lamb 230 pounds for 200 acres in 1743, later sold this land for 2,000 pounds. The Salisbury land speculation boom was so intense that even the town's first clergyman, Reverend Jonathan Lee, who was a cousin and a tutor of Ethan Allen, became known as the richest minister in Connecticut thanks to his real estate dealings.[8]

After the Connecticut General Assembly chartered the town in 1741, many people throughout the colony traveled north to inspect Salisbury. Two individuals who visited the town in 1748 were young Thomas Chittenden and his father, Ebenezer. They liked what they saw. On May 1, 1749, Ebenezer Chittenden joined with Samuel Turner of Guilford and bought 162 acres in Salisbury from Nathaniel Skinner. The land they bought was a portion of Lot 22, 4th Division.[9] Their purchase included a small farmhouse and a barn located on Prospect Hill Road, a few miles north of Salisbury village.[10]

Following their wedding, Thomas and Elizabeth Chittenden moved into the small farmhouse his father had purchased in Salisbury. Within two months Thomas was elected to his first public position. At a town meeting held on December 14, 1749, he was chosen to serve as one of the three listers in Salisbury for the year ensuing.[11] The fact that he was only nineteen years old when he won his first election to public office served as a harbinger of his later political career. People appeared to recognize his leadership qualities from the very outset.

A few weeks after Chittenden's election, Sylvanus Evarts of East Guilford and his brothers John and Nathaniel bought a tract of land in Salisbury for 2,800 pounds. Sylvanus Evarts was married to Thomas Chittenden's sister, Elisheba, and over the next two decades two of Thomas Chittenden's brothers, Timothy and Bethuel, would also move to Salisbury.[12]

On October 7, 1750, the Chittendens' first daughter, Mabel, was born, and two months later Thomas continued his fledgling political career when he was elected as one of the surveyors of highways at the Salisbury town meeting. On April 27, 1751, his father bought a portion of the lot he had purchased in Salisbury from his partner Samuel Turner, and on May 9, 1751, Ebenezer deeded all of the land he owned in Salisbury to Thomas. When making this gift, Ebenezer stated it was "in consideration of Love, Good Will, and Affection to my Loving Son, Thomas Chittenden, for and towards his advancement in the world, accounting it to the value of 550 pounds Old Tenor toward his part of my estate." [13] At the time, Ebenezer and Mary Chittenden had a family of seven children, including four sons. Under prevailing custom, the four boys would normally share in the bulk of Ebenezer's estate, and it appears that Thomas received his share at the age of twenty-one in the form of this gift from his father.

During the 1750s Thomas and Elizabeth Chittenden's family grew in size. During the remainder of the decade three more children were added. They were Noah, born on September 26, 1753; Hannah, July 13, 1756; and Mary, September 18, 1758.[14]

As the family prospered, Thomas began to buy additional land adjacent to his farm as well as in other parts of Salisbury. By 1760 the Salisbury records of taxpayers reveal that Chittenden's tax bill of 130 pounds was the seventh largest among the town's 235 property owners.[15]

On August 8, 1756, Thomas Chittenden's father, Ebenezer, died. Two years later, in March 1758, his younger brother, Timothy, bought a lot for his own home in Salisbury. The following month, on April 20, 1758, Timothy married Rebecca Skinner. They lived in Salisbury for the next fifty-eight years, where Timothy became a successful clock and watch maker and a prominent citizen. A decade after Timothy arrived in Salisbury, Bethuel Chittenden, the youngest brother of Thomas, also moved to the town and was elected as one of the surveyors of highways in both 1767 and 1769 before leaving for the town of Tinmouth in the New Hampshire Grants, where he started to farm in 1773.[16]

In addition to farming and raising a family, Thomas Chittenden resumed his service in local government in Salisbury in 1756 after a five-year hiatus. Minutes of the town meeting held on December 13 reveal that "it was voted . . . that Mr. Thomas Chittenden is constable for the year ensuing; sworn according to law." As the town's constable he was responsible for enforcing the edicts of the town meeting and the justice court, and he often doubled as the town tax collector.[17]

During the course of the next eighteen years Thomas Chittenden continued to serve in a wide variety of town offices. The Salisbury town minutes from 1756 through 1774 indicate that at different times he was a constable; tax collector; school committee member; third, second, and first selectman; and even a tithingman "responsible for maintaining sabbath day order and decorum." His various negotiating assignments are of special interest. In 1763, for example, he was elected to serve as the town's agent to secure a new highway, a position he also occupied for another highway in 1771. In September 1771 he was elected to serve on a five-member committee to negotiate the settlement of a large and long-standing delinquent debt that Thomas Chipman, Jr., had incurred against the town of Salisbury and the Colony of Connecticut.[18]

Thomas Chittenden's consistent advancement in responsibility from his initial work as a town lister to his service as first selectman indicates he was an astute natural politician who demonstrated very strong leadership skills in handling local town affairs. The record further indicates that his leadership transcended the arena of town government. In the fall of 1763 the men of Salisbury elected Chittenden to serve as a captain in their militia company, and then, in October 1764, they chose him to serve as one of the town's two representatives in the Connecticut General Assembly. The records of the colony of Connecticut reveal he was reelected as a representative from Salisbury for six additional terms between 1766 and 1772.[19]

It was at this time that Chittenden first became involved in the political events that led up to the Revolutionary War. At his first meeting in October 1764 the assembly voted overwhelm-

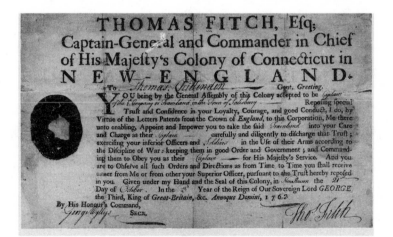

In October 1763 Thomas Chittenden received a commission as a captain in the Connecticut militia after being elected to this post by the townsmen of Salisbury. The following year they elected him to serve in the Connecticut General Assembly as a town representative. (Vermont Historical Society)

ingly to oppose the imposition of a stamp tax by the British Parliament. The following year, however, the Stamp Act went into
effect despite widespread colonial opposition. Governor Fitch, a
conservative, took an oath to support the tax. This led to the
initial split between the conservative and radical elements in
Connecticut. Reverend Jonathan Lee, the wealthy orthodox Congregational minister in Salisbury, supported Governor Fitch, but
Chittenden, who was Salisbury's member on the county committee of correspondence, opposed the governor. Governor Fitch
was defeated in the next election, largely as a result of the actions
of the Sons of Liberty, and Chittenden "assumed an increasingly
prominent stature within the town." [20]

At its October 1767 session the assembly voted to reorga-
nize Connecticut's militia, and it specified "that the towns of
Cornwall, Sharon, Salisbury, Canaan, and Norfolk shall be one
entire regiment, distinguished and called by the name of the
Fourteenth Regiment. . . . This Assembly do appoint Thomas
Chittenden, Esq., to be a Major in the Fourteenth Regiment of
the militia of this colony." Less than three years later, in May
1770, the assembly appointed Thomas Chittenden, Esq., to be
a lieutenant colonel in the Fourteenth Regiment of militia in
the colony.[21]

At its session held in Hartford in May 1773 the Connecticut
General Assembly honored Thomas Chittenden again by appointing him as one of the justices of the peace for Litchfield
County for the year ensuing. As historian Robert Shalhope
notes, "with this appointment, he achieved all the influence
and prestige generally associated with members of the gentry.
Still, even though the colonial legislature [had] accorded him
the title 'Esquire,' Chittenden remained very much a man of
the people." [22]

While Chittenden became more deeply engaged in public
affairs, his family continued to grow in numbers. During the
decade of the 1760s four more children were born—Elizabeth,
on February 17, 1761; Beulah, May 23, 1763; Martin, March

Land west of the Connecticut River is labeled as part of New Hampshire in this 1755 map, even though the Colony of New York also claimed it. Many Connecticut residents bought grants to this land from New Hampshire Governor Benning Wentworth and became involved in the growing dispute with New York. (University of Vermont Special Collections)

12, 1766; and Giles, July 30, 1768. Since there were now eight children, the family could no longer fit into their small farmhouse, so Thomas and Elizabeth built a large new house up the road from their first home near the crown of Prospect Hill. This handsome brick house, which commands a stunning view of the surrounding countryside, still stands today on its original site. While living in this house in the early 1770s, Thomas and Elizabeth Chittenden had their final two children—a fourth son, Truman, who was born on September 10, 1770, and a sixth daughter, Electa, who arrived on July 27, 1773.[23]

During the years the Chittenden family resided in Salisbury, they attended Jonathan Lee's Congregational Covenant Church of Christ, but they did not appear to be very active churchgoers. The only Chittenden family baptismal record listed in the church is "Martin, 1766, under the name of Timothy Chittenden, an obvious error for Thomas Chittenden's son, Martin, who was born in 1766 and later became governor of Vermont." [24]

While the Chittendens were living in Salisbury, the town grew steadily. One of its major industries was the iron works and the famous Salisbury furnace, which later produced hundreds of cannon for the Continental Army during the American Revolution. Originally the iron ore deposits found in the area were hauled to Sheffield, Massachusetts, or Ancram, New York, to be smelted. Once deposits of limestone were found in Salisbury, the situation changed. Since vast hardwood forests existed in the area, all three resources needed for iron production were present. Wood was used to make charcoal to fuel the furnaces and limestone was available to remove impurities from the iron ore once it became molten. All that was necessary to stimulate Salisbury's iron production was a blast furnace.

In 1762 an ambitious young man named Ethan Allen from the nearby town of Litchfield turned up in Salisbury, where he persuaded two partners to provide the capital to buy the rights to an iron ore bed. They constructed a blast furnace in Lakeville, an area a few miles south of Salisbury village where water was available for a waterwheel to power the bellows of the furnace. Ethan bought a house and ninety-five acres of land in Lakeville, and he lived there for three years with his wife and two of his brothers, Heman and Ira.[25]

Although the iron operation proved to be successful, Ethan Allen, restlessly looking for new entrepreneurial challenges, sold his interest in the Salisbury furnace and invested in lead mines in Massachusetts.[26] This venture, however, was not successful, and Ethan returned to Salisbury. There he heard about opportunities to speculate in land in the New Hampshire Grants, and he decided to move north. Thomas Chittenden first met Ethan and his brothers in Salisbury, and these early meetings with the Allens were destined to have a major impact on his own future career after he moved his family to the New Hampshire Grants.

A number of factors appear to have influenced the Chittendens' decision to move to the Grants. One fact, already noted, was that Salisbury was growing. As a local historian has pointed out, "today, the village of Lakeville in Salisbury is clean, quiet, and charming, but in Chittenden's time it was quite the opposite. The blast furnace was a noisy operation—the waterwheel and the huge bellows could be heard a mile or more away. Piles of ore and limestone were everywhere with burdock and other weeds growing unchecked around them. By night the area was lit up by the burning of gasses generated by the smelting operation. The unpaved roads were either muddy or dusty, depending on the season. The brook from the lake—now crystal clear—was polluted by furnace waste."[27]

It appears, however, that Thomas Chittenden's decision to travel north was not based as much on a desire to leave Salisbury as on the attraction of the large amounts of land available in the New Hampshire Grants. During the 1770s a number of Chittenden's colleagues were already beginning to move from Salisbury to the Grants. "Once settled in the new region, the pioneers acted as magnets to friends and relatives. . . . Often it happened that a group of neighbors from some Connecticut town would decide to move together." [28] In addition to actually moving to the Grants, other Salisbury residents were following an old town tradition. Specifically, since the early 1760s they had been engaged in land speculation in the Grants. Salisbury residents involved in such speculation included John Evarts, Samuel Moore, Josiah Stoddard, Nathaniel Buell, Abiel Camp, Joseph Waterous, Joshua Jewell, Thomas Chipman, Phillip Chatfield, and Thomas Chittenden. [29]

It also appears that members of the Evarts family, who were related to Chittenden through his older sister Elisheba, played a major role in this land speculation. John Evarts, who had served with Chittenden in the Connecticut General Assembly, was a flamboyant character. He ran a tavern in Salisbury on the stage road to Albany and, according to town records, was once convicted of selling liquor without a license. [30] As early as 1760 he went north with a Salisbury associate named Elias Reed to survey two new town sites in the Otter Creek area. In keeping with his ostentatious reputation, "Evarts was so taken with the country that he eagerly plotted three towns instead of two. Together they mapped and marked a magnificent tract of over a hundred thousand acres . . . a vast forest of pine, hemlock, maple, oak, cut through the middle by a meandering stream which French explorers a century before had labeled the Creek of Otters. They hurried back to Salisbury, where the idealists and adventurers, the escapists and the speculators, readily subscribed for plots of one hundred acres, two hundred acres, [and] three hundred acres." [31]

In November 1761 Evarts secured charters from Governor Benning Wentworth of New Hampshire for three towns in the Grants, which were named Middlebury, Salisbury, and New Haven. [32] Almost all of the first proprietors of Middlebury were from Salisbury, Connecticut, and they held their first town meeting at Evarts's tavern in Salisbury. Two of the original proprietors of Middlebury were Thomas Chittenden and his eight-

year-old son Noah. In addition, Timothy and Bethuel Chittenden bought proprietary rights in Salisbury and New Haven. It
was obvious at this time that the Chittendens were more interested in speculation than settlement.[33]

Chittenden's interest in the New Hampshire Grants increased when his brother, Bethuel, and his sister and her hus-
band, Elisheba and Sylvanus Evarts, decided to move there. In
March 1773 the Evarts bought "a farm and house in Castleton,
together with one half of the valuable sawmill and water rights
at the outlet of Lake Bomoseen, then called the Great Pond."
In order to finance this purchase, they sold all of their property
in Salisbury for 300 pounds and moved to Castleton with their
two sons, Timothy and Eli.[34]

The fact that Bethuel and Elisheba had decided to move to
the Grants had a pronounced impact on Thomas Chittenden.
His interest was further encouraged by his old Salisbury friends
Ira, Ethan, and Heman Allen. By January 1773 the Allen brothers had purchased large tracts of land in the Champlain Valley,
where they joined with their cousin, Remember Baker, to organize the Onion River Land Company.[35]

Thomas Chittenden was interested in the Allen's Onion River
land. "According to a story handed down in the family, during
the 1760's Colonel Chittenden, as head of a Connecticut militia regiment, had led an expedition to rescue several captured
residents who had been taken north toward Canada. After free-
ing the captives, the men camped on their way home in a valley
on the Onion River near Mount Mansfield . Family legend has
it that Colonel Chittenden remarked, 'this is a paradise. If I
can get title to land here, I will build my house and settle it
with my sons around me.'"[36]

This last sentiment was very important. Salisbury was growing rapidly. From the mid-1750s to the mid-1770s, its population almost doubled from 1,100 to 2,000 residents. Many of
these residents were very young. Due to a heavy influx of im-
migrants, coupled with a large average family size, Salisbury's

median age was about sixteen years.[37] Thomas and Elizabeth
Chittenden like "most Grants settlers shared a commitment to
provide for the future economic security of the lineal family. . . .
How could they help their children in a society of shrinking
opportunities? When New Englanders thought of prosperity,
of opportunity, of survival, they thought of land." [38]

So the Chittendens decided to move their family north, where
land was abundant and the prices were still very cheap. Thomas and Elizabeth Chittenden decided to leave Salisbury in
1773, a few months before their youngest child, Electa, was
born. In the spring of that year, Chittenden, accompanied by
two Salisbury friends, Jonathan Spafford and Abijah Pratt, traveled to the New Hampshire Grants. On May 17, 1773, he and
his two colleagues signed a bond binding them to purchase land
in the township of Williston from the "Allens and Baker Company, otherwise called Onion River Land Company . . . [for
the] . . . sum of Five Hundred Pounds Current Money of the
province of New York." On this same day Ethan and Heman
Allen gave Chittenden and Spafford a bond in the sum of 2,000
pounds to guarantee that they would each receive a deed of
600 acres of beautiful intervale land in the township of Williston
with "the same right to the said different pieces of land as the
grantees under New Hampshire originally had." Pratt received
206 acres.[39]

Almost a year later, on March 29, 1774, Chittenden and
Spafford secured a deed from Heman Allen for an additional
thirteen and one-third rights, or shares, in Williston, which they
agreed to sell at their discretion, with the proviso that one half of
the money arising from such sales would be paid by Chittenden
and Spafford to Heman Allen and Company. This second deed
provided them with another 4,017 acres of land, bringing their
total holdings in Williston to 5,253 acres. Early accounts indicate Williston became "one of the best agricultural towns in the
state, containing no mountains within its borders, it is beautifully diversified with large tracts of level land. A great variety of

soil exists. . . . The pastures are not excelled in their verdancy and freshness; and the intervales along the banks of the Winooski and the upland meadow, are unrivaled." [40] Although "one-eye" Tom Chittenden, as his associates sometimes called him, may have experienced some problems with his sight, he had no difficulty spotting a very attractive land deal whenever he saw one. [41]

Even before Chittenden obtained rights to this second deed of land, he had become an intimate member of the Allens' inner circle. "On March 23, 1774, the proprietors of the Townships of Colchester and Burlington . . . [met] at the dwelling house of Capt. Samuel Morris, Innkeeper in Salisbury in Litchfield County and Colony Connecticut in New England." According to the minutes, the proprietors voted Colonel Thomas Chittenden moderator of this meeting. [42] Thus, Thomas Chittenden, who owned a large amount of the Allens' Onion River land in the nearby town of Williston, was elected to serve in his first governmental post in the Grants as the moderator of the proprietors' meetings of both Colchester and Burlington.

In the spring of 1774, a few months after the meeting took place, Thomas and Elizabeth Chittenden, accompanied by their ten children, including their one-year-old baby daughter, Electa, left Salisbury, Connecticut, and set out on a difficult journey through the wilderness to their new frontier homesite on the Onion River.

CHAPTER III

The Arrival of Thomas Chittenden
(1774–1777)

⫷⫸

The Chittenden family's trip from Salisbury to Williston in the spring of 1774 covered approximately two hundred miles. The first half of the trip up to the headwaters of the Otter Creek in the Manchester-Dorset area was passable by ox-carts and wagons over rough roads. The party then probably continued north until they reached Middlebury Falls, where Ira Allen had blazed a trail and a bridle road the previous summer to connect Otter Creek with the Onion River. After completing this road, Ira had bragged, "thus in a short time, I led a people through a wilderness of 70 miles; about the same distance that took Moses 40 years to conduct the children of Israel." [1]

Despite the relative brevity of their travel, the Chittendens, like the Israelites, must have experienced an arduous journey. Once they reached Middlebury, the family could have used two different routes to travel north. One was Ira's blazed trail, which would have posed a difficult challenge. As Salisbury historian Julia Pettee commented, "imagine the party which included a woman with a year-old baby and other small children. Horses were provided to carry the provisions and equipment, but a mother with a small child atop a horse would be mercilessly whipped by undergrowth as her horse wound its way between the marked trees." [2]

An alternative route would have involved a journey west to Lake Champlain, possibly to the area around Chimney Point, where they may have boarded a boat. According to one account, "in May, 1774, Governor Thomas Chittenden and Jonathan Spafford came down the Lake in a bateau, and following up the Winooski River, they located at Williston." [3] In the absence of any confirmatory information, it is difficult to determine which route the Chittendens actually followed.

Once they reached Williston, the Chittenden family was virtually isolated in a sparsely inhabited location. At the time "when Colonel Chittenden removed into Vermont, nearly the whole country from the Connecticut River to Lake Champlain was a dense wilderness. . . . There were about forty families, all told, on the river and lake shore, and a small block-house in Jericho, on the opposite side of the river below Col. Chittenden's, had been flung up and garrisoned." [4] Among those early settlers are the familiar names of Ira Allen, Remember Baker, Thomas Chittenden, John Chamberlin, Jonathan Spafford, and Amos Brownson.

Political Factions

More than two years passed after the Chittendens arrived in Williston and began the hard work of clearing the land on their new farm before Thomas Chittenden became involved in the political affairs of the Grants. The settlers in the Grants were divided into a number of different factions. The most energetic group lived in Bennington and nearby towns. They were engaged in an escalating conflict with the colony of New York over the issue of land ownership.

A quarter of a century earlier, beginning in 1749, Governor Benning Wentworth of New Hampshire began to grant towns in a large area west of the Connecticut River that was claimed by the colony of New York. "In all, between January 1749 and June 1764, Governor Wentworth wrote grants for 129 towns, plus six smaller military grants, in the area that is now Vermont. . . ." [5] In July 1764, however, it appeared that New York had won jurisdiction over the entire area when King George declared the western bank of the Connecticut River to be the boundary between New York and New Hampshire.

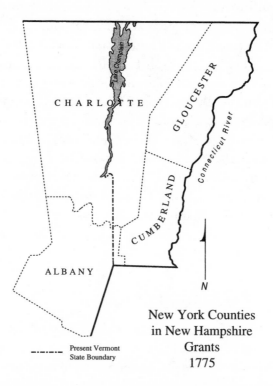

New York Counties
in New Hampshire
Grants
1775

In an effort to reinforce its claim to the New Hampshire Grants, New York established three new counties—Cumberland, Gloucester, and Charlotte. At the outbreak of the Revolutionary War in 1775, New York's counties covered the entire area of present-day Vermont. (Map by Bradley Rink)

The trouble began over the interpretation of the decision that New York's boundary was "to be" the western banks of the Connecticut River. Many of the settlers already living in the New Hampshire grants argued that this decision covered future grants, but it did not apply to land they had already purchased under previous grants made by Governor Wentworth. The colony of New York, however, claimed jurisdiction over the entire Grants area west of the river, and it began to issue land patents of its own, some of which overlapped with the lands already granted by New Hampshire. In addition, the New York authorities required the Wentworth grantees to apply for New York patents and pay new fees to secure their New Hampshire land titles.

Many of the settlers who had purchased Governor Wentworth's earlier New Hampshire grants were outraged. During the late 1760s residents of Bennington, the largest and wealthiest town on the west side of the Green Mountains, organized a militia group to keep the "Yorkers" from encroaching on their lands. In the summer of 1770 Ethan Allen was elected colonel commandant of this militia group, which became known as the Green Mountain Boys. From 1770 to 1775 the outspoken Allen took the lead in opposing New York. Once the Revolutionary War broke out, Allen, accompanied by Benedict Arnold and a small force of Green Mountain Boys, captured Fort Ticonderoga in a surprise attack against the unwary British. As a result, he became an instant military hero throughout the Grants.

Surprisingly, however, Ethan Allen received a major setback only a few months later. On July 26, 1775, representatives from the western towns in the Grants met at a convention in Dorset to elect officers for the newly organized Green Mountain Rangers regiment. Although Ethan Allen nominated himself and Seth Warner of Bennington as the field officers of the regiment, the convention overwhelmingly rejected Allen. Instead, they chose Warner to serve as lieutenant colonel of the regiment by a lopsided vote of 41 to 5. Bitterly disappointed, Allen blamed his defeat on "the old farmers . . . who did not incline to go to war." [6]

It appears, however, that the situation was much more complicated than this. One of the reasons Ethan Allen was rejected grew out of his leadership style. Although he had been effective at keeping the Yorkers at bay, Allen was a rash, flamboyant, mercurial leader, and many of the delegates at Dorset did not have confidence in his reliability.

Allen's radical religious views also worked against him. The town of Bennington had been settled by Samuel Robinson and groups of religious evangelists from Hardwick, Massachusetts, Norwich, Connecticut, and Amenia, New York. Many of the men who resided in the southwestern towns were radical "New Light" separatists who had defied the elitist leaders of the other colonies. They were quite strict, however, in their support of the orthodox Congregational Calvinism that Jonathan Edwards had advocated in the "Great Awakening" religious revivals that swept New England during the 1740s. They did not look kindly upon Ethan Allen's outspoken deism, which some interpreted as outright atheism. As Donald Smith's research has revealed, the Green Mountain Boys "derived their radical politics from religious dissent, not from Ethan's deistic, liberal Enlightenment thought. Far from being irreligious, they belonged to the Great Awakening's radical religious persuasions—the Separates, Separate Baptists, and the New Lights." [7]

As a result of his defeat for leadership of the Green Mountain regiment, Ethan Allen joined General Schuyler's northern invasion of Canada. In the fall of 1775 Allen made an ill-advised attack on Montreal, where he was captured by the British. He spent the next two-and-a-half years as a prisoner-of-war. Once Allen was removed from the scene, there was no obvious leader to take control of the Bennington faction. The nominal leader was Nathan Clark, the head of the Church Party and Committee of Safety in Bennington. Clark was elected chairman of the Grand Committee, which was made up of the local committees of safety of twenty-five southwestern towns. At age fifty-seven, however, he was not a dynamic personality. Samuel Robinson, the original settler of Bennington, was an even older sixty-eight. Most of the other potential leaders were young men. Seth Warner, who had replaced Ethan Allen as head of the militia, was only thirty-three, and he was basically a military man. Other leading Bennington figures were also young: Jonas Fay was thirty-nine, Moses Robinson was thirty-four, Joseph Fay was thirty-three, and John Fassett was thirty-two. Within the Allen family, Heman was thirty-five, Heber was thirty-two, Levi was thirty, Zimri was twenty-seven, and Ira was a mere twenty-four years old.[8]

A second key political faction in the Grants, called the "Yorkers," were directly opposed to the Bennington group. Most of the settlers within this second faction lived in the southeastern corner of the Grants in Cumberland County, adjacent to the Connecticut River. Many of them had moved north from central towns in Massachusetts and Connecticut to establish farms, and they were willing to pay the price of stability by buying confirmatory grants from New York to back up their New Hampshire grants. Some of the most important Yorkers were Judge Thomas Chandler, Sr., of Chester, Judge Samuel Wells of Brattleboro, and James Clay of Putney, the chairman of the Cumberland County Committee of Safety.

A third important faction was located in northeastern Gloucester County adjacent to the upper reaches of the Connecticut River. This group, known as the "New Hampshire Party," was championed by General Jacob Bayley, who has been described as "one of the most sagacious and upright characters in the Grants."[9]

Bayley, who was born in Newbury, Massachusetts, had served as a colonel in the New Hampshire militia during the French and Indian Wars. In 1763 he bought six square miles of land on the northern frontier under a Benning Wentworth grant and founded the town of Newbury on the Connecticut River.

Bayley also purchased a confirmatory grant for this land from New York, and he served as a colonel in charge of a New York militia regiment. Hence, he was sympathetic to New York, but he was also interested in joining the central and northern Connecticut River towns in the Grants with adjacent towns across the Connecticut River in New Hampshire, where many of his friends and closest associates lived. Bayley had explored this idea unsuccessfully in 1771 with Benning Wentworth's successor, Governor John Wentworth, but he still maintained an interest in establishing a link between the Grants towns and their neighboring towns in New Hampshire.[10]

Finally, a fourth group was known as the "College Party." This group was headquartered in the town of Hanover, New Hampshire. Its key leaders were the Reverend Eleazar Wheelock, founder and first president of Dartmouth College, which had received a royal charter in 1769, and his astute son-in-law, Bezaleel Woodward, who served as a Dartmouth faculty member, librarian, and administrator. Wheelock and Woodward, who were close to Jacob Bayley, favored creating a new centralized colony in the Connecticut River Valley that would encompass towns from both sides of the river, with the town of Hanover serving as its capital.

The differences between these four factions were further complicated by some difficult personality conflicts that divided the easterners from the westerners. Two of the key eastern leaders—General Bayley of Newbury and Colonel Stone of Windsor—were not on good terms with the Allens.[11] Bayley was a member of the orthodox church, and he had two brothers who were ministers in the church. Thus, he abhorred Ethan Allen's anti-orthodox religious views. When Bayley secured his confirmatory charter for Newbury from New York in 1772, he traveled through Bennington, where he found "very outspoken free thinkers and avowed disbelievers of the Bible." Bayley expressed his strong dislike to President Wheelock of Dartmouth in a letter dated January 15, 1771, when he referred to the Bennington party as:

> . . . avowed enemies to the cause of Christ, at least by practice . . . but God overrules all things, and deliverance will come to his people some way most to His glory.[12]

The "New State" Conventions

In light of all the political factionalism in the Grants, it was obvious that it would be necessary to create some type of centralized government to exercise jurisdiction over the entire region in order to successfully defend the original Wentworth land claims. The impetus for creating just such a centralized authority came from western leaders in the Bennington party. Once the Revolutionary War broke out against Great Britain, they had a rationale for taking such an action, not initially to deal with their land claims but rather to provide adequate protection against possible British attacks. They decided to hold conventions of local towns to coordinate defenses, and these conventions served as the mechanism to discuss political, as well as military, affairs.

Following the first Dorset meeting, when they had elected their militia officers, the leaders of the western towns held a second convention at Dorset in January 1776. At this second convention they astutely combined their military and political ambitions. They voted to send a Remonstrance and Petition to the Continental Congress to recognize them as an independent government by securing their militia to serve in the Continental Army as citizens of the New Hampshire Grants, and not as inhabitants of the province of New York. In an effort to gain recognition from the Congress, they dispatched Heman Allen to Philadelphia to deliver this petition.

During the spring and summer of 1776 conditions on the northern border became increasingly more threatening. The withdrawal of Continental forces from Canada left the Champlain Valley wide open to invasion. As a result, Thomas Chittenden journeyed south to seek out a safer homesite, and since he was near Dorset, he served as a delegate at the third convention, which assembled in that town on July 24, 1776.

This convention marked Chittenden's first formal participation in the political affairs of the Grants. Its agenda extended well beyond the earlier Dorset conventions in two important respects. First, it was a much larger gathering of forty-six delegates, representing thirty-one western and northern towns and one eastern town. Joseph Bowker of Rutland was appointed to chair the meeting. Other delegates representing the northern towns were Thomas Chittenden (Williston), Ira Allen (Colchester), Isaac Lawrence (Hinesburg), Lemuel Bradley (Burlington), Brown Chamberlain (Jericho), and Heman Allen (Middlebury). In addition, for the first time, two delegates attended from an eastern town. They were Josiah Fish and Captain Samuel Fletcher of Townshend. At the time Fletcher was serving as a member of the Cumberland County Committee of Safety.[13]

Second, this convention considered a larger agenda than the previous Dorset meetings. One of the reasons for calling this third convention in Dorset was to hear a report from Heman Allen regarding the petition to the Continental Congress. The reaction of the New York congressional delegation against the petition had been so strong that Allen withdrew it on May 8 rather than risk its defeat in a congressional vote. Only one week later, on May 15, 1776, Congress passed a resolution recommending that "where no government sufficient to the exigencies of the affairs has been hitherto established," the colonies should adopt their own governments "as shall . . . best conduce to the happiness and safety of their constituents."[14] Hence, although the members of Congress favored creating governments within the thirteen existing colonies, they refused to provide any type of recognition for the Grants. In essence, Vermont lacked a colonial precedent on which it could base its claims to statehood.

This inaction by the Continental Congress resulted in a new surge of activism on the part of the western leaders. As soon as the delegates at the third Dorset convention heard Heman Allen's report, they orchestrated a response to the congressional rebuff. Although this was his first appearance at any of the conventions, Thomas Chittenden immediately found himself in the middle of events, and he was appointed to serve on four important committees during the next two days. On the first day of the convention, July 24, 1776, he was named to a committee to examine the report of Heman Allen and make recommendations thereon. The next day, after hearing the committee's report, the convention voted "that application [should] be made to the inhabitants of [these] Grants to form the same into a separate District." The delegates, cleverly alluding to the Continental Congress's call for the colonies to form their own independent governments, voted to approve an Act of Association, which read:

> This Convention being fully sensible that it is the Will and Pleasure of the honorable Continental Congress. . . . We the subscribers inhabitants of the District of Land commonly called and known by the name of the New Hampshire Grants, do voluntarily and solemnly engage under all the ties held sacred amongst mankind, at the risque of our lives and fortunes to defend by arms the United American States against the Hostile attempts of British Fleets and Armies until the present unhappy controversy between the two countries shall be settled.[15]

The Act of Association was approved by a vote of forty-nine to one (Thomas Brayton of Clarendon was the only dissenter). In an effort to put some muscle into the resolution, the convention then voted unanimously that any person or persons inhabiting the New Hampshire Grants who shall in the future subscribe to any association other than the one adopted by this convention "shall be deemed enemies to the Common Cause of the New Hampshire Grants." [16]

During the second day of the convention, Chittenden was appointed to three more committees. Specifically, the convention voted that he and Colonel Seth Warner be a committee to present a petition to the commander-in-chief of the northern department of the Continental army requesting his assistance in defending the Grants. In addition, Chittenden was appointed to serve on a nine-member Committee of Appeals to decide matters relating to hostilities with Britain. This group was the forerunner of the Committee of War first appointed in September 1776 and later known as the Board of War. The final committee Chittenden served on was a three-member group that prepared instructions for a larger committee designated to discuss the act of association with people on the east side of the Grants and to secure their support if possible. The other two members of this group were Dr. Jonas Fay and Lieutenant Ira Allen.[17]

Thomas Chittenden's debut as a political leader at the third Dorset convention was very impressive. Some of the delegates were not appointed to serve on any committees, so Chittenden's four assignments indicate that he was already being considered as a potential leader in any new government the westerners could create in the New Hampshire Grants.

The fourth, and final, Dorset convention took place two months later on September 25, 1776. Forty-four delegates attended from twenty-five towns west of the Green Mountains. Of even more importance, eleven additional delegates attended from eight towns east of the mountains and two other eastern towns sent letters to the convention. Three of the most important eastern delegates were Dr. Reuben Jones of Rockingham, Colonel Benjamin Carpenter of Guilford, and Ebenezer Hoisington of Windsor.

Once the proceedings started Thomas Chittenden was appointed to serve on an eight-member program committee that presented a series of recommendations to the main body of delegates. The most important of these instructed the convention "that suitable application be made to form that District of Lands, commonly called and known by the name of the New Hampshire Grants, into a separate district." After the delegates approved this recommendation, they moved more cautiously by passing a provisional recommendation that stated:

> we do therefore vote that any Law or Laws, Direction or Directions, we may, for the time being, receive from the State of New York will not in future be accepted neither shall we hold ourselves to be bound by them.[18]

Both of these votes provided momentum for the so-called "New State" independence movement. The delegates were aware that they still faced a profound political problem, however. Although fifty-eight delegates from thirty-five different towns attended this fourth Dorset convention, it could hardly claim to be representative of the inhabitants in the Grants. Most of the delegates to these conventions were either self-selected or were chosen by a local committee without a popular vote by town residents. In addition, the census estimates of the inhabitants of the Grants in 1776 ranged from 14,000 to 25,500.[19] Most of these people lived in the southeastern towns of Cumberland County, which had sent only a small number of delegates to any of the Dorset conventions because support for New York was still very strong in this area. Consequently, the delegates at Dorset constituted only a tiny fraction of the total population in the Grants, and technically they were acting without any formal authority.

Nevertheless, in an attempt to build more widespread public support for their actions, the delegates appointed a committee of four members, including Thomas Chittenden, to draw up a covenant that emphasized their claim to legal authority. This covenant read:

> We, the subscribers, inhabitants of that district of Lands commonly called and known by the name of the New Hampshire Grants, being legally delegated and authorized to transact the public and political affairs of the aforesaid District of Lands, for ourselves and our constituents, do solemnly covenant and engage that, for the time being, we will strictly and religiously adhere to the several resolves of this or a future Convention constituted in Said district by the free voice of the Friends to American Liberties, that shall not be repugnant to the resolves of the honorable Continental Congress relative to the General Cause of America.[20]

Despite the fact that none of the four Dorset conventions had, as yet, received any broad base of public support, the delegates were bold enough to take a number of actions to indicate they were intent on exercising some of the major functions of government. They appointed a "Board of War" (which included Thomas Chittenden as a member), adopted a code of rules for discipline of the militia, and even provided for the building of a jail at Manchester "for securing Tories," with Lieutenant Martin Powell as the jail keeper. This latter action is most intriguing. Here was a group of entrepreneurial state builders whose first act of capital construction was a log jail and whose first civil service appointment was a military jail keeper.

In a further effort to broaden their base of public support, the delegates took a final action aimed directly at northeastern Gloucester County. They had been unable to secure backing from Jacob Bayley of Newbury, and "the lack of his support meant the lack of the support of Gloucester County . . . [since] . . . without him they were without the strongest moral force to be found in any single character on the Grants." [21] In an attempt to flatter Bayley, the convention asked him to serve on a joint committee to request inhabitants of Gloucester County to sign the Association covenant. In August 1776 Jacob Bayley had been appointed to serve as a brigadier general in the New York militia, and he was not interested in becoming involved with the Grants "New State" independence coalition.

When the fourth Dorset convention adjourned, the delegates agreed to reconvene in the eastern town of Westminster on October 30, 1776. In September, however, the settlers in the Grants became greatly alarmed as a result of the movements of the British fleet on Lake Champlain. On September 28 "a council of war was held at the home of Col. Chittenden in Williston," and the small garrison of officers agreed to abandon their stations on the Onion River and march south to the Otter Creek area.[22] The northern frontier had become too dangerous, and the Chittenden family fled to safety in the south. According to one account, they traveled on foot, with their provisions and clothing carried on two horses. They followed marked trees on a trail down to Castleton, where presumably they met with Chittenden's sister, Elisheba Evarts, and her family. From Castleton they went to Danby.[23]

Thomas Chittenden missed the next convention, which was held in Westminster in October 1776. Only seventeen delegates from six western and nine eastern towns managed to attend. At the time of the meeting the inhabitants of the territory were in turmoil because of the defeat of the small American naval force commanded by Benedict Arnold on Lake Champlain and an expected attack by the British on Ticonderoga. As a result, the Westminster session was brief, and, since the turnout was so low, the delegates did not attempt to take any major actions. They did agree to publish a pamphlet to set forth their case for a separate state.

It was not until January 15, 1777, that another convention was held in Westminster. Attendance remained low because of the difficult military situation, but Thomas Chittenden managed to attend along with twenty-three other delegates from six western and eleven eastern towns. This convention was extremely significant because the delegates declared their independence as a new state for the first time, only six months after the original thirteen colonies had taken this same action. On the opening day of the convention, a three-member committee of Leonard Spaulding of Dummerston, Ebenezer Hoisington of Windsor, and Thomas Murdock of Norwich reported that "we find by examination that more than three-fourths of the people in Cumberland and Gloucester counties, that have acted, are for a new state; the rest we view as neuters." [24] It was not clear exactly how this figure was derived, but since all three members were from eastern towns, this report provided the impetus for the delegates to the convention to draft a Declaration of Independence.

A five-member committee consisting of Colonel Thomas Chittenden (still listed as being from Williston), Nathan Clark and John Burham of Bennington, Jacob Burton of Norwich, and Ebenezer Hoisington of Windsor was appointed for this purpose. The committee drafted a resolution, which read in part as follows:

> This convention whose members are duly chosen by the free voice of their constituents in the several towns, on the New Hampshire Grants, in public meeting assembled, in our own names, and in behalf of our constituents, do hereby proclaim and publicly declare that the district of territory comprehending and usually known by the name and description of the New Hampshire Grants, of right ought to be, and is hereby declared forever hereafter to be a separate, free and independent jurisdiction or State by the name of NEW CONNECTICUT. [25]

Thus, the delegates voted to make a clean break from New York by declaring the creation of a new state. In addition to serving on the committee that drafted the Declaration of Independence, Thomas Chittenden was appointed—along with Heman Allen, Reuben Jones, and Jonas Fay—to serve as a delegate to take the new state's request for recognition to the Continental Congress in Philadelphia. Jacob Bayley was also invited to serve in this delegation, but he declined the invitation.

The fact that Chittenden was asked to make this trip indicates how quickly he had taken on a major leadership role in the Grants. There were no other obvious candidates who were as mature and experienced as Chittenden. Ethan Allen was a prisoner-of-war in England, and once Jacob Bayley declined to serve on this delegation, Chittenden became the senior member of the group at the age of forty-six. Chittenden was the only delegate at the January convention in Westminster who had extensive political experience. His town government service in Salisbury, his work as a member of the Connecticut General Assembly, and his service as a colonel in the Connecticut militia prepared him to meet the challenges facing the leaders of the Grants.

Perhaps even more important than his age and experience was the fact that Chittenden was acceptable to all the major factions in the Grants. He knew the Allen family from their days together in Salisbury, so they trusted and respected him. Chittenden's religious views were also acceptable to the Bennington area New Lights, as well as to the older eastside leaders such as General Bayley. "Thomas Chittenden was thrust to the fore by the old-timers as a compromise candidate for leadership. It was clear that General Bayley would not support any one of the leaders of the Green Mountain Boys, whom he cordially detested. Chittenden, however, as a newcomer had had no part in the earlier riotous activity, although they knew him well enough to believe him 'safe.' He did not betray their expectations." [26]

The Vermont Constitution

Two important developments in the spring of 1777 were destined to have an impact on the future of the Grants. First, although the four delegates were unsuccessful in gaining congressional recognition for the new state when they traveled to Philadelphia on April 8, 1777, they were able to meet with Dr. Thomas Young, an old friend of Ethan Allen and a prominent Pennsylvania radical. Young gave the four men a copy of the new Pennsylvania Constitution. He urged them to use this as a model when they returned home to write their own state constitution. In addition, he suggested that "New Connecticut" was a poor choice for a name. It was already being used by a group of settlers in the Wyoming Valley area of northeastern Pennsylvania, so Young urged the delegates to call their new republic Vermont.[27]

A second significant event took place on May 8, 1777, when the New York legislature adopted a very conservative state constitution that perpetuated property qualifications for voting. In addition, this new constitution disregarded the towns and established electoral districts. "If there was one article in the Yankee's political creed to which he was attached, it was that each town was an independent entity, and as such, entitled to have its own representative in the general legislative body." [28] Instead, the New York Constitution limited the Grants to only nine of the seventy members in the state assembly and to only three of the twenty-four state senators. Finally, and "far more threatening, the constitution affirmed all land grants of the colony of New York, invalidating the deeds held by nearly every settler in Vermont." [29]

Members of the Bennington Party, with their usual political astuteness, quickly managed to circulate copies of New York's "aristocratic" constitution to the populist settlers throughout the Grants. The results were disastrous for New York. The impact in Gloucester County was particularly important because it caused General Jacob Bayley to finally withdraw his own political support from New York. In June Bayley wrote the following letter to the New York Assembly:

> Gentlemen: I acknowledge the receipt of an ordinance from you for the election of governor, lieutenant-governor, and senators and representatives, etc., but I am happy to think that our people will not choose to sit in the State of New York. The people before they saw your constitution were not willing to trouble themselves with a separation from New York, but now, almost to a man, they are violently for it.[30]

On June 4, 1777, seventy-two delegates from twenty-two western towns and twenty-six eastern towns gathered for a convention in Windsor. For the first time Jacob Bayley of Newbury was in attendance. Thomas Chittenden was there, as were both Ira and Heman Allen. Once again, Joseph Bowker of Rutland served as chairman, and Jonas Fay was the clerk. The minutes of this first Windsor convention are very fragmentary, but it is clear that, at this time, the delegates changed the name of the state from New Connecticut to Vermont, and they also agreed to schedule a Constitutional Convention in Windsor in July.

One month later, on July 2, 1777, the second convention assembled in Windsor to adopt a formal state constitution and to take any other measures deemed to be necessary. At this point General Burgoyne was in command of a force of 8,500 British soldiers and Hessian mercenaries that was advancing down Lake Champlain in a major assault designed to split the American colonies in two and thus end the Revolutionary War with a British victory. As a result, only thirty-eight delegates from twenty-six towns, fairly evenly divided between the east and west sides of the Green Mountains, were able to attend. Joseph Bowker again served as chairman and Jonas Fay was the clerk. Thomas Chittenden, Ira Allen, and Heman Allen were again

From July 2–8, 1777, "new state" town delegates met in Windsor to adopt the Vermont Constitution. Known today as "Constitution House," local sources indicate that this building was Elijah West's tavern. It was later restored as a historic site and museum. (University of Vermont Special Collections)

in attendance. Key leaders from the eastside towns were Jacob Bayley of Newbury, Benjamin Carpenter of Guilford, Joseph Marsh of Hartford, Thomas Chandler, Jr., of Chester, Ebenezer Hoisington of Windsor, Reuben Jones of Rockingham, and Samuel Fletcher of Townshend.

Once again, the records of this convention are incomplete, but it is clear the delegates were working under tremendous pressure because of the British invasion in the west, which led to the evacuation of Fort Ticonderoga. According to Ira Allen's account, the delegates were ready to leave Windsor when a severe thunderstorm struck. Trapped by the storm, the delegates got back to work and approved the constitution, which was read paragraph by paragraph. Once they completed this task, the convention appointed a Council of Safety to act as Vermont's new government during the recess. [31]

There are no complete records of the convention debates, but we do have precise copies of the constitution that was adopted in July 1777. Thomas Chittenden, Heman Allen, Jonas Fay, and Reuben Jones, the four men who had visited with Dr. Thomas Young in Philadelphia, almost certainly helped to draft the Vermont constitution, as it was based on the Pennsylvania model that Dr. Young had suggested. Ira Allen also played an important role. [32]

Although Pennsylvania's document provided its foundation, the Vermont Constitution contains "twenty-seven substantive changes from the Pennsylvania original. Many sections were the same, word for word. Both constitutions provided for a single assembly, an executive council, and a supreme court. But the Vermont Convention altered the provisions for all three branches, and the changes were more numerous and important than usually recognized." [33]

Over the years some of the changes have served as a source of pride for Vermont, particularly the opening declaration of rights, which abolishes slavery and eliminates property qualifications for male suffrage. Other changes were more controversial. It proved to be very significant that the Vermont framers eliminated the Pennsylvania prohibition on continuous reelection of statewide officers, as well as the prohibition against any one individual holding multiple offices at the same time. The Vermont Constitution also omitted Pennsylvania's section on the organization of the judiciary.

In addition, although the Vermont Constitution provided "the supreme legislative power shall be vested in a House of Representatives," it did not clearly enumerate these legislative powers. Instead, Section XIV created a special executive body known as the "Governor and Council" and granted it the power of legislative review by stating "to the end that laws, before they be enacted, may be more maturely considered . . . all bills of public nature shall be first laid before the Governor and Council for their perusal and proposals of amendment . . . before they are read in the General Assembly for the last time." [34] This provision increased the power of a relatively small group of executive officers, who were able to gain, and maintain, control over the entire government.

The Council of Safety

Although the constitution provided for elected officers of government, General Burgoyne's invasion and the British advance down through the Champlain Valley made it impossible to hold any elections at the time the constitution was adopted. Instead, members of the convention decided to delegate the entire authority of the new government—executive as well as legislative and judicial—to a small group of twelve men known as the Council of Safety. The convention delegates designated this body to rule Vermont until the election of officers could take place at some unspecified later date. In the interim, the powers of the council were unlimited and absolute. "Its acts and orders for the time being had the force of laws; it was itself the executor of them . . . it exercised judicial powers; it served as a board of war; it punished public enemies, or reprieved them; it transacted business civil and military with other states and Congress . . . it was THE STATE." [35]

The council's secretary, Ira Allen, left enough records to indicate that this group was dominated by members from western Vermont. Nine of the twelve members who served on this body were from towns west of the Green Mountains. They were Thomas Chittenden, Jonas Fay, Moses Robinson, Ira Allen, Joseph Fay, Jeremiah Clark, Nathan Clark, Heman Allen, and Matthew Lyon. Once Thomas Chittenden, Matthew Lyon, and Ira Allen moved south, they were able to maintain continuous contact with the Fays, the Clarks, and Moses Robinson, who were all living in Bennington. These men dominated the council. The only three council members from towns east of the Green Mountains were General Jacob Bayley of Newbury, Paul Spooner of Hartland, and Benjamin Carpenter of Guilford, who replaced Benjamin Spencer of Clarendon after he deserted to the British in December 1777. [36] Despite their geographical diversity, the members on the council shared a common frontier background and heritage. As historian Aleine Austin has noted, "the men who gained control of political power were 'new men' in the sense that they lacked the social status generally considered a prerequisite for political office in the colonial period." [37]

The task the Council of Safety faced was extremely daunting. It had no source of revenue at its command, and the military situation was deteriorating. After taking Fort Ticonderoga and defeating Seth Warner's forces at Hubbardton, Burgoyne's invading army advanced rapidly toward New York State. At its first organizational meeting, held in Manchester on July 11, 1777, the Council of Safety elected Thomas Chittenden as president, Jonas Fay as vice president, and Ira Allen and Joseph Fay as secretaries. Less than one year after he attended his first convention in Dorset in July 1776, Thomas Chittenden emerged as the major governmental leader in Vermont. During the next eight months the Council of Safety met at the Catamount Tavern in Bennington, which served as the seat of Vermont's official government.

First and foremost, the Council of Safety was responsible for financing and coordinating the defenses necessary to insure the survival of the new state. In addition to organizing the militia, it directed troop movements, acquired supplies, obtained foodstuffs, oversaw the building of fortifications, and helped coordinate the work of local councils of safety. In order to support the militia and raise a regiment—which was to play a crucial role in the Battle of Bennington—Ira Allen is credited with proposing that revenues should be raised by sequestration of the personal property of Tories and other enemies of Vermont. "The Council of Safety appointed at least thirteen men to act as commissioners of sequestration and sale during July and August, 1777. . . . After trial by at least thirteen Committee of Safety members from nearby towns, movable property [not real estate], appraised by an outside authority could be sold to pay whatever judgment was exacted." These actions taken against the "enemies" of Vermont also helped to solidify the authority of the Council of Safety by stifling dissenters and opponents of the new government. [38]

On August 16, 1777, the military pressure on western Vermont was partially relieved at the Battle of Bennington, where Colonel John Stark's New Hampshire troops, reinforced by Colonel Seth Warner's Vermont militia, defeated a force of British and German dragoons under the command of Colonel Freidrich Baum. This unexpected defeat was a stunning setback for the British, and it provided the first clear sign that General Burgoyne's invasion force was in serious trouble. Less than two months later Burgoyne's army suffered a crushing defeat at Bemis Heights near Saratoga. The immediate British threat to the northern frontier temporarily disappeared when Burgoyne surrendered to General Gates on October 17, 1777.[39]

Although the British military threat had temporarily eased, during the fall and winter of 1777–78 the Vermont Council of Safety was forced to deal with an astonishing range of issues, as this brief sampling of its official dispatches indicates:

Bennington Nov. 16, 1777
Mary Reynolds is permitted to Send for her Gray horse and keep him in her possession until further orders from this Council.
Joseph Fay Sec.y

Bennington 20th Dec.r 1777
This day given Colonel Chittenden an order to Take one

Cow belonging to this State Now in the Custody of John
Conner of Manchester which Cow is to be appraised and an
acc.t Returned to this Council.
By order of Council
Joseph Fay Sec.

Bennington January 3, 1778
Resolved that Captain John Fasset Jr. be & he is hereby ap-
pointed a Commissioner of Sequestration for the Town of
Arlington. Commission Instructions Dilivered
By order of Council
Joseph Fay Sec.y

Bennington 30 January 1778
This day Major Jeremiah Clark is permitted to Transport
nine bushels of wheat out of this State
By Order of Council
Thomas Chittenden [40]

In addition to discharging its daily responsibilities, the Council of Safety also considered more lofty affairs of state. On December 24, 1777, the council called for a second constitutional
convention in Windsor, where a preamble was added to the
original document that had been approved during the previous
July. According to a number of accounts, this preamble was
drafted by Ira Allen and Thomas Chittenden. On February 6,
1778, Thomas Chittenden issued a proclamation to the people
of Vermont announcing that the state constitution would be
distributed prior to the election of state officers and members
of the Vermont General Assembly, which was scheduled to take
place on the first Tuesday in March.

During the eight months of its existence prior to the election of March 3, 1778, the Council of Safety realized many
significant achievements. Of most importance, it had secured
the defense and survival of the new state. During the winter of

1777–78 conditions in the Grants were incredibly harsh, and as a result of the British invasion the previous summer, many homes were burned to the ground and settlements left in rubble. Feeding the people was one of the council's most difficult problems . "The people who had been driven from their homes were so destitute of grain, both for food and for seed, that the council prohibited, under heavy penalties, the transportation of any wheat, rye, corn, flour, or meal out of the state without a permit, except Continental stores. Suffering privations that can now be scarcely understood, these people struggled through the long and bitter winter." [41]

The Council of Safety also provided a training ground for a small group of governing elite, who gained valuable leadership experience. All but one of the twelve members of the council were later elected to positions of leadership in the new state government. The only exception was Heman Allen, who became ill at the Battle of Bennington and died in May 1778. By working together, the members of the council gained an understanding of the nature of political power, which they later used with great effectiveness. The experience of the council members proved to be essential in helping Vermont deal with a variety of external and internal threats during the next several years. Although Burgoyne's army had surrendered after its defeat at Saratoga, there was no guarantee the British would not attempt a second invasion down the Lake Champlain corridor in the future.

The new state government also needed experienced leaders to face a variety of thorny problems at home. New York remained adamantly opposed to the new state, and it was able to pressure the Continental Congress to refuse any official recognition of Vermont. There was widespread dissent within the Grants, especially in the southeastern towns, where some extremely vocal Cumberland County residents expressed a strong desire to retain their ties with New York. The Brattleboro town meeting, held on March 3, 1778, the day of the first statewide

Vermont elections, voted to send a protest to the new assembly of the "pretended state of Vermont" for disavowing allegiance to New York as an act tending to "disunite the friends of America in the present important contest with Great Britain." [42] At the same time that many residents in the southeastern towns were expressing their allegiance to New York, a number of towns in the northern Connecticut River Valley were anxious to unite with nearby New Hampshire.

A little more than a week after the first state elections, the Council of Safety issued its final order:

> State of Vermont In Council: Windsor, 12 March 1778
> This Council do recommend to the Several Gentlemen appointed by the freemen of the Several Towns within this State to Represent them in General Assembly, to Assemble to the Town house in this place immediately & to form a house of Assembly by choosing a Speaker & Clerk and make Report of your proceedings hereon as Soon as may be to this Council
> By order of Council
> Thos. Chittenden Pr.t [43]

The newly elected representatives met in Windsor on March 12 and formed themselves into a general assembly. Unfortunately, their names were not entered into the journals of that session. According to Benjamin Hall's history, "it is certain that fifty or more were present; twenty-three were representatives from nineteen towns in Cumberland County. Agreeable to the Vermont Constitution, a committee was chosen to count the votes of the people, and Thomas Chittenden was declared Governor. At the same time, Joseph Marsh was elected Deputy Governor, and Col. Ira Allen Treasurer. Twelve Councilors were also chosen, and were formed into a body known as the Governor and Council." [44] Thus, Thomas Chittenden was designated to continue in the role he had performed on the Council of Safety as the executive leader of the new government.

The challenges this government faced were made even more difficult by the revolutionary ideology upon which Vermont based its existence. This ideology was articulated in the preamble to the Vermont Constitution, which asserted that the people had a right to establish their own government. Although Ethan Allen was still being held in England as a prisoner, much of the credit for this idea must be given to Allen's early defense of the New Hampshire Grants from the encroachments of New York. As soon as the Revolutionary War began, Ethan Allen seized the opportunity "to annihilate the old quarrel with the governor of New York by swallowing it up in the general conflict for liberty." [45] As Michael Bellesiles points out, "Allen's greatest political accomplishment proved [to be] his carefully wrought linkage of the American cause and republican ideology with the Grants settlers' claims to their own land and institutions. Allen clothed the Grants cause in the language of American resistance to Parliament and King, equating the struggle of the Sons of Liberty with that of the Green Mountain Boys." [46]

The major difference between Vermont and the other new American states grew out of the fact that Vermont had never existed as a colony established under the authority of the British Crown. As a result, Vermont's leaders based their claim to statehood on the radical argument that it had been created by the will of its people from a state of nature. Since Vermont's constitution was never formally ratified by the people, some observers have questioned this claim. [47]

This revolutionary idea—that the people could form their own government—became known as the Vermont Doctrine. Under the best of circumstances, the Continental Congress was not about to recognize Vermont as a new state in light of New York's opposition. In addition, the concept of the Vermont Doctrine created fear among many conservative congressional leaders, who were suspicious of any broad exercise of popular democracy. Such fear was particularly strong in the southern states, which faced perceived threats of separatist movements within their own borders. "When a South Carolina Congressman assured the New York delegation of his state's support in opposing Vermont's application, he explained that he and many of his southern colleagues believed that 'the consequences of their [Vermont's] holding their independence would be a means of producing fifty new states, and therefore must not be allowed.'" [48]

In March 1778, when its first assembly gathered in Windsor, the new Republic of Vermont, not as yet an official state within the Union, was involved in three different revolutions, one external, one internal, and one ideological. It was obvious that the leaders of Vermont would have to exercise a very high degree of political skill and diplomacy in order to survive such a difficult series of challenges.

CHAPTER IV

Defending the Republic
(1778–1779)

W̶hen Thomas Chittenden was elected governor in March
1778, it seemed there was little likelihood that Vermont
would ever become a viable state.[1] In light of the volatile political situation within the state, western leaders saw the March
1778 elections as a calculated gamble. They knew that Vermont would not be recognized, internally or externally, on the
merits of a constitution alone. In order to legitimize Vermont
in the eyes of Congress, the government had to be elected by
the people in the Grants. This was a risky challenge, because
Vermont's leaders had to create the appearance of consensus
when one did not, in fact, exist.

Elections in eighteenth-century New England were based
on the smallest political unit, the town. This aided the western
independence movement. If a referendum of all settlers in the
Grants had been the test of statehood in 1778, it might well
have failed. Instead, it was much easier to gain a consensus of
towns. By fostering alliances during the earlier conventions,
western leaders had secured representation from many eastern

towns by convincing only a handful of men to participate in state affairs.

A good example was the town of Guilford in southeastern Vermont. Most Guilford residents favored honoring New York's claims to the land in the Grants. These Guilford Yorkers joined with members of seven other nearby towns and signed a protest arguing that "the pretended state of Vermont" would: "weaken the authority of the Continental Congress, disunite the friends of America, and stimulate a spirit of separation and sedition which may end in the ruin of the United States. We think it the duty of every friend to the independence of America, more especially in the 'Grants,' to use their strenuous efforts to suppress or check this offspring of anarchy in its infancy." [2]

Despite this intense opposition, a small group of Guilford settlers, led by Benjamin Carpenter and John Shepardson, forged an alliance with the western leaders. These two men organized their own town meeting, and Carpenter ended up representing Guilford at the first session of the Vermont General Assembly after the initial Vermont elections were held in March 1778.

Following a bitterly cold winter, on Tuesday, March 3, 1778, thirty-eight towns elected forty-nine representatives to the Vermont General Assembly and entrusted them to deliver sealed ballots for governor, lieutenant governor, a twelve-member executive council, and a treasurer. Only fifteen of these towns were western, while twenty-three towns were from the east side of the Green Mountains. Although election records are nearly nonexistent, it was probable that a higher percentage of inhabitants voted in the west than in the east, but the east won more seats in the first assembly by virtue of the number of towns represented. According to the Vermont Constitution, towns with eighty or more taxable inhabitants could send two representatives to the assembly. Six of the eleven towns that sent two representatives were east of the Green Mountains, giving the east an even larger majority.

The elections singled out the most ardent supporters of Vermont's independence movement for the top offices. As has already been noted, Thomas Chittenden was chosen governor and Ira Allen was elected treasurer. Other western leaders who were elected to the Governor and Council were Jonas Fay, Jeremiah Clark, and Moses Robinson of Bennington, Joseph Bowker of Rutland, and Timothy Brownson from Sunderland. Easterners on the council were Benjamin Carpenter of Guilford, Paul Spooner of Hartland, Jacob Bayley of Newbury, Benjamin Emmons of Woodstock, and Peter Olcott and Thomas Murdock of Norwich. When no candidate obtained a majority of votes, the assembly appointed Joseph Marsh, an eastern leader from Hartford, as lieutenant governor with the concurrence of the Governor and Council. In addition, the assembly appointed Nathan Clark of Bennington, a former member of the Council of Safety, as its speaker.[3]

On March 12, 1778, the various town representatives met at the opening session of the Vermont General Assembly in Windsor. Only five days later the assembly divided the state into two counties—Bennington, west of the Green Mountains, and Unity to the east. On March 26 the assembly passed an important act that authorized the confiscation of Tory estates. Prior to this time, confiscation had been limited to moveable property, such as cattle, crops, clothing, household goods, and farm equipment. At this point, however, the legislature decided to grant the Governor and Council the extraordinary judicial power to seize the real estate of Tories as well. The Governor and Council divided itself into two courts of confiscation, one for each side of the state. Governor Chittenden and the six western councilors formed one court, while Lieutenant Governor Marsh and the six eastern councilors constituted the other court.[4]

The western court, chaired by Governor Chittenden, turned out to be much more aggressive. According to Sarah Kalinoski's analysis, "in the six months from March to October, 1778, when [only] one parcel of confiscated land was sold in Cumberland

County, the west-side council sold thirty-seven. . . . By November [1780], the commissioners completed at least ninety-eight additional sales. Of these, seventy-five were in Bennington County." [5]

Thus, Chittenden and the new government were ruthless in their attempts to punish the Tories. They also went after the Yorkers in Cumberland County, who they considered to be enemies of the state because they supported New York. Paradoxically, however, the first major challenge facing the state came from New Hampshire towns to the east rather than from New York. When the assembly reconvened in June 1778, regional divisions between the eastern and the western towns quickly became apparent.

The First Eastern Union

Developments within the state of New Hampshire brought about the first power struggle in Vermont politics. New Hampshire settlers along the Connecticut River border felt too far removed from the state's seaboard government in Portsmouth. Organizing around the College Party at Dartmouth, many New Hampshire residents boycotted their own state elections and seized upon the idea of annexing New Hampshire's frontier towns to Vermont.

The inhabitants of the northern Connecticut River Valley towns on both sides of the river welcomed the opportunity for such a union. Many area settlers, such as Jacob Bayley of Newbury, Vermont, and John Hazen of Haverhill, New Hampshire, were close friends.[6] The leadership within the union movement did not come from General Bayley, however, but from Eleazar Wheelock, the President of Dartmouth College; his son-in-law and principal aide, Bezaleel Woodward; and Elisha Paine of Cardigan, New Hampshire. On the eve of Vermont's initial legislative session, the leaders of the College Party organized a coalition of sixteen New Hampshire towns. Agreeing that a union with Vermont was advantageous, they sent a delegation to

Windsor on March 13, just as the Vermont General Assembly was considering its first order of business.

The issue of annexing the New Hampshire towns split the assembly. The conflict it sparked provides clear insights into how Thomas Chittenden and the western leaders managed to gain control of the political agenda in early Vermont. From the outset, they were skeptical about an eastern union. They feared it would hurt the case for Vermont statehood by making enemies in both the New Hampshire government and the Continental Congress. In addition, they realized this move would dilute their own power in the assembly. The proposed union with the New Hampshire towns would shift the political center of the Grants well to the east of the Green Mountains and out of their reach. Western leaders wanted to drop the issue, but their eastern counterparts threatened to withdraw from the assembly if they did so. The two sides compromised by agreeing to submit the matter to the people by holding a referendum on the issue among the Vermont towns.

At this point it was becoming obvious that the western leaders had a formidable opponent in the College Party. The great strength of the western leadership was its incredible cohesion. Not only were a large percentage of its leaders from the Bennington area, but many of them were united by blood or marriage. Another strength of western leaders was their ability to organize. The College Party's leaders also knew how to organize, however. President Wheelock had developed a coalition of sixteen towns that voted to sever political connections with Portsmouth. By uniting friends and family on both sides of the river, the College Party had transformed the border towns of Vermont and New Hampshire into a potent political force. In an effort to counteract this force, the western leaders scheduled the adjourned June session of the assembly in their own stronghold, the town of Bennington.

The strategy proved to be unsuccessful. When the adjourned session met on June 4, 1778, the western leaders suffered their

The Catamount Tavern in Bennington, which was built by Captain Stephen Fay, served as the headquarters for the Green Mountain Boys and as the seat of Vermont's first governmental body, the Council of Safety. The Vermont General Assembly assembled here in June 1778, when the western leaders were unsuccessful in their efforts to block the first East Union. (University of Vermont Special Collections)

first major defeat. The result of the referendum confirmed the eastern union. This result was not a tally of individuals, but of towns. Representatives from each town had used the interim between March and June to convene town meetings, which had voted to either accept or reject the proposed union. The vote was thirty-seven towns for the union and only twelve towns against, which indicates that even some of the western towns supported this proposal

The impact of the state's powerful new eastern majority was felt immediately as a result of the referendum. Although representatives from the sixteen New Hampshire towns would not arrive until the next legislative session in October, the eastern representatives used the referendum as a mandate to pass a series of new laws. The assembly formally approved the union on June 11. Four days later, the assembly "voted to take the incorporated university of Dartmouth under the patronage of this State." In addition, the assembly appointed Reverend Doctor Eleazar Wheelock as a justice of the peace and Bezaleel Woodward, Esquire, Colonel Peter Olcott, Major Joseph Tyler, Patterson Piermont, and Major Isaac Griswold as judges of the superior court.[7] The western leaders had been bypassed—they had completely misjudged the strength of the Unionists. By the time the assembly adjourned on June 18, Governor Chittenden and his western colleagues had become the victims of a major coup d'état by the eastern towns.

The western leaders saw their control of the state slipping away, and they feared that Vermont's chance for recognition in Congress was being jeopardized. Chittenden had lost the initial conflict with his eastern foes, but he was shrewd enough to realize that the final battle was not yet over. On August 22, 1778, Meshech Weare, president of New Hampshire's state council, wrote Chittenden a letter protesting Vermont's meddling in the internal affairs of his state. In response, Chittenden convened a meeting of the Governor and Council.

No formal record was kept, but this meeting probably consisted strictly of westerners. The Governor and Council prepared a response to New Hampshire, and Governor Chittenden decided to send Ethan Allen, lately freed from two years of British captivity, to Congress. While in Philadelphia, Ethan Allen ascertained the prevailing congressional opinion about Vermont's eastern union. Later, eastern legislators and councilors would complain that they had not been informed of this meeting and had not authorized Ethan Allen's mission. It is apparent that Thomas Chittenden and other western leaders were planning a counterattack of their own.

By this time the College Party dominated the Vermont General Assembly through the eastern legislative majority. State elections were held again on the eve of the October 1778 session, the official start of the new legislative year. These elections did little to change the state's executive leadership. Thomas Chittenden was reelected governor and Ira Allen continued as treasurer. The legislature admitted fifteen new representatives, however, with seven from western towns, two from the southeast, and six from the northeast. In addition, ten of the sixteen towns from New Hampshire sent representatives to the October session. This gave the eastern Unionists twenty-six towns and thirty members out of a total of seventy-four legislators. Several additional swing votes from western and southeastern towns gave the Unionists a majority, and the assembly elected the ambitious Dartmouth representative, Bezaleel Woodward from Dresden, as its clerk.

When the October 1778 session convened in Windsor, Ethan Allen dropped the first bombshell on the legislature. Ethan, having just been elected as a representative from the town of Arlington, obtained permission to address "his Excellency the Governor, the Honourable the Council, and the Representatives of the freemen of the State of Vermont." He explained that Vermont's annexation of the New Hampshire towns aided Vermont's enemies in Congress, chiefly the State of New York. He argued that although he could refute most of New York's claims, he was at a loss to justify the east union. He then offered one stirring bit of advice:

> I am sufficiently authorized to offer it as my opinion that, except this state recede from such a union immediately, the whole power of the confederacy of the United States of America will join to annihilate the state of Vermont, and vindicate the right[s] of New Hampshire. . . .[8]

Allen's unwillingness to justify the eastern union to Congress infuriated the Unionists in the council and assembly. In a carefully orchestrated follow-up, Governor Chittenden revealed that the letter he had received from Meshech Weare, president of the New Hampshire Council, directly supported Ethan Allen's claims. The easterners were rocked by this onslaught by Allen and Chittenden, but they managed to hold their union together. On October 20 the assembly appointed committees to prepare letters to both Congress and New Hampshire defending the eastern union. The western leaders had weakened the union, but it still posed a considerable threat to their power.

On October 21 the assembly seemed to have returned to normal. The eastern legislators sought to cement their gains by extending county government to the sixteen New Hampshire towns east of the Connecticut River. They brought a vote to the floor to determine "whether the counties, of this state, shall remain as they were established by the Assembly of this state in March last." When this vote was approved by thirty-five yeas to twenty-six nays, the eastern representatives were stunned. They had assumed the assembly would modify the previous March vote and enlarge Cumberland County to encompass the New Hampshire towns.

They immediately proposed a second vote: "Whether the towns east of the river included in the Union with this state, shall be included in the County of Cumberland." This vote was closer, but the Assembly rejected the proposal, this time by thirty-three nays versus twenty-eight yeas. The easterners, in disbelief, immediately asked for a third vote, once again re-phrasing the question: "Whether the towns on the east side of [the] Connecticut River who are included by union within this State shall be erected into a distinct county by themselves." The outcome was exactly the same—thirty-three nays to twenty-eight yeas. Not one legislator had changed his vote.[9]

The eastern legislators were outraged. Twenty-four of them signed a resolution chastising the assembly for failing to pro-vide any county government for the sixteen New Hampshire towns. They claimed that this omission violated the sixth ar-ticle of the Declaration of Rights of the 1777 Vermont Con-stitution, which specified that government is, or ought to be, instituted for the common benefit, protection, and security of the people.

At this point the eastern Unionists attempted to cripple Vermont's government by resigning en masse from the assembly. On October 23 Lieutenant Governor Joseph Marsh of Hartford, council members Peter Olcott and Thomas Murdock, both of Norwich, and many other legislators from Connecticut River Valley towns in both Vermont and New Hampshire withdrew. They assumed that their resignations, which left the assembly without a quorum, would force it either to dissolve in accordance with the provisions of Vermont's 1777 constitution, or to readmit the New Hampshire towns and provide them with a county government. Since seventy-four members had answered the roll at the beginning of the session, fifty were required for a quorum. After the mass withdrawal of the easterners, only Speaker of the House Thomas Chandler, Jr., of Chester and forty other members remained. These remaining members voted to continue the October session, however, where they enacted some very important business.

In retrospect, it is easy to see how the western leaders managed to destroy the first eastern union. During deliberations on the three county government resolutions, representatives from a number of the southeastern towns switched their votes to join the western camp. Then, on October 24, the final day before adjournment, the remaining assembly members elected a committee to choose five hundred and ninety six proprietors to share in a large tract of land called the Two-Heroes (later to become the towns of South Hero, North Hero, and Grand Isle). This gigantic town was the first large grant of land made under the authority of the State of Vermont. Governor Chittenden, Speaker of the House Thomas Chandler, Jr., members of the Governor and Council (minus Joseph Marsh, Peter Olcott, and Jonathan Murdock), and virtually all of the forty other assembly members who had voted to continue the session were named as proprietors of this new town. In this manner, Vermont's western leaders rewarded those who had supported their position in the assembly.[10]

Once Governor Chittenden and his colleagues had regained control of the assembly, they quickly asserted their authority over the judicial branch as well, naming Moses Robinson of Bennington, John Shepardson of Guilford, John Fassett of Arlington, Thomas Chandler of Chester, and John Troop of Pomfret as superior court judges. Unlike the judges who had been appointed in June, all of these men were veterans of the state's independence movement.

The actions of the western leaders during the first eastern union episode provide a perspective into their political priorities and strategies. It is reasonable to assume that Governor Chittenden and his colleagues were astute enough to be aware of the risks involved in abruptly ending the eastern union. In order to rid Vermont of the College Party, they made a calculated gamble to sacrifice valuable alliances with the northeastern towns. Their action was analogous to that of a surgeon amputating an infected arm—the patient would suffer the loss of an arm but would live. In essence, the western leaders did what they felt was necessary to protect Vermont, even if it meant taking liberties with the state constitution. After all, they reasoned, what good is a constitution without a state?

They did pay a heavy price for their victory, however. Their actions divided Vermont more deeply than ever before. Joseph Marsh, Vermont's former lieutenant governor, provided his version of events to Congress and New Hampshire. On October 23, 1778, he penned a protest defending the position of the Unionists. He also cited the assembly's violation of the constitution by continuing to conduct business despite the lack of a quorum following the departure of the eastern representatives. Marsh believed that a minority in the assembly had overthrown constitutional government in Vermont. He invited "every Town in the Grants on both sides of [the] Connecticut River, whether united with the State of Vermont or not," to send delegates to a convention to consider whether to create a new state in the Connecticut River Valley.[11]

The western leaders moved just as quickly as Marsh to fortify their own position. Governor Chittenden instructed Ira Allen to rush to Portsmouth, New Hampshire, where Allen argued Vermont's case before the New Hampshire Council against Jacob Bayley and Davenport Phelps, who represented the Unionists. Each side claimed they represented the majority of Vermonters. Meshech Weare and the New Hampshire Council considered the confusion of claims and counter claims. Their decision was less than favorable to either group. New Hampshire, as a purely "friendly" measure, laid claim to the entire State of Vermont. Weare explained that this claim would apply only if Vermont was not granted independence by Congress, and then only to save it from New York. This startling verdict was ominous enough, however, to discourage Joseph Marsh and the easterners from taking any further action.

The 1779 Session

Vermont's western leaders used the lull created by the eastern walkout to resume the business of building a state. On February 11, 1779, the assembly reconvened for a very productive follow-up session in Bennington. In addition to formally voting to dissolve the eastern union, the assembly "adopted the common law, as it is generally practiced and understood in the New England states . . . as the common law of this state." [12] Thus, in the future, Vermonters were subject to the precedents of the common [i.e. judge-made] law, as well as the statutory law passed by the Vermont General Assembly. As one observer noted when the assembly first convened, "it began its work under great difficulties. There was not a lawyer . . . to draft bills and criticize the work of unskillful hands. . . . There was no state library, with precedents in printed acts, reports, and legislative journals." [13]

It has already been noted that when Vermont's leaders drafted the 1777 constitution, they had looked to Pennsylvania for their model. In part this was due to the advice of Dr. Thomas Young, but it also reflected the fact that many colonies, including Connecticut and Massachusetts, had not as yet created their own state constitutions. Massachusetts did not ratify its state constitution until 1780, and Connecticut waited until 1818 before it adopted a state constitution. Long before this, however, the Connecticut assembly had passed a large body of statutory law under its original charter of 1662, and Vermont's statutory laws were derived from the laws of Connecticut. Governor Chittenden and many of the other western leaders had lived in Connecticut and were familiar with its laws. And, according to one account, "there is proof of only one book in possession of the first Vermont legislature; and that was the statute book of Connecticut—furnished, I would venture to guess, by Governor Chittenden." [14]

During its 1778–79 legislative sessions, the Vermont General Assembly adopted a host of statutes using the 1769 Connecticut law book as a guide. The assembly copied many of these laws verbatim with little or no debate. On Monday, February 15, 1779, for example, the assembly passed acts concerning bastards, branding, burglary, cattle, divorce, dowries, grand juries, lands, licensing, marriages, replevins, signs, skins and hides, stallions, strays, and taverns. It also passed acts against barratry, breaking the peace, burglary, defamation, forgery, fraud, gaming, lying, murder, manslaughter, perjury, and unseasonable night walking. Interestingly, the final act passed on that day governed the appointment and regulation of attorneys. [15]

Since the Connecticut laws were modeled on the early Massachusetts Bay statutes, penalties for crimes were very severe. Persons found guilty of adultery, polygamy, incest, burglary, counterfeiting, and manslaughter were subject to branding with a hot iron, as well as whipping. Those found guilty of murder, homosexuality, sodomy, arson, rape, high treason, and "highhanded" blasphemy could be put to death. [16]

The assembly passed 102 laws in twelve days during the February session. In the aftermath of the walkout, the members of the assembly increasingly depended on the Governor and Council for advice and expertise. Governor Chittenden and the eight remaining councilors were the state's only full-time leaders. As a result, they created the assembly's agenda, wrote necessary legislation, revised and published laws, raised the militia, and appropriated money. This policy was pragmatic, but it failed to conform to the state's constitution, which required that bills originate in the assembly. At the end of the February 1779 session the assembly attempted to legalize this practice with "An Act for Making the Laws of this State Temporary." [17] In addition, the assembly misinterpreted the constitution when it gave the Governor and Council power to revise and alter laws after they had been passed.

The legislative responsibilities of Thomas Chittenden and the other western leaders were exceeded only by their war powers. Many of them believed the eastern union had been a costly distraction from Vermont's most immediate and important goal: securing the frontier against the British. With the union dissolved, the assembly turned to these leaders to help face military challenges. The assembly appointed the Governor and Council as a court to try "enemies who have assisted or joined the enemy," and, if they were found guilty, to confiscate their estates for the defense of the northern frontier. In addition, the quorum requirement was reduced from seven to four. The assembly also designated the Governor and Council as a Board of War with the exclusive right to direct the war effort, from paying soldiers to building fortifications. The quorum for the Board of War was also changed from seven to four, giving Governor Chittenden and only three other councilors greater ability to quickly respond to crises.[18]

These measures were designed to ensure the defense of the state. They also firmly anchored the state's governmental and war powers in the hands of Thomas Chittenden and a few of his western colleagues. On February 26, 1779, following the adjournment of the assembly, Governor Chittenden expressed his confidence by means of a special proclamation:

WHEREAS the virtuous efforts and laudable exertions of the good people of this State have . . . procured the inestimable blessings of a free and independent government . . . I do hereby strictly require and command all magistrates, justices of the peace, sheriffs, constables, and other civil officers, to be active and vigilant in executing the laws . . . without partiality, favor, or affection.[19]

Despite Chittenden's optimism, Vermont continued to face very challenging problems. It had not as yet received recognition as a state from the Continental Congress, and internal dissension was still widespread in many of the towns in Cumberland County.

The First Cow War

A New York poll of settlers in the towns of Guilford, Brattleboro, Halifax, Marlboro, Wilmington, Dummerston, Newfane, Westminster, Springfield, Weathersfield, Vernon, and Putney conducted in August 1778 had found 480 inhabitants favored New York, 320 supported Vermont, and 185 were indifferent. Enforcing Vermont law in this type of atmosphere was extremely difficult.[20]

In April 1779 a dispute erupted that directly tested Vermont's ability to exercise its jurisdiction in the southeast portion of the Grants. In Putney a militia captain named Daniel Jewet, who held his appointment by the authority of the State of Vermont, chose several Yorkers to fill a militia quota. The Yorkers simply ignored the order. Captain Jewet imposed the customary fine, but the fine was ignored. He then sent his sergeant to confiscate two cows from the offenders, but the Yorkers, outraged by this insult, began gathering at a nearby tavern just before the sale of the cows. When nearly a hundred people assembled they confronted the sergeant and took back the cows.

Colonel Samuel Fletcher, who was in charge of Jewet's regiment, immediately appealed to Governor Chittenden for help.

Chittenden felt obligated to answer the call. Having weathered the walkout from the Vermont General Assembly the previous year, Chittenden and his western colleagues needed to prove that their government was still a viable force throughout the Grants. Governor Chittenden turned to his old friend, Ethan Allen, to intimidate the dissident Yorkers. Ethan's reputation preceded him. Given command of one hundred state militia, he set forth again at the head of a group of Green Mountain Boys. The lessons of the earlier struggle with New York had not been lost on either Chittenden or Allen. Both men understood that Vermont's credibility lay in its ability to respond more quickly and decisively than New York.

Members from nine southeastern towns met in a convention at Brattleboro on May 4, 1779, in anticipation of Allen's raid. The convention pleaded with New York's Governor Clinton to protect the loyal citizens of New York who lived in Cumberland County. The petitioners complained not only about the arbitrary rule of Vermont but also about the divisions within their own communities. These internal differences, amplified by the support of western leaders, had caused "anarchy," harassment, and the loss of property. A committee appointed by the convention urgently sent a letter to Clinton:

> Our situation is truly critical and distressing, we therefore most humbly beseech your Excellency to take the most speedy & efficient Measures for our Relief; otherwise our Persons and Property must be at the disposal of Ethan Allen, which is more dreaded than Death with all its terrors.[21]

The horror of Allen's raid was magnified by the humiliation the southeastern Yorkers felt over their reversal of fortune. Allen, a man they regarded as an outlaw, now possessed the ability to seize their property and jail "respected" citizens under the guise of law and order. Allen played his hand well. After many stirring stump speeches and sword-rattling threats he arrived in the Brattleboro area on May 24. He then helped the local sheriff apprehend forty-four individuals, all of whom held military commissions from the State of New York.

The object of Chittenden's policy was not to punish the Yorkers, but to demonstrate Vermont's authority. Those arrested were housed in the Westminster jail and tried by the state's newly appointed superior court. On June 3, 1779, Governor Chittenden issued a Proclamation of Pardon to all those who had been arrested in Cumberland County. The following day a grateful assembly, meeting in Windsor, elected Ethan Allen brigadier general to command the state militia. At the same time, the assembly elected Ira Allen as surveyor-general of the state. This was the first elected statewide position for Ethan, but not for Ira, who continued to occupy many other public offices.[22]

Shortly after the Cumberland County incident, Governor Chittenden settled in a new home in a southwestern town. On June 10, 1779, John Fassett, the commissioner of confiscation in the probate district of Manchester, Bennington County, signed a deed to Thomas Chittenden providing for the sale of a house and 617 acres of land in Arlington, Vermont, which had formerly been owned by a loyalist named Jehiel Hawley. Chittenden paid the sizable sum of 3,000 pounds for this confiscated house and land, and he and his family moved into Hawley's house, where they were destined to live for the next decade before returning north to Williston.[23]

The Vermont Issue in Congress

Thomas Chittenden's pardons of the Cumberland County insurgents did not prevent New York from continuing to plan the demise of Vermont. Governor Clinton had failed to prevent Vermont from enforcing its authority over southeastern

Yorkers, but he successfully used the Cow War incident to discredit Vermont before Congress. In order to gain the most advantage from the situation, Clinton sent John Jay, his most capable statesman, to Congress. Upon his arrival in Philadelphia, Jay was immediately elected president of Congress.

Jay quickly realized that most congressmen either supported, or were indifferent to, Vermont's claim of independence. In a letter to Clinton, Jay listed the public and private reasons congressmen refused to deal with the Vermont issue. It was generally believed that Congress lacked both the authority to interfere and the resources to enforce New York's claims. The prevailing opinion did not hinge on the legitimacy or illegitimacy of the State of Vermont, but rather on the limitations of the Continental Congress, whose primary goal was winning the Revolutionary War. Many in Congress feared that action against Vermont would weaken the already tattered northern frontier and might even drive Vermonters into the hands of the enemy. In addition, there were personal concerns. Influential men, both inside and outside of the Grants, had speculated in discounted Wentworth land after 1764, and they were gambling on Vermont's success. These men thought that the longer Vermont existed separately from New York, the more likely it was that the state would be confirmed after the war. Vermont had also become a political wildcard in Congress. The addition of representatives from Vermont would strengthen New England and the small middle states against New York and the larger middle and southern states.

Events in the New Hampshire Grants produced a flurry of petitions from various parties: New York, New Hampshire, Connecticut Valley Unionists, Yorkers, and Vermonters. Under the pretense of sorting out these confusing claims, Congress, under Jay's leadership, appointed a committee on June 1, 1779, "to repair to the inhabitants of . . . the New Hampshire Grants, and inquire into the reasons why they refuse to continue as citizens of the respective states [i. e. New York and New Hampshire]." [24] This four-man committee was composed of two congressmen from Connecticut, one from New Jersey, and one from Pennsylvania, three of whom were required to officially carry on the inquiry. Governor Clinton was outraged—instead of censuring Vermont and Ethan Allen, Congress implicitly recognized Vermont as a party in the dispute. Jay assured Clinton, however, that the resolution of Congress was part of a long-range strategy for New York to regain the New Hampshire Grants.

Jay wanted Congress to appear equitable as he built a base of support for New York. The committee Congress sent to the Grants was established by Jay not to gather information, but to trick Vermonters into believing that Congress would respect their interests. In a private letter to Governor Clinton, Jay defended this subterfuge:

> Why [is] Vermont made a party? The reason is this: that by being allowed a hearing, the candor and moderation of Congress may be rescued from asperation; and that those people [Vermonters], after having been fully heard, may have nothing to say or complain of, in the case the decision of Congress be against them, of which I have no doubt. [25]

Vermont's leaders were unaware of Jay's plan, and they viewed the committee as a way to counter the threat of civil war and anarchy within Cumberland County. Although New York thought it could manipulate Congress, not all congressmen were willing to turn on Vermont. Two of the committee members— Reverend John Witherspoon of New Jersey and Samuel Atlee of Pennsylvania—met with Governor Chittenden at his home in Arlington in late June 1779. Reverend Witherspoon, as a representative from a small state, was not a friend of New York. Of more importance, he owned land in Vermont. Before he emigrated to New Jersey from Scotland, Witherspoon had been granted the town of Ryegate by Benning Wentworth in 1763. Witherspoon was appointed president of the College of New

Jersey (now Princeton University) in 1768, and he sold half of Ryegate in 1776 to John Whitelaw, another Scotsman. He still owned the other half of the town, however, when he traveled to Vermont to meet with Governor Chittenden in 1779.

Reverend Witherspoon and Samuel Atlee were convinced that Vermont's leaders were the best able to organize the region's defenses. During their private meeting in Arlington, Governor Chittenden assured them that if the militia quota was filled in the southeast, the state government would not persecute the Yorkers. Witherspoon and Atlee left Arlington without traveling to any other part of Vermont, refusing to follow their instructions to interview other inhabitants of the Grants, including Yorkers east of the Green Mountains. The two congressional committeemen from Connecticut arrived only hours after Witherspoon and Atlee had departed. They set out after their colleagues, but when they caught up with them they could not convince them to return to Vermont. Witherspoon in particular seemed to follow an agenda distinct from that of Congress or at least from that of John Jay and Governor Clinton. He may have even warned Chittenden that Jay and Clinton were working together to overthrow self-rule in Vermont.

During their visit Witherspoon and Atlee had asked Chittenden eleven questions about the origins of the dispute between New York and the inhabitants in the Grants. Chittenden used this opportunity to reiterate Vermont's unyielding independence. The two committeemen then asked, "if the Property of your Lands were perfectly secured to you would you be willing to return under the Jurisdiction of New York?" An indication of how deeply Chittenden had come to identify himself with the cause of Vermont can be seen in his response: "We are in the fullest sense as unwilling to be under the Jurisdiction of New York as we can conceive America would [be] to revert back under the Power of Great Britain." [26]

During the summer New York's government and congressional delegates continued their attempts to turn opinion against

Vermont. On August 27, 1779, the New York legislature sent an address to Congress that made conciliatory gestures to Vermont. The move was calculated to impress Congress, not Vermont. John Jay praised the New York address, which demonstrated the state's "moderation, justice, and liberality." On the other hand, he argued, "the law of Vermont for whipping, cropping, and branding our magistrates made an impression greatly to their disadvantage." [27] Jay was confident that the disturbances in Brattleboro, Putney, and other southeastern towns could work in New York's favor. He also warned delegates from the larger states that if Vermont's independence was confirmed, such a precedent could incite frontier rebellions within their own borders.

Since Vermont did not hold a seat in Congress, it adopted a policy of directly appealing to state legislatures. Ethan Allen used his literary skills to bash New York in "A Vindication of the Opposition of the Inhabitants of Vermont to the government of New-York, and of their Right to Form an Independent State." [28] This "Vindication" was sent to Congress, the legislatures of every state, and the generals and other principal officers of the Continental Army.

Despite Ethan Allen's impassioned defense, his "Vindication" failed to produce results in Congress. John Jay not only wanted to turn opinion against Vermont, but at the same time he hoped to create the framework whereby Vermont would relinquish independence voluntarily. Specifically, Jay wanted a decision in New York's favor, but did not want to divide the United States or weaken the country's defenses.

On September 24, 1779, Congress passed a resolution that called upon it to resolve the controversy of the New Hampshire Grants once and for all by February 1, 1780. The situation was not optimistic. Jay had convinced Congress to vote against immediate recognition of Vermont. In the interim, Massachusetts and New Hampshire, each assuming Vermont would lose in the upcoming February vote, resurrected their own long dead claims in hopes of getting a few scraps from New York's table.

To make matters worse, the congressional resolution sought to undermine Vermont's sovereignty during the interim period before the final vote in February. Article twelve asked all parties to "abstain [in the mean time] from exercising any power over any of the inhabitants of the said district. . . ." [29] This statement was directly aimed at Vermont's leaders. No power other than the Vermont leadership had enforced its jurisdiction over the Grants since the beginning of the war. It was easy for New Hampshire, New York, and Massachusetts to comply with article twelve, but for Vermont, whose very survival was threatened equally from within and from without, compliance would fatally weaken the state. Article thirteen specified that no unappropriated or confiscated property should be sold within the old New Hampshire Grants.[30] This article was equally damning because it removed Vermont's primary source of revenue.

Prior to the passage of the September 24 resolution, Governor Chittenden and his colleagues had hoped that recognition by Congress would solve a host of problems. Such congressional recognition would have quelled internal turmoil by forcing both the Yorker and Unionist factions to acknowledge Vermont's sovereignty once and for all. It would have stopped Vermont's neighbors from plotting to annex the state's territory. It would have allowed for greater cooperation between Vermont and the Continental Congress in defending the northern frontier against the British.

Now, however, the reality was very different. The failure of the Continental Congress to recognize Vermont meant the state was closer to destruction than ever. Thomas Chittenden, who had already completed more than two strenuous years as Vermont's leader, was extremely frustrated by the continuing impasse. He realized it would be impossible for Vermont to survive unless it pursued a drastically different course of action. At this desperate point, when Vermont's existence was literally hanging by a thread, Governor Chittenden and his colleagues decided that the only way to defend the state's interests was by going on the offensive.

CHAPTER V

Vermont on the Offensive
(1779-1782)

⨳⧸⫤⧹⨲

There were two major reasons Vermont's leaders concluded that it was necessary to shift from compliance to defiance toward the Continental Congress. The first was simple pragmatism. The young republic was facing many difficult problems. Funds were running out and military defenses in the northern frontier were breaking down. Within Vermont, the Yorkers in the southeast and the Unionists in the northeast remained hostile. In addition, New Hampshire and Massachusetts were now joining with New York to claim some of Vermont's territory. Without any formal recognition from Congress, the future looked extremely bleak.

There was also a second factor at work. As a result of dealing with an almost constant series of crises for more than two years, Vermont's leaders had gained enough confidence to pursue an independent course of action. Governor Chittenden, now approaching his fiftieth birthday, demonstrated this new attitude in his defiant opening address to the Vermont General Assembly on October 14, 1779, which praised Vermont's constitution and government:

The Legislature having constitutionally met, I cannot for-
bear expressing to you my highest satisfaction in the many
great and important advantages arising from the due execution and careful administration of the laws . . . and cannot
but rejoice when I reflect on the infinite difference between
a state of anarchy and that of a well regulated government;
the latter which we daily experience.[1]

Chittenden's rationale for the new policy of resistance to Congress was based on the premise that Vermont could not sacrifice the stability provided by a well-regulated government. In
his address he clearly indicated that if Vermont complied with
the September congressional resolution, anarchy would result.
A criminal could break the law on the pretense that he did not
recognize the state that enacted it. Vermont's leaders concluded
Congress had overstepped its bounds, and they set about the
difficult task of persuading the members of the assembly to
support their position.

They faced a daunting task. As Ira Allen pointed out in his
History of Vermont, "the influence of Congress at that time was
great, being considered as a pillar of liberty. . . . When the Assembly convened, nine-tenths were for suspending the sale of
confiscated property and the granting of lands until after the 1st
of February, the time assigned by Congress." [2] In the words of
John Williams, the editor of the Chittenden papers, "this was a
critical period in the history of the new State of Vermont. . . .
The Vermont leaders, were able to convince the legislators that
an aggressive plan was safer than following a policy that would
almost certainly lead to a decision adverse to Vermont." [3]

Vermont could not afford to alienate Congress in the middle
of the war, but the state's leaders reasoned that Congress could
not afford to alienate Vermont either. Chittenden and the council members labored for a week before they convinced the assembly members to challenge Congress. Finally, on October
21, 1779, the assembly approved two resolutions:

> Resolved unanimously, that it is the opinion of the Com-
> mittee of the Whole [i.e. joint session] that this State ought
> to support their right to independence, at Congress, and to
> the World, in the character of a free and independent State.
>   Resolved that this Committee recommend to the Assem-
> bly, to make Grants of all, or any part of the unappropriated
> lands within their Jurisdiction, that [do] not interfere with
> any former Grants, as their wisdom may direct.[4]

In the first resolution the state's leaders were attempting to counter the impression, fostered by John Jay and the New York delegation, that Congress had the authority to nullify Vermont's sovereignty. The second resolution opened up a large tract of land along the spine of the Green Mountains that had not been already been granted by Benning Wentworth.

On October 23, 1779, Governor Chittenden, the Vermont General Assembly, and the council convened a joint session to consider immediate grants of some of this land. Despite confiscation sales, the state was low on funds to pay its militia, and the land grants were seen by Vermont's leaders as a means not only to frustrate New York but also to compensate soldiers. For example, the assembly granted the township of Eden in equal shares to militia officers and soldiers (Seth Warner and seventy-one associates). Raising state taxes to pay the militia was not an option considering the desperate financial situation of most Vermonters, many of whom had been forced to abandon their homes. Granting land was the most logical way to pay the militia, because it incurred no cost to the state. In addition to granting the town of Eden, members of the assembly confirmed the grant of the Two-Heroes, and they also approved grants for the towns of Bethel, Isle of Mott, Royalton, and Fair Haven on the last day of the October 1779 session.[5]

In addition, the assembly directed Ira Allen to visit several state capitals during the fall and winter of 1779–80 to build alliances prior to the February meeting of Congress. When Ira arrived in the capitals of Pennsylvania, New Jersey, Delaware, and Maryland, he faced opposition that had been fostered by New York. One of New York's arguments was that Vermont had used receipts from confiscated estates for the benefit of its settlers alone, rather than supporting the American war effort. Allen retorted that Vermont had used its resources to defend all of the states, because Vermont was America's northern frontier. He endeavored to unite the smaller states over the issue of western lands. The small states feared New York and other large states would expand into undefined western borders and grow even bigger to dominate any future government of the United States. The small states wanted the large states to give up their western land claims for the creation of new states. Vermont, Allen argued, would be a valuable addition to the cause of the small states.

After the assembly adjourned, the Governor and Council voted on December 10 to circulate a new document written by Stephen Row Bradley, a young lawyer from the town of Westminster, in an attempt to build up support for the state. Bradley called his document "Vermont's Appeal to the Candid and Impartial World." The Vermont General Assembly had elected Bradley, along with Moses Robinson and Jonas Fay, to serve as Vermont's agents to the February meeting the Continental Congress had scheduled to reconsider Vermont's petition for statehood.

The agents from Vermont met in Philadelphia on February 1, but there is no record of any action taken on that day by Congress. In fact, it was not until four months later, on June 2, 1780, that Congress resumed consideration of the Vermont issue at the urging of New York. The reason the New York delegation waited until June may have been because John Jay, its key delegate, had resigned as president of Congress to become ambassador to Spain. At the June 2 meeting, Congress chastised Vermont for violating the September 1779 resolution by selling confiscated estates, enforcing its laws over Yorkers, and granting lands. It criticized Vermont's actions as being "highly unwarrantable and subversive of the peace and welfare of the United States." Lacking a quorum, however, Congress could not act. After meeting again on June 9, Congress decided to postpone any further consideration of the Vermont issue until the second Tuesday in September.[6]

Governor Chittenden was outraged by this latest congressional criticism. He could barely contain his anger in a July 25 letter to Samuel Huntington, the new president of Congress. In his letter Chittenden blasted hand-bills and public(k) papers circulated by New York, arguing that they served "only to . . . revive a languishing flame of a few tories and scismaticks in this state who have never been instrumental in promoting the common cause of America." He reminded Huntington that "Vermont, being a free and independent state, (has) denied the authority of Congress to judge their jurisdiction," and he speculated "it is altogether probable that there have been proposals for dividing [Vermont] between the state of New-Hampshire and New-York, the same as the King of Prussia, the Empress of Russia, and the Empress of Hungary divided Poland between those three powers; with this difference only, that the former are not in possession of Vermont."

After referring to the "unjustly treated people over whom I preside," an exasperated Chittenden warned Huntington that Vermont "will take such . . . measures as self-preservation may justify." [7] It was abundantly clear that Chittenden was fed up with Congress. At this point he, the members of the Governor and Council, and the assembly decided to move ahead even more aggressively by using land, the state's most valuable resource, to broaden their base of political support.

Vermont's Land Policy

Land was the primary asset available to Vermont's government. The state used its authority to create new towns and granted individuals the proprietary right to settle on a parcel of land. The initial proprietors could sell their shares, but before they settled on the land, they were required to defray the costs of surveys and roads and the construction of sawmills or grist-mills. There were time limits to settle the land, but most time restrictions were waived during the war. Once the proprietors (or their heirs or purchasers) settled in a town they would pay the state a fee, or quitrent, which finally conferred outright ownership. The revenue from the earliest land grants was usu-ally not substantial, but the true value of these grants was not dependent on fees. Vermont was packaging a resource that was in very high demand throughout the United States.

Vermont's leaders used land both as an incentive and as a source of revenue. Land grants gave people throughout the United States a piece of Vermont and thus, hopefully, persuaded them to support the state's independence. These grants by their very nature fostered allegiance to Vermont, because the value of the grants was contingent upon the continued survival of the state. In addition, land grants could be used to reward the state's supporters and to induce Yorkers and Unionists to re-join the state. Finally, land grants with many proprietors en-sured rapid settlement after the war.

Governor Chittenden encouraged the assembly to expedite grants, thus effectively transforming land into currency and the frontier into a vast treasury. The northern half of the state was either wilderness or a wasteland of burned and empty farms, abandoned to the depredations of the enemy. Surveys were dan-gerous, if not impossible, so in its March 1780 session, the assembly passed a bill eliminating all surveying requirements to grant land.[8] In essence, the state gave itself the ability to use grants as blank checks when the need arose.

The Governor and Council received petitions for town char-ters from all over New England, New York, and the middle Atlantic states. The petitions were reviewed and approved or rejected by the Governor and Council. They were then sent to the assembly for final approval. There was no standard statute governing the granting of land, and the Vermont General Assembly exercised considerable flexibility regarding prices and other specifics.

When Benning Wentworth issued his New Hampshire grants, he had reserved four public rights in each town charter, three of which were devoted to religious purposes involving the Church of England.[9] Normally, however, the Vermont General Assembly granted land to a named proprietor, plus a company "sixty-four in number," with five public rights, three of which were intended for educational purposes. Thus, the average charter included seventy shares in a roughly square area of thirty-six square miles (23,040 acres). Once the assembly approved the grant, Governor Chittenden affixed the seal of the state to each town charter. Since petitions were often submitted by only a few individuals, fewer than required for a town charter, the governor, the council, or the assembly would make up the difference between the number applying and the number needed. Many of the remaining proprietary shares were awarded to judges, soldiers, councilors, representatives, and to Governor Chittenden.

The Governor and Council recognized supporters of Vermont's independence within the state by adding their names to approved petitions. Petitions granted during the spring and summer of 1780 included many of the state's old western leaders: Governor Chittenden, Ira and Ethan Allen, Moses and Samuel Robinson, Jonas and Joseph Fay, John Fassett and his son John, Jr., and Joseph Bowker. Valuable old friends from eastern Vermont were also included. General Samuel Fletcher of Townshend, for example, was listed as one of the proprietors in newly granted town of Londonderry, while Stephen R. Bradley of Westminster, the author of "Vermont's Appeal to a Candid World," received shares in the towns of Montgomery and Benson.

Governor Chittenden was included in many grants. Some of these grants followed a tradition of naming the state's chief executive as a proprietor, however, and it is not clear how much land Chittenden actually retained for himself. When New Hampshire's Royal Governor Benning Wentworth granted land west of the Connecticut River between 1749 and 1764, he always set off a section in every town grant for himself, and it is estimated he accumulated approximately 3,000,000 acres in 129 towns.[10] Thomas Chittenden did not attempt to dictate a uniform policy, and he accumulated a considerably smaller amount of acreage. A few grants mention his status by using "His Excellency," but most simply include "Thomas Chittenden" in the list of proprietors, giving him one section undistinguished in size or location from any of the other grantees. Of the 128 grants the state of Vermont made between 1779 and 1791, Thomas Chittenden received a proprietor's share in forty-four towns. In Carthage (later renamed Jay), on the Canadian border, Chittenden received half of the town outright in consideration for the salary he was not paid during the war. Since the average proprietor's share was 330 acres, it is not unreasonable to assume that Chittenden may have received as many as 14,200 total acres in the forty-three towns outside of Carthage where he was named as a proprietor in the original grant.[11]

Members of Governor Chittenden's family were also listed in grants of land. In the charter for Starksboro Governor Chittenden and all four of his sons—Noah, Martin, Giles, and Truman—were listed among the grantees. Noah and Martin were the most frequent grantees in the family next to Thomas. Noah received shares in fourteen towns and his brother Martin received shares in six towns. In addition, Thomas Chittenden's wife, Elizabeth, was a proprietor in the towns of Fairhaven and Williamstown.

When the assembly met in Bennington for its October 1780 session, Vermont had received so many petitions from outsiders for town grants that its leaders realized that its receipts could "defray the expenses, in part, of the war; help to alleviate, in a considerable degree, the burdens of the people; and strengthen the frontiers against the common enemy." [12]

From July 1777 to 1780, Vermont's main source of revenue had been realized from the sales of confiscated properties. Beginning in October 1780, however, the state relied more heavily on the sale of land to produce revenues, although the sale of confiscated property still produced the most revenue for the state, yielding 190,433 pounds from March 1777 to October 1786 versus 66,815 pounds received from the sale of lands. During just four legislative days between November 4–8, 1780, the assembly approved grants for more than fifty towns.[13]

Vermont's aggressive land policy had both long- and short-term benefits in terms of building support and providing needed revenues for the state. It also had drawbacks. The elimination of survey requirements posed serious problems when settlers, years later, tried to take possession of their land. Also, some historians have condemned the land grants as an example of corruption in the state's wartime government. In reality, the wartime leaders used land, their only valuable resource, to meet the serious challenges they faced. Vermont traded its land for the chance to survive.

Greater Vermont

The second aggressive policy Vermont's leaders decided to follow involved territorial expansion, which took place after another unsuccessful congressional hearing in the fall of 1780. On September 19 Congress finally proceeded "to hear and examine into and finally determine the dispute and differences relative to jurisdiction between the three states of New Hampshire, Massachusetts-Bay and New York, respectively . . . and the people of the district commonly known by the name of the New Hampshire Grants, who claim to be a separate jurisdiction. . . ."[14]

Parties representing the various interests were all present. Ira Allen and Stephen R. Bradley attended as Vermont's agents.

Peter Olcott of Norwich represented the Connecticut Valley Unionists. Luke Knowlton of Newfane spoke for the southeastern Yorkers in Cumberland County. Delegations from Vermont's neighboring states represented New York, New Hampshire, and Massachusetts.

During the first two days of the proceedings Ira Allen and Stephen R. Bradley listened to the claims by New York that opened the hearings. On the third day delegates from New Hampshire were called upon to present their case, but Allen and Bradley declined to attend that session. Instead, on September 22, 1780, both men withdrew and sent a "Remonstrance of the Vermont Agents against the Proceedings" to the members of Congress. This remonstrance argued that "the mode of trial now adopted . . . is deviating from every principle of the laws of nature, or nations." In essence, the remonstrance charged that the other states were ganging up on Vermont and treating it unfairly. As a result, the two Vermont agents left with the caveat that they would return "at the same time any equitable enquiry should be made [with] the State of Vermont being allowed equal privileges with the other States in the dispute." [15]

It is not entirely clear whether Ira Allen and Stephen Bradley were following a strategy that had been dictated by Governor Chittenden and members of the council or whether they were acting on their own. In either case, an argument can be made that the strategy they employed was unwise. Vermont's leaders had consistently claimed they wanted to become the fourteenth state. Now, however, Vermont's agents walked out of a congressional hearing on the basis of a legalistic procedural argument. Perhaps the agents felt that members of Congress would have voted to reject Vermont's claim for statehood, but it is difficult to imagine they would have approved such a risky action in the middle of the Revolutionary War. Instead, on September 27, 1780, after Vermont's agents had left Philadelphia, the Continental Congress once again voted to indefinitely postpone further consideration of the Vermont question.

During the fall of 1780 the military situation on the northern frontier deteriorated rapidly. Many troops and provisions were redeployed from forts and supply depots in the north to reinforce Washington's beleaguered army in the south. A major problem arose when New York's state militia, which had helped to defend the Lake Champlain corridor, was unable to muster the resources needed to fill the gaps created by the withdrawal of Continental army. Leaders in Congress viewed support of Washington's forces as an absolute necessity, but civil and military leaders on the northern frontier could not help but watch in dismay as their own militias marched south.

A British invasion of the northern frontier in the fall of 1780 precipitated another crisis. The British forces devastated New York's poorly manned defenses, reaffirmed their control of Lake Champlain, and probed far down the Connecticut River Valley, leaving the region's defenses in disarray. Many of the inhabitants of the northern frontier in both New York and New Hampshire felt abandoned by Congress and betrayed by their own state leaders.

For a brief period of time, it appeared that Governor Chittenden shared this sense of betrayal following the September congressional vote to indefinitely postpone any decision on Vermont. To use Charles Thompson's terminology, he temporarily "flinched." On the morning of Friday, October 13, 1780, after his reelection had just been certified by the assembly, "His excellency the Governor requested the House verbally to accept his resignation. . . . After repeated requests of a number of the Members of Council and Assembly . . . he agreed to take the oath." [16] Perhaps Chittenden was worn out by the continuous delays of the Continental Congress, but, whatever prompted his surprising request, once back in office he never again offered to resign. Instead, he supported a bold new policy to strengthen the northern frontier by expanding Vermont's jurisdiction into eastern New York and western New Hampshire.

This second expansion, which led to the creation of "Greater Vermont," was very different from the earlier annexation of the sixteen towns from New Hampshire. Now the desperate frontier communities petitioned for Vermont's leadership. The inhabitants of northeastern New York were angered by Governor Clinton's consuming desire to regain Vermont, which hindered cooperative defense of the Champlain corridor. Several New York frontier towns sent word to Governor Chittenden that a military alliance with Vermont was their only hope of surviving, and many New Yorkers from towns located east of the Hudson River eagerly sought the jurisdiction of Vermont.[17]

Yorkers, Unionists, and the New Hampshire towns in the Connecticut River Valley were more fractured politically, but they also faced the same crisis that affected northeastern New York towns. Some Yorkers in southeastern Vermont severed their political allegiance to New York because that state had been unable to assert jurisdiction or defend Cumberland County. In the northern Connecticut River Valley, Unionists who had remained aloof from Vermont and New Hampshire also felt the need for law and defense. Thus, Vermont expanded into both northeastern New York and western New Hampshire by dissolving the political boundaries with its neighboring states in order to provide much needed military coordination and aid to the frontier communities.

In September 1780, when Ira Allen was in Philadelphia at the congressional hearing, he began to execute the first step in Vermont's expansion east of the Connecticut River. Never one to forego an opportunity, Allen approached Luke Knowlton, the Yorker from Newfane who was representing Cumberland County. Knowlton owned more than 30,000 acres of New York land grants in northern Vermont. Some Yorkers, like Knowlton, were as frustrated as the Vermont leaders with New York's delaying actions in Congress. According to Ira Allen's account, "a plan was laid" between Knowlton and himself that would unite "all parties in Vermont in a way that would be honorable to those who had been in favor of New York. . . ." [18] Although the particulars of this plan are subject to speculation, it is possible that Allen assured Knowlton that, if he defected from New York to Vermont, his New York land titles would be recognized by Vermont. Later the state actually granted Knowlton the entire town of Bakersfield in northern Vermont, only a few miles from his original New York grants.

After his meeting with Ira Allen, Luke Knowlton issued a call for a convention of Yorkers and New Hampshire residents to meet at Charlestown, New Hampshire, in November 1780. Knowlton was joined in his efforts by other former Yorkers from Cumberland County such as Micah Townsend of Brattleboro and Major Jonathan Hunt of Vernon. On November 8 these men from southeastern Vermont met with leaders from New Hampshire's Grafton and Cheshire counties at the Charlestown convention. The following week another convention met at Walpole, and it drew the attention of more Unionists from northeastern Vermont. On January 16, 1781, a third convention of delegates from forty-three towns met again in Charlestown to develop a cooperative strategy.

This third convention marked a turning point. Although there was opposition from some of the delegates, Luke Knowlton still hoped to bring a new coalition of former Yorkers and eastern Unionists into Vermont's government per his agreement with Ira Allen. Late that afternoon Ira Allen, acting as agent for Governor Chittenden, arrived, and the following day a majority of the convention voted to unite with Vermont. A fourth and final meeting was then scheduled during the Vermont General Assembly session in Windsor to negotiate the terms for a new eastern union. [19]

This second eastern union was radically different from the earlier union in 1778. Vermont's western leaders were now firmly in control of the assembly, and their influence in determining the "Articles of Union" was unmistakable. They refused to modify any of Vermont's key policies, like confiscation or granting land. They also included in the articles a provision for the dissolution of the union when the Congress admitted Vermont as the fourteenth state. On February 22, 1781, the assembly passed the "Articles of Union," and shortly thereafter Vermont expanded eastward and admitted thirty-five towns from New Hampshire. On the same day the assembly divided Cumberland County into Windham, Windsor, and Orange counties and created Rutland County to the west.[20]

Governor Chittenden also recommended that the state should lay claim not only to western New Hampshire, but to some of the towns in northeastern New York as well. Final action on the western union was put on hold, however, pending the outcome of a bill then before the New York legislature.

Governor Chittenden dispatched Ira Allen to travel to Albany in February 1781 to deliver his letter proposing a resolution of the long-standing controversy between the two states. In the wake of the most recent British invasion in the fall of 1780, the New York legislature, meeting in Albany, was well aware of the region's vulnerability. Several influential men in New York sought to officially end that state's claims to Vermont. General Philip Schuyler was a key supporter of Vermont's independence. The pro-Vermont party in the New York government cited a need for cooperation rather than antagonism in light of the British threat. With the support of these New Yorkers, the assembly in Albany drafted and passed a bill that would end the long dispute between the two governments. The bill, which relinquished claims of jurisdiction over Vermont, passed the lower house and was sent to the state senate, where it also met with approval.

Governor George Clinton was so upset he sent his personal secretary to the senate and threatened to dissolve the legislature if the Vermont bill was considered further. His threat convinced the senate to set the bill aside. Clinton complained that Vermont's leaders nearly outmaneuvered him. He noted "some of our monied gentlemen have been induced to speculate in lands and solicit grants under the government of Vermont, and by this means become warmly interested." Clinton was able to intercept the Vermont bill in the state senate, but he was powerless to stop New York's powerful "monied gentlemen" from becoming "warmly interested" in Vermont's survival. In the end, however, his actions postponed the final agreement between New York and Vermont by more than a decade.[21]

Although "Greater Vermont" had no official standing, Vermont's second union with nearby New Hampshire and New York towns was part of a political offensive launched by Governor Chittenden and his associates in 1781–82 in an effort to ensure the state's survival. (Map by Bradley Rink)

Governor Chittenden and the assembly had already considered the state's options if the New York bill failed. On April 11, 1781, the Vermont General Assembly agreed to accept the New York towns by a vote of forty-eight to thirty-nine.[22] On July 19, 1781, Governor Chittenden issued a formal proclamation that recognized fourteen towns from northeastern New York as part of Greater Vermont. By expanding Vermont's territorial jurisdiction into both New Hampshire and New York, the state's leaders provided clear notice to the Continental Congress that its claims to statehood could not be taken lightly.

The Haldimand Negotiations

At the same time that Governor Chittenden and his associates were orchestrating the expansion of Greater Vermont, they were also engaged in an incredibly bold policy initiative that involved secret exchanges of communications with British leaders in Canada. These exchanges, which later became known as "the Haldimand negotiations," were among the most controversial actions carried out during Chittenden's long service as Vermont's governor.

The exchanges had begun back in August of 1780, when Ethan Allen was approached by a disguised British courier as he was walking down the highroad in Arlington. The courier gave Allen a letter from Colonel Beverly Robinson, a prominent Virginia Loyalist, who commanded a Tory regiment known as the Royal Americans. Robinson's letter was very straightforward:

Sir - I have often been informed that you and most of the inhabitants of Vermont are opposed to the wild and chimerical scheme of the Americans in attempting to separate the continent from Great Britain, and to establish an independent state of their own; and that you would willingly assist in uniting America again to Great Britain. . . . If I have been rightly informed, . . . I beg you will communicate to me without reserve whatever proposals you would wish to make. . . .[23]

Ethan dismissed the courier without an answer, but "within ten minutes" he brought the letter to the attention of his brother, Ira, and Governor Chittenden. In Ethan's words, for the time being the three men "agreed after mature deliberation, and considering the extreme circumstances of this state, to take no further notice of the matter." [24]

Within a short period of time, however, Ethan Allen drafted a letter from Governor Chittenden to Frederick Haldimand, the Governor-General of British Quebec, suggesting a prisoner exchange. Many Vermonters, both settlers and soldiers, had been captured by the British since the beginning of the war. Vermont, on the other hand, had two large jails on either side of the Green Mountains that housed British and Loyalist prisoners of war. Governor Chittenden agreed with Ethan and Ira Allen that a prisoner exchange would lessen the hardships on both sides. Having failed to convince General George Washington to initiate such an exchange, Governor Chittenden sent the letter to General Haldimand on September 27, 1780, just when the British forces were launching another military offensive down the Champlain Valley.

The letter bore fruit in late October, when Governor Haldimand instructed Major Charles Carleton, who was occupying Crown Point, to transmit his reply back to Chittenden. Under a flag of truce Major Carleton met with General Ethan Allen and Major Nathan Clark. According to Haldimand's instructions, Major Carleton suggested a truce for the rest of the season, and he suggested another meeting to discuss a prisoner exchange in May. Ethan Allen agreed to comply, but he requested that the truce apply to northern New York as well, to which Carleton assented.

Vermont's leaders suspected that the British were not as eager for a prisoner exchange as they were to win over Vermont. The British hoped to capitalize on Vermont's struggles with New York and with Congress and convince the Grants' inhabitants to reconcile with the Crown. If successful, the British could drive a wedge—started by their control of Lake Champlain—even deeper between New England and New York.

On October 31 Governor Chittenden advised the Vermont General Assembly that "he had [written] to Gen. Haldimand by advice of his Council making proposals to exchange prisoners," and on November 2 Ira Allen and Joseph Fay were appointed to negotiate these exchanges.[25]

Thus, a truce was arranged for the winter of 1780–81, which turned out to be fortunate for Vermont. "The winter that year was one of the worst in Vermont's history. The cold arrived early and stayed long, and in December a great snow fell that kept life slowed nearly to a standstill over much of the Grants until early May. Indeed, so severe was the winter . . . that spring planting had to be put off until June, and with the growing time of crops so shortened, a critical food shortage resulted that forced many of the westside settlers to turn to the resources of the forest in order to keep alive until the harvest of the following year." [26]

Despite the wretched winter conditions, communications were kept open between the British and the small southern Vermont town of Sunderland, five miles north of Arlington, where Ethan and Ira Allen lived. On May 1, 1781, Ira Allen, on his thirtieth birthday, traveled north from Sunderland to Isle aux Noix on Lake Champlain to negotiate a prisoner exchange with Major Francis Dundas and Captain Justus Sherwood, the agents of Governor-General Haldimand. Major Dundas was instructed by Governor Haldimand to negotiate an exchange of prisoners, but Captain Sherwood received different instructions.

Captain Justus Sherwood was an old friend of Vermont's leaders. He had settled New Haven in the old New Hampshire Grants in 1774, later moving to Shaftsbury. During these early years he was an active member of the Green Mountain Boys. Although Captain Sherwood decried the rule of New York, he refused to forsake the rule of King George. He was denounced as a Tory and his property sold. Fleeing to Canada, he raised a company of Loyalists. His personal friendship with Vermonters and his understanding of the state's long-standing conflict with New York made him the perfect candidate to negotiate with Vermont.

Lord George Germaine, the British Secretary of State for Colonial Affairs; Sir Henry Clinton, commander-in-chief of British forces in North America; and Quebec's Governor-General Frederick Haldimand all wanted to see Vermont become a British province. Governor Haldimand indicated he could guarantee Vermont unprecedented autonomy within the Empire. Governor Chittenden, on the other hand, had sent two sets of instructions with Ira Allen. It was widely known that Governor Chittenden was planning a prisoner swap, but only seven other individuals—Ira Allen, Moses Robinson, Samuel Safford, Ethan Allen, Timothy Brownson, John Fassett, Jr., and Joseph Fay— were aware of Ira Allen's secret instructions. Allen was told to encourage Governor Haldimand's agents to believe that Vermont's key leaders desired a reunification with Britain.

Governor Chittenden had repeatedly warned Congress that, unless Vermont was accepted as an equal member of the United States, it would remain outside of congressional jurisdiction. He had even stated outright that Vermont's independence enabled it to accept terms from the British. These threats had gone unheeded by Congress as the crisis on the northern frontier deepened in the summer and fall of 1780. When the governor and other key Vermont leaders embarked on the covert part of the Haldimand negotiations, they did not feel that they were forsaking America. Instead, they believed America had already forsaken them. Vermont's leaders wanted to join the Americans rather than the British, but they also feared that without military aid or cooperation from America, Vermont would become a conquered territory of Britain.

Vermont pursued a policy of delay in the Haldimand negotiations while the state expanded its territory and consolidated the region's defenses against another British invasion. Ethan

Allen sent the two letters from Loyalist Colonel Beverly Robinson to Congress. With no commentary by Allen, the letters spoke for themselves. It was in America's interest to conciliate Vermont.[27]

During the seventeen days Ira Allen remained at Isle aux Noix, he refused to make any commitments. Captain Sherwood sought assurances from Allen about a date when a union with the British could be effected. Allen restated the willingness of Vermont's leaders to form a union, but protested that the time was not ripe. Vermont was in the process of extending its borders into New York and New Hampshire. When this plan was completed, by the summer perhaps, the state would be in a better position to negotiate. Allen also advised Captain Sherwood that many of Vermont's inhabitants were staunch patriots and would not easily forsake the American cause. He asked for more time to win these people over and proposed that the truce remain in effect lest the British engender new animosities among Vermonters. Despite the impasse, plans for the prisoner exchange proceeded favorably, and the two parties parted amicably.

Ira Allen traveled straight from Isle aux Noix to Governor Chittenden's home in Arlington, where Chittenden and a few of his closest advisors convened a meeting to consider Allen's report. British spies failed to learn what transpired in this three-day meeting, although they later observed that Moses Robinson and Samuel Safford did not approve of the Canadian correspondence. The only glimpse into Governor Chittenden's policy was a statement Matthew Lyon made to a British agent:

> Governor Chittenden would settle with Britain if the present leading Men in Vermont were allowed to continue . . . under Britain, their old and new Grants confirmed—the East and West new territories confirmed—all their Laws and Acts confirmed, and nothing revoked. . . . The Governor said those were the only Terms Vermont would agree to, and if General Haldimand would not agree to them, it was the

business of Vermont to spin out this Summer in Truces, and in the mean time fill their Magazines as fast as possible with arms, ammunition, and provision, by which, with the continual increase of the Inhabitants, he hoped to be able next Summer to defend Vermont against invasion from Canada.[28]

This is second-hand testimony, but it may afford the only glimpse into Thomas Chittenden's true intentions. Although this testimony gives the impression that Governor Chittenden considered joining the British, the long list of demands seemed to preclude a speedy settlement.

Perhaps the best clue to Chittenden's position is found in the fact that from the beginning of the truce with the British, he and the other members of the Board of War did not prepare for capitulation. Instead, they prepared for war. Starting in October 1780 the assembly passed bills to provision and regulate the militia as well as broaden the powers of the Board of War. The board was given all the necessary powers to raise and pay an army and call the militia for eleven months. During the winter of 1780–81, the board redirected forces; built stores, barracks and new forts; called the militia to reinforce frontier defenses; raised one regiment of infantry; and paid troops in the field.

When the Vermont General Assembly convened in Bennington in June 1781, its agenda reflected a policy of military preparedness. For the first time representatives from both the eastern and western union were present, making for a total of 123 legislators. The assembly considered new measures to streamline defenses all across the territory of Greater Vermont. At both its April and the June sessions the members consolidated the unions by appointing two boards of war to make the military better able to respond in emergencies. Addressing a scarcity of supplies, the assembly approved Governor Chittenden's proposed embargo on the export of food stuffs. In its April session the assembly passed a bill authorizing 25,515 pounds in bills of credit and backed it up by passing a tax bill to raise the necessary revenues to outfit the state's defenses. In addition, a new batch of land grants were approved. Despite such support for this military buildup, a number of assembly members were alarmed by rumors surrounding Ira Allen's mission to Isle aux Noix.

Ira Allen, when called on by the assembly to explain his mission, protected the secrecy of the Haldimand negotiations. Ira had to exert the utmost tact, because there were surely British spies in the gallery. He told of the prisoner exchange and Governor Haldimand's generous offer of reconciliation, but he did not expose any plans Governor Chittenden and his councilors had at the time. In a statement made famous through retelling, Ira, in his *History of Vermont*, boasted "is it not curious to see opposite parties perfectly satisfied with one statement, and each believing what they wished to believe, and thereby deceiving themselves!" [29]

Although Vermont's leaders escaped detection, the British did not. A letter exposing British designs on Vermont was widely published in America in the summer of 1781. The French, allies of the American cause, had captured a British ship. Among the booty was a letter from Lord George Germaine in England to Sir Henry Clinton, commander of the British forces in America. The letter made its way to America, where it was published. In his letter Germaine discussed the importance of returning the people of Vermont to their allegiance to the king. Germaine noted that the possession of Vermont would bar any American attempt to invade British-held Quebec. Now it was Congress, alarmed at Vermont's territorial expansion and its flirtations with the enemy, that had to make an apparently dramatic shift in policy.

Congressional Maneuvering

Congress, shocked by the information in Lord Germaine's letter, moved to resolve the Vermont question. In August 1781 the Vermont General Assembly chose Ira Allen, Jonas Fay, and

Bezaleel Woodward as Greater Vermont's agents. Before the three men arrived in Philadelphia, Congress appointed a committee to determine "on what terms it may be proper to admit [Vermont] into the federal union of these states." [30] At this time General George Washington sent a special messenger to Governor Chittenden. The messenger interviewed the governor, who admitted candidly that Vermont would join the British rather than submit to New York, but also asserted that he and the inhabitants of Vermont desired above all to join the American states. When Vermont's three agents arrived in Philadelphia, they proposed that Congress should officially recognize Vermont, admit its delegates, and determine boundary disputes later under the mode described in the Articles of Confederation.

On August 20, 1781, Congress finally approved a plan—New York was the only dissenting vote—whereby Vermont would be recognized under the condition that it relinquish the east and west unions, returning its jurisdiction to its original self-proscribed boundaries of the Connecticut River on the east and a line twenty miles east of the Hudson on the west.[31]

Vermont's leaders did not take any immediate action on this plan. During the fall of 1781 they were forced to engage in a series of adroit maneuvers to deal with growing impatience from the British authorities. Governor Haldimand cited "delays and obstacles" thrown in the way of negotiations by Vermont leaders. He speculated that they were delaying a union in order to see the outcome of General Washington's fall campaign in the south. Haldimand noted that Vermont could not remain on the fence, waiting to see which side would be the victor. If the Americans won the war, Governor Haldimand speculated, Vermont could not expect recognition by Congress. If the British won before Governor Haldimand and Vermont's leaders came to terms, then Vermont would be treated the same as the other conquered colonies. "In short," he stated, "I do affirm, (and I hope I shall be believed,) that, if it is the intention of Vermont to trifle with me, she will find herself deceived." [32] Despite his doubts about the Vermont leaders' sincerity, Governor Haldimand and his superiors in the British ministry were too attracted by the potential outcome of the talks to end their negotiations. Haldimand hoped that a defeat of General Washington in the south would draw even more men from the defenses of the northern frontier, opening the way for a proclamation declaring Vermont a British province.

In the interim Governor Haldimand decided to send a British force down Lake Champlain to issue a proclamation. Realizing their bluff was being called, Chittenden and his closest associates agreed to actually invite Governor Haldimand to issue such a proclamation in an effort to buy one more delay. In a letter to Haldimand Ira Allen and Joseph Fay assured him that the popularity of Congress was plummeting and they expected the state elections in early October to bring a shift in government that would favor a union with the British. [33] Ira Allen suggested that if Haldimand issued the proclamation in the fall and then gave Vermont until the spring of 1782, a majority within the state's government would support a reconciliation with the British. Governor Haldimand agreed, hoping that a defeat of Washington's army in the south would drive Vermont into his hands. Vermont's leaders, on the other hand, were gambling that his proclamation would convince the members of Congress to recognize Vermont quickly and settle boundary disputes later.

In early October 1781, before Haldimand issued his proclamation, an incident occurred that almost derailed the negotiations. A small group of Vermont militia scouts fired on some British troops. The Vermonters were captured after one of their number, Sergeant Archelus Tupper, was mortally wounded. Since the truce had just taken effect, the British commander wrote a letter of apology to Vermont General Roger Enos, advising him that he gave Sergeant Tupper a military burial. He also sent Tupper's clothes and effects to General Enos, who forwarded the letter and clothes to Governor Chittenden at an assembly session in Charlestown, New Hampshire. The messenger, unaware of the delicacy of the situation, talked openly about the curious events in the north, where the British were burying Vermont soldiers with military honors. Some members of the assembly, especially General Jacob Bayley and other old Unionists, seized upon the messenger's account as additional evidence that Governor Chittenden and other western leaders were engaged in treasonous negotiations with the enemy.

Governor Chittenden was forced to exercise the utmost skill to avoid immediate condemnation. Demanding time to consider the contents of the letter, which had remained sealed, Chittenden convened a meeting of the Board of War. The governor and his associates then took the questionable step of fabricating a revised letter to read to the assembly.

Fortunately for them, totally unexpected news arrived from the south. On October 19, 1781, General Washington's army captured 6,000 British regulars under General Cornwallis at Yorktown. Washington's victory instantly changed the tactical landscape on the northern frontier. Ira Allen wrote to Governor Haldimand to inform him that the events at Yorktown had emboldened Vermont's patriots, making it untimely for Haldimand to issue his proclamation. Although the conflict on the northern frontier was not yet fully resolved, it appeared the British had lost not only at Yorktown, but also in their gamble to annex Vermont.

The American victory at Yorktown was stunning and decisive, but few realized at the time it was the last major conflict of the war. For the time being, Governor Chittenden and his advisors did not end the covert Haldimand negotiations, nor did they falter in their military and political union with the towns from eastern New York and western New Hampshire.

In the late fall of 1781 New York and New Hampshire tried to reassert their jurisdiction over Vermont's eastern and western unions. After New York's militia failed to expel Vermont from its western union, General Peter Gansevoort tried to muster a force to invade Vermont in order to reestablish New York's authority. Unable to convince General Stark to give him aid, Gansevoort attempted to raise troops on his own. It is a clear reflection of Vermont's popularity and the desperate condition of New York's defenses that he could only enlist eighty men. Discouraged, he disbanded and turned back.[34]

During this same period, the New Hampshire legislature moved to reassert jurisdiction over Cheshire County. News that hostilities might begin in the eastern union arrived just as Vermont's leaders were dealing with General Gansevoort in the western union. Governor Chittenden alerted Vermont's commander in the eastern union, "to protect the civil authority and inhabitants against the menacing insults of New Hampshire, and if attacked, to repel force by force."[35]

New York's Governor Clinton, unable to force Vermont to retreat, began a virulent campaign to discredit Vermont's leaders by supplying Congress with the testimony of individuals who claimed to have intimate knowledge of Vermont's treasonous negotiations with the British. As a more direct blow to Vermont, Clinton encouraged the Yorkers in southeastern Windham County who were still loyal to New York to disrupt Vermont's government and to expect outside help.

In the midst of all this turmoil, in a letter dated November 14, 1781, Governor Chittenden appealed to America's most esteemed patriot, George Washington. Governor Chittenden accused Vermont's neighboring states of using "every art they could devise to divide [Vermont's] citizens, to set congress against her, and finally to overturn the government and share its territory among them." He candidly spoke of Vermont's prisoner exchange with Canada and the intent of Vermont's leaders in encouraging the Haldimand negotiations. He did not apologize for Vermont's policies, arguing that the failure of Congress to act had moved his state to extreme desperation. The solution lay not in any recriminations against Vermont, but instead in the need for Congress to provide recognition to Vermont.[36]

General Washington feared that Vermont might turn out to be the catalyst for a civil war. In a letter dated January 1, 1782, Washington wrote to Thomas Chittenden "in confidence" that he believed the act of Congress on August 20, 1781, had implicitly recognized Vermont. In his letter to Chittenden, Washington stated:

> . . . the dispute of boundary is the only one that exists, and that being removed, all other difficulties would be removed also, and the matter terminated to the satisfaction of all parties. You have nothing to do but withdraw your jurisdiction to the confines of your old limits, and obtain an acknowledgment of independence and sovereignty, under the resolve of the 20th of August, for so much territory as does not interfere with the ancient established bounds of New York, New Hampshire, and Massachusetts.[37]

By this time three factors made it possible for Vermont's leaders to accept General Washington's advice. First, it appeared that the British would not launch another northern campaign in the winter of 1782. Second, the threats from New York and New Hampshire had subsided. Third, General Washington's victory at Yorktown allowed troops and supplies to return north, greatly enlarging the military base on the northern frontier and providing the foundation for a more adequate defense.

Governor Chittenden and the council called an emergency meeting of the assembly in Bennington to carry out their plan to dissolve the unions. After Governor Chittenden submitted General Washington's letter and other correspondence to the joint session held on February 21, 1782, the assembly voted the August resolution of Congress constituted sufficient assurance to dissolve the eastern and western unions, provided "in the faith and wisdom of Congress that they will, immediately,

enter into measures . . . whereby this state may be received into
. . . a federal union with the United States of America as a free,
Independent and Sovereign State." [38]

Vermont's leaders were careful not to burn all their bridges
with the easterners as they had done after the dissolution of the
first eastern union in 1778. The assembly pledged to continue
aiding towns in the dissolved unions, and on February 23 the
assembly approved a new slate of land grants. Many eastern
union leaders were conspicuous among the list of proprietors
of the twenty towns and gores established before the end of the
session. For example, Bezaleel Woodward from Hanover, New
Hampshire, was the chief proprietor in the gore of Norfolk,
followed by Peter Olcott of Norwich, Paul Spooner of Hartland,
and John Strong of Woodstock.[39]

In April 1782 Vermont applied to Congress for admission as
the fourteenth state. Governor Chittenden and his advisors were
confident that with the preliminary requirement of dissolving
the unions, plus the support of General Washington, Vermont
would soon be invited to join the United States, but new issues
took the stage in Congress early in 1782. Following the victory
at Yorktown, the attention of Congress was diverted by the issue of western lands. Now that the war was ending, Congress
again delayed admitting Vermont as the fourteenth state.

Governor Chittenden and his colleagues were bitterly disappointed and utterly frustrated at what they considered to be
this failure of trust. As a result, they continued to correspond
with Governor Haldimand to ensure that peace was maintained
on the northern border. On April 4, 1782, the British Cabinet
suspended hostilities in America. Although Vermont had still
not been recognized by Congress, the territory of Vermont was
ceded to the United States by the British in the Treaty of 1783.

In the final analysis, Governor Chittenden and his colleagues
insured the state's survival by shifting Vermont's policies to the
offensive during the extremely difficult and challenging war
years from 1779 to 1782. The use of land grants and territorial

expansion—coupled with the Haldimand negotiations—had secured precious time when Vermont and the whole northern frontier faced imminent destruction.

Now, as the war drew to a close, it was necessary for these leaders to turn their attention to internal matters. In light of the inaction by Congress, Vermont would be forced to act on its own. As historian Peter Onuf astutely pointed out, "in the aftermath of the war, only Vermont could govern Vermonters." [40]

CHAPTER VI

Reform and the Rise of Rival Leaders
(1782–1786)

~~≫⧊≪~~

In 1782, as the Revolutionary War drew to a close, Governor Chittenden decided to remain at the confiscated house and land he had purchased in Arlington rather than exposing his family to the rigors of frontier life by immediately moving back to his farm in Williston. At the time, Vermont still faced one significant domestic challenge, which involved the continuing unrest among Yorker settlers in the southeastern towns of Windham County.

The Guilford Insurrection

During the spring of 1782, encouraged by Governor Clinton of New York, a Yorker group in the town of Guilford became involved in a new confrontation with the state. In a repeat performance of the first Cow War in Putney, this conflict concerned another beleaguered cow. On May 10 the selectmen of Guilford levied a fine on a Yorker for refusing to serve in the Vermont militia. A sheriff's deputy confiscated a cow from the dissident Yorker but was intercepted as he passed a local tavern. A crowd encircled the deputy, denounced Vermont, and released the cow. The Yorkers then called a meeting to ask New York's Governor Clinton for aid.

Vermont's Governor and Council and assembly passed a law on June 21, 1782, to punish the Yorkers. The law, entitled "An Act for the Punishment of Conspiracies against the Peace, Liberty and Independence of this State," provided for either imprisonment or banishment of the offenders.[1]

The assembly and the Governor and Council each assumed it was their own responsibility to deal with the Yorkers. The assembly chose an ambitious, college-educated young lawyer, Isaac Tichenor of Bennington, for the job. Governor Chittenden, on the other hand, sent the equally ambitious and industrious Ira Allen to assess the situation. When Tichenor's negotiations failed to prevent another mob from intimidating a Windham County sheriff on August 29, Chittenden, using Ira Allen's information, moved to crush Yorker resistance with old-style swiftness and severity. The executive council quickly empowered the governor to raise a military force to assist sheriffs in the execution of the law. On September 2 Chittenden turned once again to his old friend Ethan Allen, who was authorized to lead a special militia force into Windham County.

When Allen mobilized the force in Bennington on September 8, he issued an ultimatum: "I, Ethan Allen, do declare that . . . unless you, the people of Guilford, peaceably submit yourselves to the authority of Vermont, I will lay it as desolate as Sodom and Gomorrah, by God." [2] After Allen's force reached Guilford, they helped the local sheriff round up sixteen Yorkers to be tried by the superior court. Eleven of them were fined and five were sentenced to banishment, never to return to Vermont upon pain of death.

Six months later, in December 1782, when some of the Yorkers threatened a new uprising, Governor Chittenden expressed his frustration by arguing he would rather "hang the Yorkers one by one until they are all extirpated from the face of the earth." [3] Despite these threats, sporadic resistance continued in Guilford for the next few years, and the last meeting of Yorkers in Guilford was not disbanded until 1784.

Since Guilford was Vermont's largest town, the government's success in crushing the insurrection was an important step in the state's effort to establish its internal authority. There were also a number of important side effects from this action. The area around Guilford suffered severely, with many farms being despoiled and much property confiscated. In February 1786 four residents of Guilford petitioned the New York legislature for relief, and New York eventually granted them and the other "sufferers" a total of 48,000 acres of land in south central New York State in Chenango County on the Susquehanna River. They organized a town in that area originally named Jericho, and later changed to Bainbridge.[4] In addition, Vermont subsequently made a $30,000 payment to the sufferers in Windham County, although the Guilford bicentennial history complained that this only partially compensated for "the gross injustice of this outrage." [5]

The most serious consequence of the Guilford insurrection resulted from the fact that the state's tough actions provided a new rationale for New York to stir up opposition against Vermont in the Continental Congress. On December 5, 1782, Congress charged that the acts of Vermont authorities were "highly derogatory to the authority of the United States, dangerous to the confederacy, [and] require the immediate and decided interposition of Congress for the protection and relief of such as have suffered. . . ." It passed a resolution requiring the people of Vermont to make restitution to the banished Yorkers without delay and stated, "the United States will take effectual measures to enforce a compliance with the aforesaid resolution in case the same shall be disobeyed by the people." Congress then ordered General Washington to forward the resolutions to "Thomas Chittenden Esq. of Bennington." [6]

This congressional threat infuriated Governor Chittenden. On January 9 he sent the president of Congress a lengthy remonstrance, written by Ira Allen and Thomas Tolman, the deputy secretary of the Governor and Council. The remonstrance attacked "the impropriety of the claim of Congress to interfere in the internal government of this state," and concluded by stating that it was probable Vermont would appeal to the justice of His Excellency General George Washington for help.[7]

Although General Washington did not hold any official position in Congress, he was by far the most respected individual in the United States. Alarmed by the danger involved in attempting to overpower Vermont, he expressed his own concerns in a letter he sent on February 11, 1783, to Joseph Jones, a congressman from Virginia. Washington warned Jones that Vermont is "very mountainous, full of defiles, and extremely strong." He went on to express grave doubts whether an army composed of men from the other New England states would be willing to invade Vermont on behalf of New York, and he concluded by stating, "I shall only lament that Congress did not, in the commencement of this dispute, act decidedly." [8]

Later in February the Vermont General Assembly once again petitioned Congress to admit Vermont to the union and advised that Moses Robinson, Paul Spooner, Ira Allen, and Jonas Fay had been elected as agents to negotiate an agreement. At the same time, however, the assembly elected a new seven-member Board of War to prepare for any external invasion. Although Congress did not take favorable action on Vermont's request, it declined to grant a request from Governor Clinton of New York for troops that might be used in an invasion against Vermont. The following excerpt of a July 23, 1783 letter from Alexander Hamilton to Governor Clinton indicates Hamilton felt that New York could not win this battle:

> The Vermont question is a business in which nobody cares to act with decision. . . . I much doubt the perseverance of Congress if military coercion should become necessary. . . .

The present dissatisfaction of the army is much opposed to any experiment of force. . . .[9]

No invasion ever materialized, and Vermont continued to defend its own interests. Finally, on May 29, 1784, a committee of Congress reported in favor of recognizing Vermont as a new state, but the committee's resolution could not gain the necessary support from nine of the existing thirteen states. This was the last time the Continental Congress considered the issue of Vermont's statehood.

At this point Vermonters decided not to press the issue any further. With their own constitution, Vermonters felt they could steer a course independent of the United States. Actually, Vermont's economic condition was much better than that in the thirteen states. Vermont had not accumulated any debt during the war, while the other states were staggering under huge war debts and incredibly inflated Continental currency. In September 1777 one hundred Continental Bills of Credit had been worth one hundred Spanish milled dollars, but three years later, in September 1780, it took 7,200 Continental Bills to equal one hundred Spanish dollars. The frugal Vermonters decided they would be better off on their own, at least for the time being.[10]

The Rise of Opposition

By 1784 the rivalry between Vermont's executive and legislative leaders was becoming considerably more heated. One of the central issues creating friction involved a series of divisive debates about the Betterment Act that polarized the assembly and the Governor and Council into opposing political factions. The Betterment Act focused on land. More specifically, it determined who should benefit from betterments (i.e. improvements such as surveying, clearing, and cultivation) that the early settlers had made to increase the value of land. Once peace returned to the northern frontier, thousands of new settlers moved to the Champlain and Connecticut River valleys. Since the settlement of land in Vermont followed a very different pattern than that of colonial New England, this created problems that plagued the state government.

States like Connecticut had seen an incremental expansion of the frontier, accompanied by surveys with local courts to settle disputes. Vermont land, however, was granted by four separate governments (New Hampshire, New York, Vermont, and Massachusetts) in many different stages. Further confusion involving Loyalist claims resulted from the fact that once Vermont's leaders began the Haldimand negotiations, they let the committee of sequestration lapse and did not interfere when Loyalists returned to Vermont to reclaim their old properties. "This change in policy created an administrative and judicial morass . . . when the courts and legislature were inundated by a deluge of conflicting claimants seeking restitution of their losses." [11]

The final problem resulted from the fact that a vast wilderness area in Vermont was divided with few accurate surveys. Ira Allen, the state's first surveyor-general, mixed reports from his official state surveys with the private surveys he made for the benefit of his Onion River Company. "Hence, the greater part of the lotting done by Allen, or under his direction, dating from 1772 down to the close of the Revolution . . . has slight value as a record." [12] With overlapping claims and a lack of clear and definitive surveys, great confusion existed over the validity of land titles. To compound the problem even further, the courts were not able to settle disputes, because the state's leaders had banned debt and land cases during the war in order to protect the state's soldiers from the costs of litigation.

As a result of this confusion, many new arrivals bought deeds only to find that other earlier settlers already occupied "their" land. While some of these early settlers were squatters, others held what they thought were valid titles and surveys, and they had worked hard to improve the land.

Governor Chittenden was moved by the plight of these "ancient settlers," who were forced to move off land where they had made betterments. He felt they should not be punished for circumstances beyond their control. Thus, back in 1781, he had urged the assembly to make "such resolves as will in equity quiet the ancient settlers" by passing a bill to assure that they would be reimbursed by "so much money as judged equitable" for the improvements they had made on the land. The assembly approved this bill, known as the Betterment Act, on October 27, 1781, and it had remained on the books until it became the object of a legislative revolution.[13]

This legislative revolution was nurtured by a new group of leaders who had recently moved to Vermont. These new leaders were younger than Chittenden, and they tended to come from the more settled areas of southern New England, New York, and New Jersey. They had studied at colleges such as Princeton, Yale, and Harvard, and many of them were lawyers. This new group of leaders had an attitude toward government that was profoundly different from that of Chittenden and his colleagues, which led to an ongoing clash of values. The reformers felt that they possessed the education and knowledge necessary to refine what they considered to be a crude frontier government.

In his memoir Daniel Chipman wrote that Governor Chittenden was a man whose governing was "rather patriarchal than constitutional." [14] During the war, Chittenden had demonstrated time and time again that he felt an almost paternal responsibility for the welfare of Vermont's people, "his people." What the governor lacked in formal education, he made up for in his practical life experience. He was a pragmatist who believed that the letter of the law was secondary to the spirit of the law. The Betterment Act, for example, had been tailored to meet the needs of a desperate group of frontier settlers, but it had no legal precedent, nor was it framed in proper legal language. By challenging the Betterment Act, the new reform leaders were questioning the ability of the older leaders to formulate state policy. It was a clash between two different world-views—between the old frontiersmen, like Chittenden, who took a more flexible, pragmatic view of government, and the strict constructionist reformers, who viewed the mandates of the law as being supreme.

Isaac Tichenor was one of these new opposition reformers. Born in Newark, New Jersey, in 1754, he graduated from Princeton in 1775 and studied law before he entered military service and was posted in Bennington. In 1781 he became a permanent resident, practicing law and serving as Bennington's representative in the assembly. In 1783 he was elected speaker. Tichenor's college education gave him a view of the state quite different from that of Thomas Chittenden. Although Tichenor's venue for political change was the assembly, he believed government should be led by an educated elite, and he saw strict enforcement of the law and the constitution as the only means to control the powers of office holders. Since Tichenor was a relative newcomer from New Jersey, he earned the unflattering epithet of "Jersey Slick" from some of Vermont's older political leaders.[15]

There were others who shared Tichenor's vision of a more "legal" Vermont. Micah Townsend also attended Princeton. Born in 1749 on Long Island, Townsend moved to Brattleboro and married the daughter of a prominent Yorker and Tory. He was among those arrested in the first Cow War, but he later switched his allegiance to Vermont. He was reported to be the first lawyer admitted to the bar under the authority of the State of Vermont. In 1781 he was elected secretary of state by the assembly, a position that he held for the next seven years.

Stephen R. Bradley, another lawyer, was admitted to the bar in 1779. Bradley was the same age as Tichenor. He graduated from Yale, attained the rank of major in the war, and moved to Westminster in 1778. As already noted, Bradley aided the statehood movement by writing "Vermont's Appeal to Candid and Impartial World." He was also a leader in the state militia that suppressed the southeastern dissidents in the second Guilford insurrection. Although Bradley's views were often in accord with the political philosophy of Thomas Chittenden, he gave weight to many of the reformers' policies after he was elected to the assembly in the October 1784 session.

Nathaniel Chipman was also elected to the assembly in 1784. He was born in Chittenden's old home town of Salisbury, Connecticut, in 1752. After graduating from Yale in 1777 he served as a lieutenant in the Continental Army. In 1779 he followed his father to the town of Tinmouth, where he started his own legal practice. When he came to Vermont, Chipman bragged to a friend, "I shall be *rara avis in terris,* for there is not an attorney in the state. . . . What a figure I shall make when I become the oracle of law to the state of Vermont." [16] Chipman was mistaken, of course—he was not the first lawyer certified in Vermont.[17] In 1781, however, Chipman was elected state's attorney in Rutland County, and he helped Governor Chittenden during the Haldimand negotiations. That appears to have been an alliance of necessity brought on by the war, because once Chipman was elected as a member of the assembly, he consistently opposed Chittenden and became Tichenor's partner in politics, sharing Tichenor's views of strict legal interpretation, strong constitutional government, and fiscal conservatism.

Nathaniel Niles, who served as assembly speaker during the October 1784 session, was older than these other new legislative leaders. His education and his impact on Vermont state government added weight and legitimacy to the reform movement, however. Niles attended both Harvard and Princeton, where he studied medicine, law, and theology before becoming a minister in his native Rhode Island. After moving to Fairlee in 1779 he continued to preach, and he also began a political career.[18]

As these men reformed and strengthened the assembly, they attracted other men with similar ideas. Jonathan Brace, a long-time member of the Connecticut Supreme Court, moved to

Vermont, where he became a trusted consultant. Others who supported Tichenor and Chipman included lawyer and former Tory Samuel Knight of Brattleboro, lawyer Israel Smith of Rutland, Samuel Mattocks of Tinmouth, and Judge Increase Moseley of Clarendon, a distinguished former representative in the Connecticut assembly. Once they entered politics, these lawyers helped to streamline and empower the legislature.

Since 1778 the Governor and Council had prepared the agenda for each assembly session and had been given the responsibility of revising the laws. In 1784 the new legislative leaders succeeded in appointing two new joint committees from the executive council and the assembly to do this job. The assembly also reduced the power of the Governor and Council by eliminating the executive council entirely from the process of revising laws. The assembly chose Micah Townsend and Nathaniel Chipman to review and revise laws, and in order to better fulfill their responsibility, they were given their pick of books from the confiscated law library of a southeastern Yorker, Charles Phelps. The lawyers began to rewrite the labyrinth of acts originally written by councilors or assemblymen, few of whom had any legal training.

The new assembly leaders also brought greater definition to the lawmaking powers they shared with the Governor and Council. In February 1784 the assembly passed a bill to clarify the legislative confusion of the earlier period. Isaac Tichenor and Micah Townsend wrote this new law, entitled "An Act directing the Form of Passing Laws," which helped to standardize the passage of laws and prevented the Governor and Council from exceeding its limited legislative powers. One of the law's principal innovations was to prohibit the Governor and Council from holding bills for extended periods of time. If a bill was sent to the Governor and Council and no action was taken within three days, the assembly could pass it into law.[19] These reforms also reduced the power of the executive council by stipulating that it could only submit "opinions" that the assembly was at liberty to accept or reject.

Once they had completed work on procedural reforms, the new members of the 1784 assembly turned to substantive policy issues. One of their first targets was the Betterment Act, which the earlier assembly had passed in 1781. During the February 1783 adjourned session, legislative leaders began to call this law into question. The young lawyer who took the most direct interest in rescinding the Betterment Act was Nathaniel Chipman. He argued that under the precedents of the English common law, the so-called "ancient settlers" were no more than illegal trespassers who should be ejected from land they did not own.

In October 1784 the Governor and Council joined the assembly in a Committee of the Whole to consider the issue. Governor Chittenden, chairman of the Committee of the Whole, was anxious to protect the intent of the original Betterment Act, and he appointed a subcommittee to amend the act. Significantly, he stacked the committee in his favor, even appointing himself as a member, but the subcommittee's proposed bill was defeated in the assembly, with Speaker Nathaniel Niles, Isaac Tichenor, Nathaniel Chipman, Samuel Mattocks, Stephen R. Bradley, and Samuel Knight all voting against the bill. Governor Chittenden then agreed to resort to the will of the people by putting the question to a statewide referendum.

The referendum supported the Betterment Act by a vote of 756 to 508, but the young reform legislators, especially Nathaniel Chipman, refused to give up. In the end the assembly agreed to an amendment proposed by Chipman that reduced compensation for improvements to "one half of what such lands have risen in value," and on October 27, 1785, the revised Betterment Act was finally enacted into law.[20]

Both sides learned important lessons from the Betterment Act debate. The new assembly leaders realized the will of the people as expressed in a referendum could not be ignored, and the Governor and Council found they could no longer dictate state policy. The debate also revealed the ideological gulf separating the young reformers from Governor Chittenden and his colleagues. As historian Aleine Austin observed, the reformers' "approach was rigidly legalistic in contrast to the flexible, pragmatic attitude adopted by the adherents of the act who favored making new laws to meet the requirements of a new situation." [21] As a result of this gulf, Governor Chittenden realized he could not rule Vermont by executive fiat alone. It would take all of his considerable political skills to provide leadership in the years ahead.

During the 1785 session the drumbeat of opposition continued in the legislature. After the Revolutionary War, Governor Chittenden and other western leaders continued to negotiate with British Canada in the hope that they could gain special trade concessions for Vermont from Quebec. In the October 1784 session they had convinced the assembly to pass "An Act for the Purpose of Opening a Free Trade to and through the Province of Quebec." The Governor and Council chose Ira Allen and Joseph Fay to negotiate on behalf of Vermont. In June 1785 Ira Allen returned from Quebec and optimistically advised the assembly, meeting in Norwich, that he had been successful in instituting negotiations with Great Britain through his meetings with Quebec's lieutenant governor. A week later, however, Isaac Tichenor proposed "an act repealing an act for the purpose of opening a free trade to and though the Province of Quebec," which the assembly eventually referred to the next session. [22] Tichenor argued that all Vermonters would have to pay for the negotiations but only a few men would benefit from a Quebec trade agreement.

In retrospect, the Governor and Council had been unwise to select Ira Allen for this assignment because he had become the focus of very intense scrutiny and scathing criticism from the new legislative reformers. They viewed Allen as the symbol of, and the scapegoat for, all of the perceived failings of the Chittenden administration. Although Thomas Chittenden's glowing wartime reputation made him politically unassailable, Ira Allen's overreaching ambition and his willingness to mix private with public business made him vulnerable to attack. During the war Allen had occupied as many as four important state offices at the same time. He spread himself so thin he was forced to neglect some of his official duties. All the while he was amassing holdings for his Onion River company so that, by the end of the war, he owned large stretches of land throughout a vast area of northwestern Vermont.

In a direct slap at Allen, the 1785 assembly passed an act that "annuled all of Ira's town surveys. Charging that his slovenly efforts had produced innumerable boundary disputes, the act also prohibited him from undertaking any further surveys in Vermont." [23] In 1786 Allen was forced to resign as treasurer, and he was succeeded by Samuel Mattocks, a colleague of Nathaniel Chipman from Tinmouth. The young reformers had managed to severely weaken Allen, and it became clear that Thomas Chittenden had to fight vigorously if he hoped to remain as Vermont's governor.

The Constitution of 1786

In July 1786 Governor Chittenden launched his counter-attack, but the most significant conflicts did not take place in the assembly. Instead, the battleground was the state Constitutional Convention in Manchester where, despite some major gains made by the reformers, Governor Chittenden was very successful in enlisting the support of the small frontier towns to strengthen his own political position.

When the Vermont Constitution was adopted in 1777, its very last provision, Section XLIV, stipulated that every seven years a thirteen-member Council of Censors would be elected to review the constitutionality of the laws already enacted by the legislature. They would then call a convention to consider any proposed amendments to the constitution they deemed to be necessary.

In order to gain support for constitutional reform, a person using the pseudonym Cato sent letters to the *Windsor Vermont Journal and Universal Advertiser* as early as the winter of 1785. By using the name of an early Roman republican statesman, Vermont's Cato managed to maintain his anonymity, but some researchers have concluded the letters were written by Stephen R. Bradley. In the spirit of the reformers of the time, Cato wanted to shape public opinion by redefining Vermont's wartime political record:

> Not only many laws were made, but our constitution was formed, at a time of the greatest political fermentation. It is no reflection on the wisdom of these patriots who formed them to say, they are not perfect. They are as perfect as the necessities and circumstances of the times would admit. There is no nation, however respectable, but what will find, many of their proceedings, in their rude state, were entirely inconsistent with every principle of liberty and true policy.

Thus Cato, without directly slandering any of the wartime leaders, carefully exhorted people to vote cautiously and maturely for change. In his next letter, which was written at the same time Ira Allen was being vigorously attacked, Cato condemned "crowding a multiplicity of offices upon the same individual" as the most urgent danger to liberty, and he outlined the state offices that should not be held simultaneously.

In later letters Cato directed the public's attention to the Council of Censors. He chided Vermonters for being ignorant of the purpose of the council and quoted the section of state constitution that created it. He also noted that the election of censors was scheduled to take place on the last Wednesday in March 1785, and he drew a profile of an ideal candidate for the Council of Censors:

Good sense, with common honestly, and an acquaintance particularly with our laws, public situation, & political interests, and generally with the laws of nature and the constitutions of other governments, is sufficient. In order for this, a good education is certainly necessary.[24]

Cato's letters appear to have had an impact on the election of the Council of Censors. In March 1785 eleven of the thirteen members who were elected came from the most populated towns in the southern part of the state, which were large enough to warrant two representatives each in the assembly.

The members chosen were a mix of oldtimers and younger lawyers. Oldtimers included Benjamin Carpenter of Guilford; Joseph Marsh of Hartford; Ebenezer Curtis of Windsor, a former member of the Committee of Safety; Ebenezer Marvin, a Tinmouth physician ; and Lieutenant Colonel Elijah Robinson of Weathersfield, who had served on the Board of War. Other oldtimers were John Sessions of Westminster, who had been a delegate to the 1777 Windsor Convention, and Ebenezer Walbridge of Bennington, a brigadier general in the state militia.[25]

The council members who tended to side with the reformers were three young lawyers—Jonathan Brace of Manchester, Stephen Jacob of Windsor, and Micah Townsend of Brattleboro. A fourth young member, Lewis Beebe of Arlington, was the Bennington County clerk. Another member was Jonathan Hunt of Vernon, a Yorker whose land had been confiscated, but who later returned to serve as a legislator from Vernon. Finally, the senior member of the group and the most experienced, was seventy-three-year-old Increase Moseley of Clarendon, who had served in the Connecticut legislature for thirty-six years and became chief judge of the Rutland County court after he moved to Vermont in 1779.

Although the council was fairly evenly divided between oldtime and more recent Vermont settlers, its strong tilt toward the reform position became obvious when Increase

Moseley was elected to serve as president and Micah Townsend as secretary. In addition, eight of the members resided on the eastern side of the state, and some of the oldtimers, such as Joseph Marsh, had engaged in bitter battles with Governor Chittenden over the first eastern union. Actually, Ebenezer Walbridge was the only council member who had served through the early struggles with Chittenden.[26]

During the course of their deliberations, the censors held three sessions in Norwich, Windsor, and Bennington. Their primary goals were to have the assembly repeal, or adjust, any acts it had passed during its first seven years that the council deemed to be unconstitutional, and to propose amendments to the constitution that the censors felt might be necessary. The council's first two sessions in Norwich and Windsor were largely devoted to reviewing prior legislation, and in October the censors submitted fifteen recommendations calling for the assembly to alter or abolish laws they had found to be unconstitutional.

In addition to being extremely critical of the assembly, the censors were grudging in their praise of the state's executive officers. Increase Moseley, president of the censors, referred to Vermont's wartime leaders with a tepid, backhanded compliment as "a few husbandmen, unexperienced in the arts of governing, [who] have been able to pilot the ship of state through storms and quicksands, into the haven of independence and safety."[27] It was obvious that Moseley viewed Governor Chittenden and his early colleagues with deep suspicion.

This suspicion was reinforced when Matthew Lyon refused to comply with an order to give the Council of Censors the public records of the court of confiscation that they had requested. On October 15, 1785, the censors voted that "Col. Matthew Lyon be impeached before the Governor and Council of this State for refusing the deliver to the order of this Board the record of Court of Confiscation." Before they took this vote, the censors met with four lawyers from the assembly for advice. They were Stephen Bradley, Nathaniel Chipman, Samuel

Knight, and Israel Smith. In response to the censors' resolution, the Governor and Council did try Lyon on October 18. He was found guilty and ordered to deliver the records of the court of confiscation to the censors, and he received a reprimand from the governor.[28]

Once they completed their legislative review, the censors began to work on the state constitution. According to President Increase Moseley, the council "principally had in view rendering government less expensive, and more wise and energetic." [29] On October 20, 1785, they made a number of very important procedural decisions. Although the Vermont Constitution authorized the censors to call a Constitutional Convention, it did not provide any guidance on how, or how many, delegates should attend. The 1777 Vermont Constitution did specify, however, that it required a two-thirds vote of the entire Council of Censors to call a convention .

At its October 20 meeting, perhaps because the council contained a number of older members who had participated in earlier conventions that were organized around towns, the censors decided that each town would be entitled to elect one delegate to the convention. They scheduled the convention to convene in Manchester, Vermont, on the last Thursday of June 1786. In addition, at this same October meeting, the council passed a resolution that was later published in Vermont newspapers:

> In the opinion of this Council, the Governor, Lieutenant Governor, Treasurer of this State, Members of the Council of the State, Council of Censors, or General Assembly, Officers who hold their Commissions during good behaviour, and other Officers who may be interested by the Alterations proposed to be made in the Constitution ought not to be elected members of such Convention.[30]

This is a puzzling recommendation. It could have been designed to eliminate possible conflicts-of-interest at the convention among active governmental leaders who were serving in office at that time. Just as possible, however, it could have represented a subtle attempt by the Council of Censors to eliminate the most experienced and knowledgeable older leaders in Vermont's government, especially Governor Chittenden, from having an opportunity to shape any revisions or amendments to the new state constitution.

The council completed its work on the constitution in October. Instead of recommending individual amendments, the council took the unusual step of preparing a complete redraft of the entire constitution, which was published in Vermont's newspapers in January 1786.[31]

On February 14, 1786, "the Council adopted an address to the freemen of the state, which was soon printed and distributed, and the severity of its censures added largely to the discontent of the people, provoking discussion in the two newspapers of the state and stirring up an active opposition to the government, aimed particularly against Governor Chittenden and Ira Allen." [32] The council was particularly severe in its attack on many laws enacted by the legislature. One analyst has pointed out that the 1785 Council of Censors enumerated a total of twenty-six actions by the legislature that it found to be objectionable. This accounted for more than half of all the objections the council would issue during its entire eighty-four-year history. As a result, the analyst classified the 1785 council as being "anti-Chittenden." [33]

It appears there was a heated response to the proposals of the Council of Censors. According to Crockett's account, "the *Vermont Gazette,* under date of March 26, 1786, printed a report from Poultney to the effect that the inhabitants of that town burned a copy of the proposed revision of the Constitution. . . . Newspaper reports indicate that Governor Chittenden was not altogether pleased with the criticisms of the Council or with some of the changes proposed." [34]

In late June 1786 the Constitutional Convention met in Manchester to consider the censors' proposals. Unfortunately, no records have been preserved from this convention. We do know from other sources that the delegates elected Moses Robinson of Bennington to serve as president and Elijah Paine of Williamstown to serve as secretary.[35] By comparing the 1786 constitution with the original constitution, we also know which of the Censors' proposals were approved and which were rejected by the convention. Finally, an examination of town records has revealed the names of thirteen town delegates, including Stephen Bradley of Westminster, who attended the convention. At least five of these delegates were serving in the 1785–6 Vermont General Assembly despite the Council of Censors' admonition that members of the assembly should not be elected as delegates.[36]

In light of the fact that Moses Robinson, Stephen Bradley, Elijah Paine, and a number of other active legislators were at the convention, it is virtually inconceivable that Governor Chittenden did not attend, especially in light of the criticism he had received from the Council of Censors. Chittenden was still living in Arlington at the time, but the town records reveal that, on June 13, 1786, voters in that town elected Captain Lemuel Buck, a former member of the assembly, as Arlington's delegate to the Constitutional Convention. [37]

Since Governor Chittenden did not represent Arlington, he may have served as the delegate to the convention from Williston. Although originally chartered in 1763, Williston was not organized as a town until March 28, 1786, only three months prior to the convention, and its records were still very incomplete. We do know that Chittenden was getting ready to move back to his Williston farm at this time, and also that he later served as Williston's delegate at the 1791 and the 1793 conventions, so it is quite possible he may have represented Williston at the 1786 convention as well.

The young reformers were able to achieve a number of notable successes at the Constitutional Convention. They won a major victory when the delegates approved adding a new section to the constitution specifying that "the legislative, executive, and judiciary departments, shall be separate and distinct, so that neither exercise the powers properly belonging to the other." [38] The delegates accepted the censors' argument that a clear separation of powers would allow each branch of government to develop independently.

The reformers scored a second major victory when the convention eliminated multiple office holding, the most cherished power of the state's old leadership. Section XXIII of the revised constitution specified that this limitation would apply to the offices of "governor, lieutenant-governor, judge of the supreme court, treasurer, member of the council or the general assembly, surveyor-general, or sheriff." [39] Using the letters of Cato and the example of Ira Allen, the reformers managed to gain widespread public support for this change. The state's wartime leaders had controlled the state's top offices for seven years. The convention delegates agreed with the censors that it was detrimental to the state for any one individual to hold more than one important governmental position at one time. Not coincidentally, this limitation opened up several positions on the Governor and Council and on the state supreme court, which were filled by the aspiring young reform leaders.

Finally, the reformers were successful in securing approval for a number of procedural changes. For example, the convention accepted several amendments that strengthened the assembly by expanding the powers of the grand committee. The convention also modified the section of the constitution outlining the shared lawmaking powers of the Governor and Council and the assembly. The rewriting of this section gave the Governor and Council a suspensory veto, but it also limited the amount of time it had to consider bills.[40]

While the reformers were enjoying their successes, they suffered two important defeats. Although no copies of the records of the 1786 Constitutional Convention have survived, it is highly likely that a large influx of new frontier towns sent delegates to this convention. Between 1779 and 1786 a total of eighty-one new towns had been granted in Vermont.[41] Although it took time before local governments were organized, many of these towns were qualified to send a delegate to the 1786 convention. In the year 1786 alone, for example, sixteen newly organized towns were added to the assembly, including Thomas Chittenden's original hometown of Williston.[42] Since the censors had authorized each town in Vermont to send a delegate to the Constitutional Convention, the growing number of small frontier towns controlled a large share of convention votes, which they used to challenge any reforms that threatened their own interests.

Governor Chittenden was revered for his leadership during the war, but it was not until the summer of 1786 that he became the leader of a distinct political faction by entering the political fray as the champion of small-town frontier interests. One of the most controversial proposals of the Council of Censors involved a dramatic change in representation in the Vermont General Assembly, which would have maximized the role of the more populous southern towns, where most of the censors and the reformers lived. Under the original Vermont Constitution of 1777, towns with eighty or more taxable inhabitants had been allowed to send two members to the assembly. Section XVI of this original constitution specified, however, that "within one septenary or seven years . . . each inhabited town may . . . choose one representative, forever thereafter."[43]

In an effort to amend this provision, the Council of Censors had proposed that the assembly should be limited to a total of fifty members. These members were to be selected by districts rather than by towns, with the districts drawn up by the assembly according to population. The censors argued that this very radical amendment was designed "to prevent unnecessary expense in legislation." [44] The political implications of this proposal were obvious. If the delegates approved this amendment, the more populous southern towns would be able to maintain, or possibly increase, their representation, while representation from the smaller frontier towns in the state would be seriously curtailed. Governor Chittenden, an extremely pragmatic politician, undoubtedly realized how such a development would endanger his own political base. First, the reformers had strengthened the legislature's powers. Now, under this proposal, they would also increase their own representation in order to dominate the assembly.

It was certainly logical for Chittenden to oppose this proposed amendment. All of the early Grants' conventions he had participated in since July 1776 had been organized by the towns, and he was a strong believer in the principle of "one town, one vote." Since both Chittenden and the small towns stood to lose power if this amendment was adopted, it is hardly surprising that the majority of delegates at the Constitutional Convention voted to reject the censors' plan. Instead of limiting the assembly to fifty members, they left the original provision intact. Every town became entitled to one representative in the assembly regardless of its population size. From this time forward, the "one town, one vote" system prevailed in Vermont, and the system remained in effect until 1966, when it was eliminated following the United States Supreme Court's ruling that this practice violated the United States Constitution. [45]

A second proposal by the censors designed to modify the executive council was also defeated at the convention. The censors recommended that the Governor and Council should consist of "one able, discreet freeholder to be chosen from each county in the state." Instead, the convention again voted to retain the original formula for a "supreme executive council . . . of a governor, lieutenant governor, and twelve persons." [46]

On July 4, 1786, the convention delegates endorsed the state's newly revised constitution. This constitution was a compromise between Vermont's old and new leaders. The ambitions of one group canceled out the ambitions of the other so that the government created by the new constitution was not controlled by any one political faction.

While many of the censors' reforms improved the institutions and practices of Vermont's government, the power struggle between Governor Chittenden and the reform lawyers turned out to be a draw. The governor continued to dominate the executive branch, and he also maintained strong support in the legislature by deriving his power base from the smaller frontier towns. The lawyer reformers, on the other hand, gained power in the legislature through procedural reforms. In addition, they won positions that opened up on the executive council when the provision to eliminate multiple office holding was adopted, and they also captured complete control of the judicial branch.

The Debtor Relief Crisis

Following the Constitutional Convention, the Vermont General Assembly held its October 1786 session in Rutland. At this time Vermont was facing an extremely serious economic crisis. The close of the war inaugurated a period of unfavorable trade relations with Great Britain. The American states were flooded with imports from Great Britain while America's lucrative exports to the West Indies were cut off by the British. The economic problems were further exacerbated by the fact that Vermont suffered from a severe shortage of money. During a brief period in 1781 Vermont had issued its own paper bills of credit, but these were all redeemed in 1782. "The capital of the richest men was mainly in land, very few being able to loan money at any rate of interest however high or on any security however good." [47]

The economic situation became even more difficult when the government began to mandate taxes. During the earliest years of its existence, Vermont had obtained its revenues by selling confiscated loyalist properties and by issuing land grants. "In 1780, the state [first] taxed the towns by requiring them to raise provisions for fighting the Revolutionary War. . . . The next year the legislature for the first time formally taxed inhabitants' property. This 1781 land tax of ten shillings on each hundred acres of land was adopted in April when the legislature met in Windsor. Its purpose was to raise money to pay the war debt of the Revolution." [48]

In addition, the Vermont legislature authorized town taxes of up to two pence an acre to build houses of public worship, school houses, and bridges, and there were further statewide property taxes in 1783 and 1785. On October 21, 1783, the assembly voted a property tax of ten shillings on each one hundred acres of land in fifty-one newly settled frontier towns.[49] These growing tax burdens placed the frontier landowners in a very precarious position, since many of them did not have money to cover their debts and taxes. As creditors began foreclosures, some of the settlers became desperate. On August 15, 1786, 200 farmers assembled in Rutland, where the court was inundated with suits against debtors. Governor Chittenden, alarmed at the growing signs of unrest, decided to seize the initiative by circulating one of his most notable communications to the people of Vermont in August 1786. The issue of debtor relief fit perfectly with his own populist beliefs. He began tamely enough by using an Old Testament reference:

> In the time of war we were obliged to follow the example of Joshua of old, who commanded the sun to stand still while he fought his battle; we commanded our creditors to stand still while we fought our enemies.

The governor then turned upon his own adversaries within the assembly, and launched a vitriolic attack on lawsuits and lawyers:

> Law suits are become so numerous that there is hardly
> money sufficient to pay for entering the actions . . . I have
> reason to believe, that the expense of law suits for two years
> past, has been nearly equal to any two years of the war, and
> for a remedy one cries a Tender Act, another a bank of money,
> and others, kill the lawyers and deputy sheriffs.
>
> A remedy arising from either of these methods, without
> other exertions, will be but temporary; it might afford some
> respit at present, but would not remove the cause.[50]

Following this outpouring of classic Chittenden rhetoric, the
governor went on to urge the public to exercise "prudence, industry and economy," in order to limit purchases on credit and
to encourage industry and agriculture. In addition, he called
for a tax on lawsuits to force "sheriffs, deputies, constables and
pettifoggers" to go to work. Finally, to address the shortage of
money, he proposed the creation of a state bank and passage of a
General Tender Act to authorize paper script as legal tender. Although Vermont was already issuing its own copper coins, they
were not sufficient to compensate for the general shortage of money.

*From 1785 to 1788 Vermont authorized its own coins. One side of the
1786 coin is inscribed Vermontensium Respublica (Republic of Vermont), but the reverse side has the words Stella Quarta Decima, indi-
cating that Vermont still desired to be admitted as the fourteenth "star"
in the United States. (University of Vermont Special Collections)*

Many of the lawyers in the legislature and throughout the state were outraged by Governor Chittenden's proposal to tax lawsuits. Some of them also feared that his plan to establish a state bank to issue paper currency could lead to devastating inflation and devaluation of money. In essence, these conservative lawyers favored creditors and hard money. Chittenden, however, placed himself on the side of the small-town frontier debtors, despite the fact that he was a major creditor who owned large tracts of land and loaned sizable amounts of money to his friends and business associates.

Nathaniel Chipman once again rose from the ranks of the reformers to play the leading role in blocking Chittenden's plan to create a state bank. Chipman called a meeting with some of his closest legislative allies. "They unanimously agreed that the popular current was too strong to be resisted . . . and that they could therefore do nothing until the passions of the people should have time to cool." [51] As a result, they convinced the assembly to call for a public referendum on this issue, to be held following the adjournment of the October legislative session. In the interim, all action on a state bank was postponed. The assembly did provide some relief to debtors, however, by passing acts prolonging the time grantees of land had to settle their debts and permitting fulfillment of contracts in kind, rather than only in gold or silver.[52]

By deferring consideration of a state bank until January 1787, when the statewide referendum was scheduled to take place, Nathaniel Chipman and his reform colleagues were able to frustrate Governor Chittenden again, just as they had done in the previous session when the assembly halved the compensation payments under the Betterment Act. In the fall of 1786 it appeared that the reformers, led by Chipman and Tichenor in the assembly, were on the verge of gaining political control of Vermont. They had already largely discredited Chittenden's key ally, Ira Allen, and they were now stifling Chittenden's policy initiatives in the legislature.

Governor Chittenden's political problems were further compounded by the fact that the reformers had seized control of the judicial branch of Vermont's government at the July Constitutional Convention. As Professor Samuel B. Hand pointed out, "at the time Vermonters wrote their first constitution, they closely associated the terms lawyer and Yorker, for in order to practice in the New Hampshire Grants, lawyers had to have been admitted to the New York Bar. . . . [As a result] when Vermont first established its courts, the legislature assumed there would be lay judges." [53]

Now, however, in the year 1786, the assembly elected the first lawyer ever to serve on the Vermont supreme court. He was Nathaniel Chipman. Thomas Chittenden had a formidable opponent in Chipman and the other lawyer reformers, but he had survived the confrontations of 1786 and the struggle was far from settled.

CHAPTER VII

The Shift of Power
(1787–1791)

~⚔~

Governor Chittenden continued to experience difficult political challenges during the period from 1787 to 1791, when Vermont finally became the fourteenth state. The reformers had managed to limit his power, and in October 1789, Chittenden suffered the only political defeat of his career when the legislature failed to reelect him as governor. The next year, however, he made a quick comeback and returned to the statehouse, where he continued to deal with important policy issues.

Civil Unrest

After the assembly failed to authorize a state bank during its October 1786 session, Chittenden hoped the statewide referendum scheduled for January 1787 would vindicate his economic policies. Widespread debtor unrest continued during the fall and winter months of 1786–87. Armed mobs assembled outside both the Windsor County and Rutland County courthouses. The uprising in Rutland County during December was particularly difficult. Jonathan Fassett, the son of Chittenden's old colleague, John Fassett, and Colonel Thomas Lee, who had recently been released from prison after taking a poor debtors' oath, led a group that occupied the Rutland County courthouse and blocked its proceedings.

Judge Increase Moseley, who had recently finished his work as the president of the Council of Censors, was presiding, and he adjourned the court overnight. The next day the Rutland County militia managed to quell the uprising. At its February session, the assembly voted unanimously to expel Jonathan Fassett, who was serving as a representative from the town of Pittsford, for his role in "aiding and assisting the mob which assembled at Rutland . . . with intention to stop the County Court from sitting in that place." [1]

The root of the debtors' unrest was grounded in the self-sufficient farm economy of Vermont. As soon as new settlers arrived and secured their land grants, they immediately faced three primary needs—shelter, food, and clothing. Initially they provided shelter with rough log cabins, and then, if a sawmill was available, they "raised" a barn for their livestock with the help of neighbors. Next came clearing the uplands since "the river valleys were usually a tangle of brush and weeds. . . . It was slow, backbreaking work; a good man might clear as little as three acres a year, or the same amount in a month, depending on whether or not he attempted to grub out the stumps, dig out the stones, and fence it in. . . . The land was broken with the wooden plow and harrow behind oxen. The rest of the work was done by hand, from planting to harvesting." [2]

The new settlers grew most of their own food—first corn, followed by wheat, rye, oats, and barley, supplemented with pork and small garden vegetables plus wild berries and game from the forest. Clothing was made from wool, flax, and furs. The only essential imports were salt (to preserve food) and rum. Thus, "the frontier farm was established to provide a living for the typically large farm family, and not to produce goods for exchange." [3]

As a result, once the farmers were faced with property tax bills on top of prior debts incurred to purchase their land, they did not have enough money to meet these obligations, and they risked the threat of lawsuits and bankruptcy. During the summer and fall months of 1786 the pages of the weekly Vermont newspapers were filled with names of delinquent taxpayers from towns such as Milton, Bolton, Duxbury, Worcester, Middlesex, Vershire, Brookfield, and Waterbury.[4]

In January 1787 the public referendum was held on the governor's debtor relief proposals. The riots and mob outbreaks in Windsor and Rutland alarmed many people and had a negative impact on the support for Governor Chittenden's proposals. Only 456 people voted in favor of establishing a state bank for the issuance of paper money while 2,197 voted against this plan. The public also voted against a General Tender Act. The only item supported in the referendum provided for the fulfillment of contracts in kind after the specified time of payment elapsed.[5]

The deadlock between the governor and the reform leaders in the legislature might have continued were it not for an alarming event that occurred in neighboring Massachusetts. On January 25, 1787, Daniel Shays and a group of farm debtors in the western part of the state attempted to capture the arsenal in Springfield. This bold move, which became known as Shays' Rebellion, sent shock waves throughout the propertied classes in all of the states, and it influenced the nation's founding fathers to revise the weak Articles of Confederation in favor of a stronger new United States Constitution. After Governor Bowdoin of Massachusetts authorized a large militia force to crush the rebellion, a number of the insurgents, including Daniel Shays, fled from Massachusetts to Vermont.

On February 17 the Governor and Council considered a petition sent from Governor Bowdoin to Governor Chittenden asking for assistance in apprehending the rebels. The petition was forwarded to the assembly, which voted thirty-six to twenty-

four to instruct the governor to sign a proclamation issued on
February 27:

> By his Excellency THOMAS CHITTENDEN, Esq.;
> Captain-General, Governor, and Commander in Chief, in
> and over the STATE of VERMONT. . . . This Proclama-
> tion, strictly commanding and enjoining it upon all citizens
> of this state not to harbour, entertain or conceal the said
> Daniel Shays, Luke Day, Adam Wheeler, and Eli Parsons.[6]

Although some historians have argued that Chittenden pri-
vately "expressed sympathy for [Shays] and his plight," the governor was not prepared to risk his credibility by harboring the
insurgents, some of whom were later returned to Massachusetts, where they were eventually pardoned.[7]

The shock of Shays' Rebellion convinced the assembly to
pass both "carrot and stick" legislation to help defray the debtor
crisis during its March 1787 session in Bennington. The "carrot" took the form of "An Act to Make Certain Articles of Personal Property a Tender." This Special Tender Act recognized
that "whereas through the scarcity of a circulating medium, it
is very difficult to satisfy all Debts in Specie. Therefore . . .
neat-cattle, Beef, Pork, Sheep, Wheat, Rye, and Indian Corn
shall be a lawful Tender if turned out by the Debtor on any
Execution. . . ." [8]

The "stick" was a second act the assembly passed for the "Pre-
vention and Punishment of Riots, Disorders and Contempt of
Authority." This act specified fines and imprisonment for various types of offenses, and it also provided legal immunity to
justices of the peace, sheriffs, and constables who were attempting to deal with public riots.[9] The passage of this latter act
marked the next phase in the wide-ranging crusade by the lawyer reformers, who wasted little time revising virtually all of
Vermont's domestic laws in an effort to "civilize" the frontier
society of Vermont.

During the March 1787 session the assembly engaged in a wholesale revision of Vermont's statutes, repealing all the acts (with certain specified exceptions) passed during the period from 1779 to 1786.[10] At this same March session, the reformers in the assembly passed tough new laws governing marriage, divorce, incest, polygamy, fornication, counterfeiting, gaming, drunkenness, and profane swearing, plus "divers Capital and other felonies" including sodomy, homosexuality, arson, blasphemy, murder, burglary, armed robbery, and manslaughter.

The statutory punishments for these misdeeds and crimes were often severe. Those found guilty of murder and armed robbery, as well as sodomy and homosexuality, were subject to death. Blasphemy against the name of God "the Father, Son or Holy Ghost" was punishable by whipping, not to exceed forty stripes on the naked body, while manslaughter was also subject to forty stripes and burning the letter "M" on the naked hand with a hot iron.[11]

The assembly also considered a wide variety of other matters. It adopted the newly revised state constitution of 1786 and passed new legislation regulating weights and measures, supporting schools and the poor, and appointing printers for the state.

In October 1787, after the assembly had completed its ambitious agenda, the reformers voted to have the governor to call upon "all good people of this State" to support this wholesale revision of the laws. Governor Chittenden had little choice but to comply, and on October 20 he issued the following proclamation:

Whereas the Statute-Laws are now completed and promulgated for the government and observance of the good people of this State; and as it is of the highest importance to the peace and happiness of all communities, that a strict regard be paid, and a due obedience given, to such laws and regulations as are established for their government. . . . I

BY HIS EXCELLENCY
THOMAS CHITTENDEN, Esq

Governor, Captain-General and Commander in Chief, in and over

the State of *VERMONT*.

WHEREAS the Statute Laws are now completed and promulgated for the government and observance of the good people of this State ; and as it is of the highest importance to the peace and happiness of all communities, that a strict regard be paid, and a due obedience given to such laws and regulations as are established for their government :

I HAVE therefore thought fit, by and with advice of Council, and at the request of the General Assembly, to issue this Proclamation, strictly requiring and commanding all the good people of this State, to render strict obedience to the laws thereof. And that all executive and informing officers be active and vigilant in executing the said laws : and all the good people of this State, of every denomination, are hereby required to take notice hereof and govern themselves accordingly.

Given under my hand in Council, at Newbury, *this* 20th *day of* October, *one thousand seven hundred and eighty-seven, and in the eleventh year of the independence of this State.*

Thomas Chittenden.

By his Excellency's Command,

Joseph Fay, *Sec'ry.*

GOD SAVE THE PEOPLE

After Governor Chittenden's young lawyer opponents had completed a wholesale revision of Vermont's statutes in 1787, he issued a proclamation calling for the "strict regard" and "due obedience" to the new laws and regulations. (University of Vermont Special Collections) have therefore thought fit . . . to issue this Proclamation, strictly requiring and commanding all the good people of this State, to render strict obedience to the laws thereof. . . .

THOMAS CHITTENDEN
GOD SAVE THE PEOPLE [12]

Governor Chittenden played a subordinate role in the revision of the statutory laws, but one item of business in the October 1787 legislative session turned out to be quite special for him. Following the Revolutionary War, as new settlers flocked rapidly into the northern areas of Vermont, the assembly created new counties primarily to discharge judicial functions. On the western side of the state, Bennington was the first county to be created, followed by Rutland County in 1779 and Addison County in 1785. Two years later, the residents of Addison County requested a subdivision. On October 15, 1787, the assembly voted "to bring in a bill for dividing the county of Addison into two distinct counties." Once this bill was passed, a committee set to work to establish boundaries and to ascertain times and places for holding courts. On October 22, 1787, the assembly considered establishing a new county whose original boundaries would stretch all the way north to the Canadian border. The committee proposed naming this county Chittenden. Despite the overwhelming support of representatives from Rutland and Addison counties, who approved the new county by a margin of twenty-two yeas to eight nays, the final vote was close—forty yeas to thirty-five nays. As Ira Allen noted, "this vote determines somewhat the strength of the Governor in the Assembly." [13] Thus, Governor Chittenden was honored by having his name affixed to what was destined to become the most populous county in the state. The assembly also voted to appoint his oldest son, Noah, as the first sheriff of the county. The only other governmental unit in Vermont named after Governor Chittenden is the Rutland County town of Chittenden, which was chartered on March 16, 1780. [14]

It turned out to be extremely paradoxical that on October 24, 1787, only two days after creating Chittenden County, the assembly granted the Honorable Jonathan Hunt and his associates a township of six square miles in northern Vermont. This grant of land was destined to have a dramatic impact on Governor Chittenden's later political career.

The Woodbridge Affair

The Woodbridge affair grew out of a complicated series of actions involving the assembly's 1787 grant of land in north-central Vermont adjacent to the Canadian border in an area that now constitutes the town of Troy. On October 26, 1781, the assembly had previously voted to grant a township of land in this area to Major Theodore Woodbridge and a group of his associates. The charter issued by the Governor and Council was soon forfeited for non-payment of fees. Two years later, on October 23, 1783, the assembly passed an act that empowered the Governor and Council "to procure such Stores, or money to purchase Stores, as may be found necessary to enable the Surveyor General to compleat a survey of the Towns in this State." [15] The next day, October 24, 1783, the Governor and Council empowered and directed Ira Allen, the surveyor-general, to dispose of the township of Woodbridge, plus thirty-five rights in the township of Jay, and to use the proceeds from these sales to purchase the stores required to complete his surveys.

Allen did not dispose of Woodbridge, however. Instead, he used his own funds to purchase the necessary stores. Another two years passed before the Governor and Council, at a meeting in Arlington on October 25, 1785, authorized a back payment to Allen for the stores he had purchased. The executive council lacked a quorum, however, since only six members were present at the meeting. As a result, no final action was taken to actually reimburse Allen for the expenses he had incurred while completing his town surveys. [16]

In the September 1786 election Ira Allen was defeated for the office of state treasurer. He then called upon Governor Chittenden to deliver him the charter of the town of Woodbridge, plus the thirty-five rights in Jay, as payment for his survey expenses. Based on the earlier votes of the Governor and Council, Chittenden complied with this request. In October 1786 he issued a charter for the town of Woodbridge to Allen and a group of his associates.[17] In so doing, Governor Chittenden once again demonstrated his belief that the letter of the law was secondary to the spirit of the law. Technically, a majority of the members of the Governor and Council had not specifically voted to grant a charter for Woodbridge to Ira Allen. On the other hand, "Governor Chittenden could not avail himself of the technical objection that Allen had no legal right but 'to dispose of' the land . . . [based on] his conviction that Allen had honestly earned it. [Chittenden] seems to have determined to sacrifice a technicality in favor of honesty." [18]

The matter rested there until October 1787, when Jonathan Hunt asked the assembly to grant him a tract of land whose description was the same as the charter of the township of Woodbridge, which Chittenden had already granted to Ira Allen. Hunt was a former Yorker from the southeastern town of Vernon who had served on the Governor and Council since 1786. Despite Ira Allen's protests, the assembly went ahead and voted to grant Hunt and sixty-four associates the tract of land consisting of "twenty-three thousand and forty acres situate and adjoining north on the Canadian line at . . . ten Pounds [hard money] for each three hundred and thirty acres." [19]

At the next legislative session in October 1788, Major Hunt expressed outrage that this same tract of land had already been granted to Ira Allen. He launched a campaign against Governor Chittenden for making an illegal grant to Allen without the approval of the assembly. The assembly appointed a Committee of Inquiry, which consisted of Stephen R. Bradley of Westminster, Phineas Freeman of Marlboro, and Ebenezer Marvin of Tinmouth. After looking into the matter the committee issued a devastating finding:

> In the opinion of your Committee, his Excellency has vio-
> lated the trust reposed in him by the Constitution, to keep
> the Public Seal of this State sacred; and that he has con-
> verted it to private, sinister views . . . in the opinion of your
> Committee, said charter was fraudulent, and ought to be
> declared void by act of Legislature. [20]

As soon as the committee issued its report, the assembly voted to have Isaac Tichenor replace Ira Allen as an agent to Congress. In addition, the assembly passed an act annulling Allen's grant and severely censuring Governor Chittenden. The executive coun-cil refused to concur. Instead, it proposed that Allen should can-cel his Woodbridge charter. The assembly finally agreed to the council's request, but in an adroit political move, it directed the clerk to enter its censorious action in its official journal, thus assuring it would be made public. The damage was done, and the Woodbridge "scandal" was used by Chittenden's opponents to discredit him in the election campaign of 1789.

Despite the scandal, Chittenden again received the most votes in this election. The final returns were Chittenden 1,263; Moses Robinson 746; Samuel Safford 478; all others 378.[21] Since Chittenden did not secure a clear majority of the votes, how-ever, the assembly was authorized to elect the new governor. On October 9, 1789, at its fall session held in Westminster, the members of the assembly chose Moses Robinson of Bennington to serve as governor. Thomas Chittenden had suffered the first, and only, defeat in his political career.

Although he was bitterly disappointed by the assembly's actions, Governor Chittenden made a gracious farewell address, noting that "since you, gentlemen, would prefer some other person to fill the chair, I can . . . sincerely wish him a happy administration for the advancement of which my utmost influence shall be exerted." The

This map of Vermont by land agent William Blodgett, issued in
January 1789, was dedicated to Governor Chittenden. Ironically,
Chittenden suffered his only electoral defeat in October of that year.
The Blodgett map shows the vast extent of the original Chittenden
County in the northwest and, as the first individual "state" map
published in the American colonies, it helped publicize the Vermont
statehood cause. (University of Vermont Special Collections)

assembly extended their "gratitude and warmest thanks" for his services. Chittenden was fifty-nine years old, and Speaker Gideon Olin wrote him "it is their earnest wish that, in your advanced age and retirement from the arduous task of public life, you may enjoy all the blessings of domestic ease." [22]

It appears, however, that domestic ease was the farthest thought from Chittenden's mind. He returned to Williston, where he plunged into a flurry of activity. In the spring of 1787 Chittenden and his family had returned from Arlington to their Williston farm. Two of his sons—Giles and Truman—established their own farms in Williston, while his two other sons—Noah and Martin—began farms in Jericho. The Williston town records reveal that, once he was back home, Governor Chittenden immediately became involved in land sales. During 1787 and 1788 he sold ten parcels of his own Williston land, totaling 1,045 acres, for 540 pounds lawful money.[23] He continued to actively buy and sell land after the legislature refused to elect him governor in 1789. In addition, he became active in the town government, and he was even appointed to preside over the division of the town (into Richmond to the east and Williston to the west) in 1790.

Thomas Chittenden's political vindication came from an unexpected source. On February 6, 1790, a special independent committee, which had been appointed to settle Ira Allen's accounts as Vermont's surveyor-general, issued a report that cleared both Allen and Governor Chittenden of any fraudulent intent with respect to the Woodbridge grant. The three members on this committee, all widely respected, were Secretary of State Roswell Hopkins of Vergennes; Speaker of the House Gideon Olin of Shaftsbury; and Lieutenant Colonel Samuel Safford, who had served under Colonel Seth Warner in the Revolutionary War and had been a member of the Governor and Council since 1784.

After Chittenden was cleared by this second committee, he was again elected governor in 1790 by a substantial majority of nearly 1,300 votes. According to Daniel Chipman's memoir, "the friends of Governor Chittenden were strongly attached to him, and being highly exasperated, accused the legislature of disregarding the voice of the people [by] turning out an old and faithful public servant against their wishes. . . . The consequence was the next year, Governor Chittenden was elected by a far greater majority than that of preceding years." [24]

The Woodbridge affair represents an ugly episode in early Vermont history. While some observers have felt that Governor Chittenden and especially Ira Allen were capable of questionable deals, most historians agree they were not treated fairly on this occasion. One of the most outspoken critics, Michael Bellesiles, expressed his views very forcefully:

> The Chipman faction gained control of the state only once in the two decades following independence, and then by stealing it. In the November 1789 election, Chittenden won again, but fell 170 votes short of the necessary fifty percent majority, throwing the election into the state assembly. The assembly ignored the wishes of the voters and appointed Moses Robinson governor, even though he had received only a quarter of the popular votes cast. At the next election the voters turned out to reverse this decision, returning Chittenden to the governorship every year. . . .[25]

Perhaps Bellesiles has overstated the case, but the evidence certainly seems to support his basic conclusion. It is difficult to assume that Jonathan Hunt, an active member of the Governor and Council, could have been totally unaware of Ira Allen's Woodbridge charter, especially after Ira Allen had publicly objected so vociferously against the award of Hunt's grant. In addition, the fact that the assembly quickly appointed Isaac Tichenor to replace Ira Allen as an agent to Congress indicates that the reformers were out to get rid of Allen at all costs. Perhaps the most distressing development of all was Stephen Bradley's willingness to sign the Committee of Inquiry's highly emotional and inflammatory report. The Woodbridge affair was confusing, but Bradley was trained as a lawyer. It is difficult to understand how he concurred with a report that charged "his Excellency has violated the trust reposed in him by the constitution to keep the public seal of this state sacred; and that he has converted it to private, sinister views. . . ." [26]

There is no question that Governor Chittenden and his colleagues could play rough in the political arena when they felt that this was necessary. By the end of the 1780s, it was apparent that their more refined lawyer opponents were also willing to employ these same rough and tough tactics.

The Fourteenth State

The most important issue facing Vermont at the time of Chittenden's defeat in 1789 involved the settlement of the controversy with New York. In the spring of 1787 Alexander Hamilton, then serving as a state representative from New York City, introduced a bill in the New York Assembly calling for its delegates in Congress to ratify and confirm the sovereignty of Vermont. Hamilton's bill set three conditions: Vermont would be limited to the area between the Connecticut River and a line twenty miles east of the Hudson River; Vermont would accede to the Union; and the New York land titles in Vermont would be preserved.

In a speech accompanying his bill, Hamilton stated he viewed "with apprehension the present situation in Vermont. . . . We have the strongest evidence that negotiations have been carried out with the British in Canada [by] the leaders of the people of Vermont." Hamilton feared that hostilities might break out between New York and Vermont. Although his bill passed in the assembly by a vote of 27 to 19, it failed in the senate. When Hamilton left for Philadelphia in May 1787 to serve as one of the New York delegates to the federal Constitutional Convention, the issue of Vermont's statehood appeared, once again, to be at a dead end.[27]

As Hamilton had noted in his speech to the New York Assembly, the leaders of Vermont—Governor Chittenden, Ira Allen, and especially Ethan Allen—had been in contact with the British in Canada during the 1786–87 trade negotiations. Some historians have argued that the Chittenden/Allen group was hostile to the United States, but there is no specific evidence to indicate that Governor Chittenden actively opposed statehood. Like other owners of large tracts of Vermont land, he was concerned that no governmental actions should be taken that threatened the legitimacy of his New Hampshire titles. In addition, since Chittenden owned sizable holdings in Williston, he was interested in maintaining good trade relations with nearby Canada. He never publicly spoke out against statehood, however. As John Kelly, a New York land speculator who visited Vermont in 1788, reported, "His Excellency and Council, as well as other influential characters with whom I conversed, are well disposed towards the new constitution of the United States, and would wish to come into the confederacy on terms which [they] conceive to be proper." [28] This latter point was very important. Governor Chittenden had always made it clear that he would consent to statehood only if Vermont were treated as an equal partner.

According to one account written by historian Chilton Williamson, Ethan Allen had much deeper doubts about joining the Union.

> On July 16, 1788, Ethan [wrote] Lord Dorchester that he was fearful that, as soon as the Constitution was adopted and a new government effectively established, Vermont might be coerced into the Federal Union. . . . Vermonters, he continued, are warmly opposed to joining the other American states because they would then be exposed to Britain's displeasure which might go so far as to prohibit or hamper the Vermont-Quebec trade. . . . If the new government should attempt to subjugate Vermont, Ethan wished Dorchester to supply him with arms. . . . If the new government did not attack, Ver-

mont would re-establish the 'Haldimand System' of neutrality and trade with Quebec upon the freest and friendliest terms until events might later make possible a public declaration by Vermont in favor of rejoining the empire.[29]

When he wrote his letter to Dorchester, Ethan Allen was living on an intervale farm in Burlington with his second wife, Fanny. By the mid-1780s Ethan had retired from the Vermont political scene, and in 1785 he published a philosophical book, *Reason: the Only Oracle of Man*, that criticized many orthodox religious beliefs. Some later critics claimed that *The Oracles of Reason*, as the book came to be called, was based heavily on the work of Ethan's old tutor, Dr. Thomas Young, the radical from Pennsylvania. It was quite remarkable that a rugged frontiersman like Ethan devoted his final energies to this type of ambitious intellectual endeavor. Ethan Allen died on February 17, 1789, after visiting his cousin, Ebenezer, in South Hero. Four days later an elaborate ceremony was held in Burlington, and Governor Thomas Chittenden served as one of the pallbearers for his old friend and colleague.

Only one day before Ethan Allen had written his July 16 letter to Lord Dorchester, another Vermonter, Nathaniel Chipman, wrote quite a different letter to Alexander Hamilton. Chipman was the ideal person to contact Hamilton. Both men were Federalists and shared similar political views. Both were college graduates and lawyers. Both were young and ambitious. Chipman was thirty-six when their correspondence began, while Hamilton was only thirty-one. In many respects, these two men represented the political wave of the future.

In his letter of July 15, 1788, to Hamilton, Chipman stressed the desirability of settling the New York/Vermont controversy. He expressed a concern that should Vermont join the Union, the federal courts would favor New York land grants over those of Vermont, and flatly asserted "For these reasons, and I presume for no others, the governor and several gentlemen deeply interested in the lands granted by Vermont, have expressed themselves somewhat bitterly against the new federal plan of government." [30] He made a number of suggestions how this matter might be resolved and asked for Hamilton's advice and help on the issue.

Hamilton immediately replied to Chipman in a letter dated July 22 with an opening comment, "Your brother delivered me your letter of the 15th inst. which I received with pleasure as the basis of a correspondence that may be productive of the public good." [31] In his letter Hamilton pointed out that the southern states were anxious to admit Kentucky to the Union, and "the northern [states] will be glad to find a counterpoise in Vermont." He made a number of suggestions on the land issue, and the two men continued their correspondence in September and early October. Hamilton backed away from the issue, however, after he took over responsibility as the first secretary of the treasury in the new national government.

On October 22, 1788, the Vermont General Assembly elected Moses Robinson, Jonathan Arnold, and Ira Allen to serve as agents to Congress. As already noted, Ira Allen was later replaced by Isaac Tichenor as a result of the Woodbridge affair. On October 25 the assembly voted, "that it be the duty of the Agents to Congress to use all due diligence to remove every obstacle to the accession of this State to the Federal government." [32]

The scene then shifted to the New York Assembly, where John Jay had switched his position and become one of the leading advocates for Vermont. In February 1789 the New York Assembly passed a bill that recognized Vermont, but this was once again defeated in the state senate. Finally, on July 14, 1789, the New York legislature approved an act naming six commissioners to negotiate with Vermont, and all six of them communicated with Governor Chittenden to advise him of their appointments. Three months later Chittenden was no longer governor of Vermont, but he kept the Vermont General Assembly fully informed about the New York initiatives. On October 14, less than a week after his defeat, "His Honor the late Governor came into the House [by request] and communicated such letters and advices as he had received from abroad touching on our situation with the Federal Government of the United States." [33]

Once the assembly had officially received the communication from the New York commissioners, it passed an act appointing Isaac Tichenor, Stephen R. Bradley, Nathaniel Chipman, Elijah Paine, and Israel Smith as commissioners to negotiate on behalf of Vermont with their New York counterparts. It was obvious that Vermont's lawyers dominated the state's negotiating sessions, but even if Chittenden had still remained as governor, this would have been a logical move in light of the legal issues that had to be resolved. Following a year of exchanges, on October 4, 1790, the New York commissioners proposed the sum of $30,000 from Vermont as payment for the relinquishment of its land titles within Vermont. The Commissioners from Vermont countered with an offer of $20,000, but on October 7 the New Yorkers restated their $30,000 offer in writing. At a session held on October 28, 1790, the Vermont General Assembly agreed to pay that sum and passed an act specifying the boundary line between the two states. [34]

When this final vote was taken, Thomas Chittenden was once again presiding as governor, having been reelected to his position as the state's chief executive only two weeks earlier. In his inaugural address he had praised Vermont's government for preparing "the way for the happy day when we shall add no small weight to the scale, and be under the protection of a new and glorious empire, which bids fair in a short time to vie in power and policy with any of the European States." [35]

Once the settlement with New York was completed, the Vermont General Assembly called a special convention to consider adopting the United States Constitution. The convention was held in Bennington beginning on January 6, 1791. A total of 109 delegates attended from towns throughout the state. Governor Chittenden was the delegate from Williston, and his second son, Martin, represented nearby Jericho. The delegates elected Governor Chittenden as the president of the convention and Moses Robinson of Bennington as vice president. The election of Thomas Chittenden for this honor illustrated the political climate within Vermont at the time. Although Chittenden had not played an active role in the negotiations with New York, he still retained his position as the symbolic leader of Vermont once he was reelected as the state's governor.

At the Bennington convention, Nathaniel Chipman was the driving force, and he gave the major address supporting Vermont's entering the Union. Daniel Buck of Norwich made one of the few speeches against ratification, arguing that the federal government possessed too much power. The next day, however, Buck modified his position, and when the delegates met again on Monday, January 10, 1790, they ratified the Constitution of the United States and petitioned Congress to admit Vermont as the fourteenth state. The vote was 105 to 4. [36]

From this time forward, the lawyer reformers in Vermont assumed the major responsibility for overseeing the state's relations with the federal government. On January 19 the assembly elected Moses Robinson and Stephen R. Bradley to serve as Vermont's first United States senators. The following day Nathaniel Chipman and Lewis R. Morris were appointed commissioners to take the necessary steps to make sure Vermont was admitted to the Union. The only wartime leader ever elected to Congress was Matthew Lyon, who served as a representative for a tumultuous four-year term from 1798 to 1802 before he left Vermont for Kentucky.[37]

Once Congress voted to admit Vermont to the Union on March 4, 1791, Governor Chittenden turned his attention to domestic affairs. He was one of only a few wartime leaders who were still active in the state's government. By this time, a number of his former colleagues had already passed away, including Heman Allen in 1777, Joseph Bowker and Seth Warner in 1784, and Ethan Allen in 1789. Despite his advancing age and the challenges posed by his opponents, Thomas Chittenden was still a man of prodigious energy who was eager to serve Vermont during the remaining years of his life.

CHAPTER VIII

The Final Years
(1791–1797)

Once Vermont became the fourteenth state, it grew very rapidly. The population in the 1791 census was listed as 85,341, with more than two-thirds of all inhabitants living in the state's four southern counties. Ten years later, in the 1800 census, the population climbed to 155,000, making Vermont the fastest growing state in the nation.

As a result of this growth, the agenda of government changed. New counties were created while the towns, the most basic providers of local services, petitioned the state legislature to approve taxes and lotteries to enlarge their revenues. At the same time, state government took on an increasing number of obligations. First, it planned internal improvements, such as establishing a state university and constructing a more effective transportation system with new roads and canals. Second, since Vermont was now part of the United States, it was forced to adjust to a new role in handling external affairs, especially with British Canada. Third, Vermont had to review its own constitution and laws to make sure they conformed with those of the federal union. Finally, it witnessed the emergence of more structured national political parties within the state.

By the 1790s the assembly met annually for a three-week fall session after the harvest was gathered. The members presented their credentials and spent most of the first day counting the votes for the state's top executive officers, including the twelve members of the executive council. The October 1791 session of the Vermont General Assembly in Windsor, which marked the fifteenth meeting of the legislature, was formally opened with an unusual ceremony. After the votes were counted and Thomas Chittenden was again elected governor, he was "received by a company of Artillery and a company of Light Infantry each corps in the most beautiful uniforms. . . . His election was announced by the discharge of fifteen cannon from the parade. A sermon suitable for the occasion was delivered by Rev. Mr. Shuttlesworth with his usual energy and pathos. In the evening an elegant ball was given . . . to a most brilliant assembly of Gentlemen and Ladies from this and from neighboring states." [1]

One of the first items of business at this 1791 session involved Vermont's new responsibilities as the nation's fourteenth state. In early October Moses Robinson had written Governor Chittenden and Speaker of the House Gideon Olin to suggest that his election as a United States Senator at the January convention in Bennington had been premature, since Congress did not formally admit Vermont as a new state until early March. He urged the assembly to reaffirm the senatorial elections as soon as possible, because Congress was scheduled to meet at the end of the month. On October 17 the Governor and Council met jointly with members of the assembly in "Grand Committee" to reaffirm Moses Robinson of Bennington and Stephen R. Bradley of Westminster as Vermont's first two United States senators. In addition, a former speaker of the assembly, Nathaniel Niles of Fairlee, and Israel Smith, a Yale graduate, lawyer, and former Yorker from Rutland, served as the state's first members in the United States House of Representatives.[2]

A few weeks later, on November 3, 1791, Vermont voted to ratify all twelve of the amendments to the United States Constitution proposed by the Congress. The first ten of these amendments, which were approved by the required number of states, were added to the Constitution as the "Bill of Rights," so-named because they were designed to protect our most fundamental freedoms. Two other amendments were not approved—they dealt with the apportionment of representation to Congress and the compensation of United States senators and representatives prior to an intervening election.

Although many of the modifications Vermont made in its own constitution and laws to comply with the requirements of statehood were beneficial, at least one was questionable. In 1793 the assembly passed a lengthy act governing all phases of the state's militia. Its second section stated that every able-bodied, free, white male citizen between the ages of sixteen and forty-five was to serve in the militia. As Marlene B. Wallace, an editor of the Vermont state papers, comments "The qualification 'white' stands out in view of the notable lack of a color bar in other areas of state government." [3] The earlier Vermont militia act of 1786 had not made any references to color or race. The United States Congress, however, had specified a white only restriction in the 1792 national militia act, and under the U.S. Constitution's "Supreme Law of the Land" clause, Vermont was forced to add this same discriminatory requirement to its own militia act. Thus, Vermont, whose own 1777 constitution was the first to abolish slavery, was obligated to organize a segregated militia after it became the fourteenth state.

In addition to dealing with issues relating to statehood, the 1791 assembly revised the state's criminal laws and redefined the powers of the state supreme court and the county courts. Finally, the legislators also considered a number of financial issues, including an inquiry into the state of the treasury to determine Vermont's expenditures in the "late war with Great Britain, as well as the ways and means to make the thirty-thousand-dollar payment to the state of New York which was required to settle its statehood obligation." [4]

Internal Improvements

A great deal of the assembly's time involved internal improvements—relating to post roads, bridges, waterways, and educational institutions—that were necessitated by the state's growing population. "Inland trade was badly hobbled by the abominable state of the dirt roads, many of which were passable only when winter filled in the trench-like ruts. Mostly they began as blazed trails, widened first to bridle paths and then to roads capable of accommodating ox carts. Exceptions were the two great military roads, Crown Point and Bayley Hazen, [but] even these highways fell into disuse after the war." [5] The situation was very serious in central Vermont, where towns scrambled to make road and bridge improvements. In the 1791 session, for example, the assembly considered petitions from towns such as Bethel, which requested a lottery of 550 pounds to erect a bridge over the third branch of the White River. Woodstock asked for a lottery of 300 pounds to repair roads across the "mountains toward Killington." [6] Within a few years the legislators had received so many requests from towns that they organized their first standing committees—one on land taxes and another on lotteries—to screen the town petitions. During the sessions the members worked very hard. They met daily, except Sundays, beginning at eight in the morning, and members who were absent a day or more without leave were subject to expulsion.

On October 25, 1791, the assembly debated an act for the establishment of a college, or seminary, within the state. A key issue involved its location. After Ira Allen pledged to provide land worth 4,000 pounds if it was located in Burlington, the assembly voted as follows: Burlington (89 votes), Rutland (24 votes), Williamstown (5 votes), Manchester (5 votes) and one vote each for Danville, Castleton, and Berlin. Governor Chittenden was designated to serve as president of the board of the new institution, and the next day ten "gentlemen" were elected as trustees, including Ira Allen. Also elected as a trustee was the Reverend Bethuel Chittenden, the youngest brother of the governor, who lived in Shelburne, where he was a minister and missionary in the Protestant Episcopal Church.[7]

At the same time the towns were building roads and bridges, larger efforts were underway to link Vermont with its neighboring states to the south. When the Allen brothers and Thomas Chittenden first settled in the Winooski River area, they looked to Canada, especially to Montreal, as a natural trading outlet. Once Vermont had joined the federal union, however, the focus shifted south. Although most of the small farm families in the state were largely self-sufficient, some external trade existed because cash was needed for taxes and for certain necessities and luxuries.

This shift of trade to the south involved the state's two major waterways—Lake Champlain on the west and the Connecticut River on the east. In the early 1790s New York began to consider plans for a canal that would link Lake Champlain with the Hudson River. Within Vermont, Nathaniel Chipman was a leading advocate for the Champlain canal. In a letter to General Philip Schuyler of New York, Chipman predicted, "it would not be extravagant to suppose that . . . this canal would in less than ten years command the trade of 100,000 people." [8] Nevertheless, the Vermont General Assembly decided to focus its immediate attention on the Connecticut River. On October 31, 1791, the assembly passed an act granting William Page and Lewis R. Morris the exclusive right to build locks at Bellows Falls. This was the first charter for a canal in the United States. During the following session the legislature granted David Sanderson the exclusive right to cart goods, wares, and merchandise through the Bellows Falls canal. Thus, while the Champlain-Hudson River canal was still on hold, the Connecticut River was made more accessible. As a result of the new Bellows Falls locks, a round trip by flatboat from Wells River, Vermont, to Hartford, Connecticut, required only about twenty-five days.[9]

The assembly also had to consider issues brought about by the increasing religious diversity in the state. Vermont was originally settled by Congregationalists from other New England states, but growing numbers of other religious groups had arrived over the years, including Roman Catholics from Quebec, plus Episcopalians (in Arlington 1767), Baptists (in Shaftsbury 1768), Quakers (in Danby 1785), Methodists (on the western circuit 1788), and Presbyterians (in Barnet 1788). The Quakers objected to paying the fees of the assembly's chaplain from general tax funds "out of tenderness of conscience toward God." When they petitioned the 1791 assembly to discontinue this practice, the legislature agreed to the request of "the Respectable people called Quakers," and a bill was passed to pay all future chaplain's fees from supreme court fines, penalties, and forfeitures, rather than from the general taxes collected by the state.[10]

At the conclusion of the 1791 session, the assembly passed an act specifying that it would meet in Rutland for its October 1792 session, and thereafter it would hold its annual sessions alternately in Windsor and Rutland for the next eight years.

The Alburgh Incident

Before the legislature was able to meet for its fall 1792 session, an incident in the northwestern corner of the state brought into focus the new role Vermont had to adopt as a member of the federal union. The June 1792 episode, known as the "Alburgh incident," provoked a fascinating exchange of letters between Governor Chittenden, President George Washington, Governor Alured Clarke of Quebec, and Secretary of State Thomas Jefferson.

The legal issues surrounding the incident were somewhat complex. Almost a half century earlier, in November 1744, the King of France made a land grant to a claimant named Francis

Focault. After the British conquered Canada in 1759 they passed on the title of this grant to Henry and John Caldwell. In 1792 John Caldwell was still living in the area with other British subjects, who had obtained their land from him.[11]

The problem arose from the fact that the town of Alburgh lay south of 45 degrees latitude, the line the Treaty of 1783 had established as the boundary separating the United States from British North America (i.e. Canada). The British army had continued to man two garrisons south of this boundary line, however, at Dutchman's Point in North Hero and at Point au Fer in New York, even though these garrisons violated the provisions of the treaty. The British justified them on the grounds that the United States had failed to fully compensate former Tories as required under the terms of this same treaty.[12]

The Vermont General Assembly had authorized the Governor and Council to grant Alburgh to Ira Allen on February 23, 1781, but it wasn't until June 7, 1792, that Governor Chittenden formally ordered Alburgh to be organized as a Vermont town. It was obvious to the Caldwells that this represented a direct threat to their land holdings. On June 8 the deputy sheriff of Chittenden County and three of his assistants traveled to Alburgh, where they served a writ authorizing them to attach the goods of a resident named Patrick Conroy in satisfaction of a debt Conroy owed in Vermont. When the deputy sheriff and his assistants began to round up some of Mr. Conroy's cattle, a group of British guards arrived and took the deputy and two of his assistants as prisoners, removing them to the guard house at Point au Fer. Two days later an armed British force seized and interrogated a Vermont justice of the peace.[13]

Governor Chittenden was outraged by these events, which he regarded as a clear violation of Vermont's sovereign authority. Assuming his previous posture as the leader of an independent republic, he rushed home to Williston and fired off three blistering letters on June 16, 1792. His first letter was addressed to Acting Governor Alured Clarke in Quebec:

Sir: A British Capt with an armed force leaving his post and penetrating eight or nine miles within the acknowledged jurisdiction of Vermont, and then imprisoning an executive officer of this government in the peaceable execution of his office . . . has an appearance both novel and extraordinary. . . . I feel myself therefore obliged immediately to request from your excellency an explanation of this unprecedente [sic] conduct and unprovoked insult upon the government of Vermont. . . .

Thomas Chittenden

Chittenden's second letter was written to Levi Allen and instructed him "without loss of time [to] repair to the city of Quebec and personally deliver to his Excellency Gov. Clarke, my letter." The third letter was written to President George Washington to inform him about the situation:

Sir: The unprovoked insult lately offered to this, and the united government by the commanding officer of a british Garrison within jurisdiction of the united States; is so flagrant a breach of the Laws of Nations, and the late treaty with great Britain; that I feel myself under obligations to give you the earliest information of it. . . . Inclosed is a copy of my Letter to the Governor of Canada. . . . As soon as I receive an answer I shall without loss of time, communicate it to you. . . . I am with the greatest respect your Excellency's very humble servant.

THOMs. CHITTENDEN[14]

All remained quiet until Chittenden received the following reply from Acting Governor Clarke dated July 5, 1792:

Sir: Your representation leading to Questions beyond the sphere of my Trust, and being unaccompanied with the Proofs to be expected with Complaints of that kind, I can only give

Philadelphia, July 9th 1792.

Sir,

I have the honor to enclose you sundry papers communicated to me by the British Minister residing here; which have been duly laid before the President of the United States, and further to solicit from your Excellency information as to the facts therein stated. and while I am authorized to assure you that the government is proceeding sincerely and steadily, to obtain by the way of negociation a relinquishment of our territory, held by the British, I am at the same time to press that no measures be permitted in your state, which, by changing the present state of things in districts where the British have hitherto exercised jurisdiction, might disturb the peaceable and friendly discussion now in hand, and retard, if not defeat, an ultimate arrangement.

I have the honor to be with perfect respect and esteem,
Your Excellency's
most obedient &
most humble servant.

Th: Jefferson

His Excellency the Governor of Vermont.

On July 2, 1792, the United States' Secretary of State, Thomas Jefferson, became alarmed over Governor Chittenden's correspondence with the British concerning the Alburgh incident. He warned Chittenden not to press measures that "might disturb the peaceable and friendly discussion now in hand, and retard, if not defeat, an ultimate arrangement." (Vermont State Archives) command for the Investigations to be obtained here on a Subject of such Importance to the Peace of the Borders. . . .

I am, Sir your very humble servant

Alured Clarke[15]

Shortly after hearing from Clarke, Chittenden received a letter from an alarmed Thomas Jefferson, the U. S. Secretary of State, dated July 9, 1792. It is obvious that Jefferson was trying to calm Chittenden while also gently advising him that the responsibility for dealing with international affairs now rested with the national government of the United States rather than with the State of Vermont:

Sir . . . While I am authorized to assure you that the government is proceeding sincerely and steadily to obtain by the way of negociation a relinquishment of our territory held by the British, I am at the same time to press that no measures be permitted in your state which . . . might disturb the peaceable and friendly discussion now in hand, and retard, if not defeat, an ultimate arrangement.

TH: JEFFERSON[16]

Jefferson then followed this up with a second letter from Philadelphia dated July 12, 1792. This time Jefferson explicitly warned Chittenden not to overreact:

Sir . . . I must renew my entreaties to your Excellency that no innovation in the state of things may be attempted for the present . . . and it would be truly unfortunate if any premature measures on the part of your state should furnish a pretext for suspending the negociations on this subject. . . .

TH: JEFFERSON[17]

At this point a frustrated Chittenden began to back off, although not before he fired a final shot across the bow by sending President Washington a hastily written second letter dated July 16:

> Sir: I now have the Honor to Transmit to your Excellency a Copy of Governor Clarke's answer to me. I shall make no Comments upon the equivocal and evasive manner in which it is written as I was Sensible that the Conduct of this garrison might Involve questions of national Importance and desarve a national discursion. . . . I Submit to your Excellency how far I have acted prudent in this Bisness or what further or different measures I should have taken. . . .
> T. C.[18]

The affair was finally resolved by Jay's treaty of 1794, when the British agreed that the town of Alburgh was located within the jurisdiction of the United States, and more specifically within the state of Vermont.[19] In the interim Governor Chittenden presented the relevant letters and documents to the fall 1792 session of the legislature in Rutland, which appointed a committee to look into the matter. On October 20, 1792, the committee concluded "Governor Chittenden had acted with that degree of spirit and propriety which ought to mark the conduct of the Chief Magistrate of a free and independent State. It further appears to us, that the letters written by Mr. Jefferson, to his Excellency the Governor of this State, must have been founded on a mistaking of the facts, which must have been received from Canada." [20]

In addition to the Alburgh incident, a number of other issues were considered during the fall 1792 legislative session. A dispute broke out during the very first week involving Ira Allen's pledge to establish the state university in Burlington. Allen's pledge had involved land worth 1,000 pounds on which university buildings could be constructed, plus another 3,000 pounds worth of outlying lands that would pay a yearly rent to the university. The disagreement arose between Allen and the

Board of Trustees over the date the university could expect the donation of the outlying lands. On October 16 the legislature recommended that the Board of Trustees should bring a legal suit against Allen if he refused to give the outlying lands whenever the trustees required it.[21]

Ira Allen's rough treatment in the legislature continued in early November. After hearing an accounting from Isaac Tichenor, the assembly passed a resolution on November 2 "that the Treasurer of this state be, and he hereby is directed immediately to call on Ira Allen, Esq. for the sum of 300 pounds," and it also approved a second resolution appointing the Honorable Isaac Tichenor, Esquire, to represent the state in a lawsuit Allen threatened to bring in federal court. The suit was subsequently dismissed due to lack of proper jurisdiction.[22]

Ira Allen and Isaac Tichenor, who were bitter political enemies, continued their feud for many years. Allen's accounts as state treasurer were brought before the assembly again in 1793, 1794, 1795, and 1796, when they were finally dismissed. In all this time, the state never made a serious attempt to collect the money that Tichenor claimed Allen owed it.

In contrast to its harsh treatment of Ira Allen, the assembly voted Governor Chittenden a salary of 150 pounds and also "resolved that His Excellency Thomas Chittenden be directed to sign a Charter to himself . . . for Twenty rights of land in the Township of Carthage [later named Jay] amounting to seven thousand six hundred acres including part of the public rights in such Township according to said resolution." [23]

Governor Chittenden had originally obtained this land in Carthage under a 1781 Vermont grant as part of his back salary, and this vote by the assembly confirmed this addition to his burgeoning land holdings. The resolution offers convincing evidence of Chittenden's continuing ability to maintain strong political support. Some of the young conservative lawyers—Nathaniel Chipman, Isaac Tichenor, and their colleagues—"contented themselves with ridiculing Chittenden as a backwoodsman who lacked polish." [24] He still commanded political respect, however, especially in the frontier towns of northern Vermont. The size of Chittenden County was cut in half during the 1792 session when the Assembly passed an act "dividing the counties of Orange and Chittenden Into Six Separate and Distinct Counties." The four new counties were named Franklin, Essex, Caledonia, and Orleans.[25]

The Constitution of 1793

On June 6, 1792, the second Council of Censors convened in Rutland to review laws and consider revisions to the Vermont Constitution. The president of the council was lawyer Samuel Knight of Brattleboro, the chief justice of the Vermont supreme court. A number of other lawyers and conservative Federalists were members of the council, including Isaac Tichenor, Elijah Paine, Elijah Dewey, Samuel Mattocks, and Roswell Hopkins, the Vermont secretary of state. The council also included some political progressives, most notably Anthony Haswell of Bennington, the publisher of the *Vermont Gazette*, and Jonas Galusha from Shaftsbury, a future governor of Vermont, who was married to Thomas Chittenden's daughter, Mary.[26]

The council completed its work on November 30. The council's major recommendation called for a new framework of government by establishing a state senate to replace the Governor and Council. The proposed nine-member senate would be apportioned by counties based on their population, with the authority to expand its size by one member for each additional 10,000 inhabitants in a county. The proposed elimination of the Governor and Council would have seriously weakened the governor, who would have had no veto power, nor even the power to suspend any laws that had existed under the 1786 constitution.[27]

On July 3, 1793, delegates from 125 towns met at the Constitutional Convention in Windsor to consider the Council of

Censors' recommendations. Thomas Chittenden represented Williston, and his second son, Martin, was a delegate from the nearby town of Jericho. As their first order of business, the delegates elected Thomas Chittenden as president. Unlike the Constitutional Convention of 1786 in Manchester, where Governor Chittenden and delegates from the small frontier towns had worked together, this time the tables were reversed as these same delegates disagreed with some of Chittenden's proposals.

A manuscript of the record of this convention was discovered in 1877, and it was later printed in the *Windsor Vermont Journal* in 1922. The manuscript shows that the delegates struggled to reach a consensus on how they should deal with the censors' proposals to establish a new state senate and to abolish the Governor and Council. On the fourth day of the convention, Saturday, July 6, a fourteen-member committee was created to resolve this issue, but they could not reach agreement. On Monday, July 8, John Fassett of Cambridge, an old-time political leader and Chittenden ally who had spent fifteen years as a member of the Governor and Council, "arose and proposed a mode to accommodate the Jarring opinions of this Convention." On the motion of General Brigham a new four-man committee was appointed. The members were John Fassett, Gershom Lyman of Marlboro, Matthew Lyon of Fair Haven, and Representative John Law of Colchester. Fassett and Lyon were political veterans, while Lyman and Law were newcomers. After Governor Chittenden was added as a fifth member to the committee it was clear the Chittenden forces were in control.[28]

When the committee reported that same afternoon, it made a number of recommendations. First, and perhaps most surprising, it "proposed that the Senate may be established. . . ." It noted, however, "the alteration with regard to Representation be rejected . . . [and] . . . the mode of electing conformable to the old mode of electing Councillors" should be retained. It also proposed that the "necessity of the Concurrence of the Senate in money bills [be] Errased."

In addition to supporting a modified senate, the committee members made a number of other recommendations. They proposed to weaken the 1786 constitutional restrictions on holding multiple offices by suggesting "that all Illegibility to certain offices [be] descarded when in their Nature they are not incompatible." They rejected the censors' recommendation that would have excluded major office holders from serving on the Council of Censors in the future. The committee also recommended that "the religious Test in the old Constitution [be] expunged," and it rejected the Council of Censors' proposal to eliminate the requirement that each town in the assembly was entitled to send at least one delegate to future Constitutional Conventions, thereby retaining the one town, one vote tradition.[29]

Once the committee had presented its report, the delegates at the convention voted on "whether they will consent to have a Senate under any modifications which this Convention may have the Right to make." The motion was handily defeated by a substantial majority of seventy-three nays to fifty yeas, despite the fact that all five of the committee members—John Fassett, Gersham Lyman, Matthew Lyon, John Law, and Governor Chittenden—voted in its favor.

The frontier town delegates from Addison and Chittenden counties, the area of Governor Chittenden's greatest political strength, voted overwhelmingly against the senate. Only two delegates from these two counties other than the committee members supported the proposal for a senate, while thirty-four delegates voted in the negative. Even Governor Chittenden's son, Martin, voted nay.

It appears that the committee may have been attempting to reach a compromise. Its members concluded that a weak new senate with no power to consider money bills was acceptable if the prohibition on multiple office holding was modified and the right of each of the small towns to send delegates to future constitutional conventions was guaranteed. It is also possible that the committee's proposals represented a significant political miscalculation by Chittenden and his colleagues. The small frontier towns' opposition to the proposal to establish a senate was probably based on the delegates' fear of losing power to the larger towns in the southern part of the state. As Daniel Chipman noted in a speech to the 1836 convention, which finally did amend the Vermont Constitution to provide for a state senate, "in the year 1793, a great portion of the towns north of the counties of Rutland and Windsor contained less than forty families, and as we had even in those days, some genuine demagogues, they undertook to render themselves popular by telling the people in that region that if the proposed amendments to the constitution should be adopted they would lose their whole might in both branches of the legislature. And so successful were they, that every member of the convention from that section of the State except two voted against the amendments." [30]

Hence, the Constitutional Convention of 1793 rejected the major proposals of the Council of Censors, and the original framework of the state government remained in place. Because Vermont was now a member of the United States, however, the convention delegates did attend to "the important task of amending the Vermont Constitution to avoid conflicts with its federal equivalent." Some of the key amendments to the state constitution involved revising Section 22, training the state militia "agreeable to the Constitution of the United States;" Section 26, which prohibited holding offices in both the federal and state government; and Section 27, which was eliminated entirely since the procedures for electing congressmen were specified in the United States Constitution. In addition to making these accommodations to the United States Constitution, the delegates voted to eliminate the religious test for office, but they did not approve any other important procedural or structural changes in Vermont's government.

Perhaps because of all the debate that had taken place about the proposed senate, there was confusion over the issue of legislative representation after the Constitutional Convention adjourned on July 9, 1793. When the Vermont General Assembly met for its October 1793 session, Joseph Hubbard of Weathersfield demanded to be seated as the town's second representative, since Chapter II, Section 7 of the 1793 constitution had retained the original 1777 language that each town with eighty or more taxable inhabitants was entitled to two representatives during the first septenary. This septenary had expired in 1786 but Hubbard argued that since this section had not been eliminated, it was still in effect until at least 1800, when the next Council of Censors was scheduled to meet.

Governor Chittenden and his political allies immediately recognized the danger of Hubbard's demand. If Weathersfield were allowed to retain two representatives, all of the larger southern towns could make this same claim, and the smaller northern towns would lose their control of the assembly. On the motion of Matthew Lyon, the assembly members voted that they would not allow two representatives from any one town—again retaining the one town, one vote tradition—and Hubbard was not seated.[31]

Political Parties

The legislative battles of the mid-1780s, when Isaac Tichenor, Nathaniel Chipman, and the other younger lawyers challenged Thomas Chittenden and the wartime frontier leaders, had involved local and regional issues. By the early 1790s, however, larger national political controversies were taking on increasing importance within Vermont. In June 1791 Thomas Jefferson and his colleague from Virginia, Congressman James Madison, made a visit to New England. According to Willard Sterne Randall's account, "for a long time Jefferson had wanted to visit Vermont. As the champion of the frontier farmer, he had come to think of the new state as the frontier ideal, a sort of unspoiled Virginia without slavery or entrenched tidewater aristocrats, a place where everyone would have a chance to own a home and land and make a good living." [32]

Jefferson and Madison described their trip as a "botany excursion," since Jefferson kept copious notes about the fish, birds, animals, flowers, trees, and other flora and fauna they observed. They traveled up the Hudson River incognito and avoided meetings with major political officials. After a two-day stay on Lake George, they boarded a ship near Crown Point on Lake Champlain, but a fierce north wind kept them from proceeding further. As a result, they backtracked and followed a land route to Bennington. When Vermont's U. S. Senator-elect Moses Robinson discovered they were in town, he invited them to dinner at his home, where they met a number of guests, including Isaac Tichenor and Anthony Haswell, the radical editor of the *Vermont Gazette*. They remained in Bennington on Sunday because of a recent state blue law that prohibited Sabbath travel. The following day they crossed over to the Connecticut River and headed south to Philadelphia. Due to time constraints, Jefferson and Madison did not see much of Vermont beyond the Bennington area, nor did they have time to meet with Governor Chittenden or other top state officials.

Jefferson and Madison's trip was the harbinger of a new surge of political activity in Vermont. Between 1783 and 1799 at least sixteen weekly newspapers appeared in the state. The two earliest papers were the *Vermont Gazette* in Bennington, a pro-Jefferson weekly edited by Anthony Haswell, and the more conservative *Vermont Journal*, published in Windsor.[33] In 1793 James Lyon, the son of the radical firebrand Matthew Lyon of Fair Haven, established the *Farmers' Library* in Rutland, The next year that paper was bought by two partners who bore the same name, Samuel Williams, and they renamed it the *Rutland Herald*.[34]

The October 1793 election indicated the political climate within the state was becoming more competitive. Thomas Chittenden was reelected governor over Isaac Tichenor, but the total vote of 3,184 to 2,712 was relatively close. Tichenor won all the counties east of the Green Mountains, but Chittenden was reelected because he secured massive majorities in Rutland and Addison counties. Whereas Tichenor and the lawyer reformers felt they possessed the knowledge to govern Vermont, the frontier settlers had a completely different mindset. They related to Governor Chittenden as one of their own, while they felt Tichenor represented an "aristocratical party." The settlers believed "genuine principles of good government were neither complex nor mysterious and men of common capacity [were] capable and better suited than others to be public officers. Tichenor's supporters were lawyers and literary people who had imbibed all their political knowledge from books. . . . If allowed to succeed, Tichenor and his party would live in idleness while the poor peasant and his family toiled away in poverty. . . . Devotion to liberty, equality and the rights of man demanded that aristocratic politicians be brought down on an average with ordinary citizens. Equality, not hierarchy, must remain the rule." [35]

At the same time that Vermont's political arena was becoming more heated, national politics were also becoming more intense. The growing conflict between Alexander Hamilton and Thomas Jefferson led to the formation of America's first two political parties—the Federalists and Jeffersonian Democratic Republicans. Alexander Hamilton, the leading Federalist, favored a strong national government that would encourage commerce and industry by creating a Bank of the United States and pursuing other centralizing financial policies, such as the assumption of state debts. Thomas Jefferson had a different vision of a more localized agrarian society based on rural yeomen farmers. In addition, Hamilton advocated an increasingly pro-British trade policy, while Jefferson, the former ambassador to France, was more sympathetic to the French. These conflicts grew out of fundamentally different visions of government. The Federalists were accused of pursuing aristocratic policies that promoted economic factionalism and favored the wealthy commercial interests over the common workers and farmers. The critics of Federalist policies feared that they would undermine the democratic promise of the American Revolution.

Within a short period of time, radical political societies formed in many states to address this concern. In addition to opposing Hamilton's policies, the members of these Democratic-Republican societies were strong supporters of France and the ideals of the French Revolution, which they believed reflected the ideals of the earlier American Revolution. In contrast, the Federalists viewed the French Revolution with increasing alarm as a dangerous manifestation of democratic excesses.

The first political societies appeared in 1793 in Pennsylvania, which ended up with nine, the most of any of the states. In February 1794 Matthew Lyon, who was playing an increasingly active role in Vermont politics, issued a call for the formation of Democratic societies, and within a couple of months Democratic societies began to spring up throughout Vermont. The first was formed in Chittenden County on April 16, 1794, the second in Castleton in Rutland County on April 23, 1794, followed by two more in Addison and Rutland counties. Vermont soon had the second-largest number of societies next to Pennsylvania.[36] Many of the members of the Vermont societies were former Green Mountain Boys, members of local committees of safety, and Revolutionary War leaders such as Isaac Clark. Interestingly, the societies drew the support of radicals as well as wealthy men such as Udney Hay, who had large land holdings in Underhill and elsewhere.[37]

In Vermont "the central issue that occupied the attention of the members of the Democratic Societies was the threat Great Britain posed to the newly established republics of both the United States and France." [38] Hence, the Vermont societies turned their attention to Canada as the most immediate issue of concern. In 1791 the British Parliament had passed a Constitution Act that divided Quebec into two separate provinces—Lower Canada (still known as Quebec) and Upper Canada (later known as Ontario). By this time, Lord Dorchester had become governor. Unlike his predecessor, Governor Haldimand, Dorchester was anxious to encourage settlement, and he issued a proclamation specifying that vacant lands would be granted in townships divided into 200-acre lots to new proprietors with no single grant exceeding 1,200 acres. Applicants for these grants were required to take an oath, but the grants were actually offered with minimal constraints.[39]

Applications for land flooded into Quebec from all over New England, including Vermont. Although many claimants had been active supporters of the American Revolution, they counted on their Loyalist friends, such as Levi Allen, to endorse their applications. "By the end of 1792, a total of three million acres of land had been warranted for survey in 150 townships. The overwhelming number of applicants were Americans; indeed, it has been estimated that nineteen-twentieths [95%] of those persons petitioning for land in Lower Canada at this time were residents of the American states." [40]

Once Vermont's Democratic-Republican societies were organized, they looked at these lands in Quebec, with its large French speaking population, and began to talk about the possibility of a military invasion to annex the lands. This deteriorating situation placed Thomas Chittenden and his old colleagues, including Ira and Levi Allen, in a very awkward position. There is no question that Chittenden sympathized with many of the populist views of the Democratic-Republican societies. During his tenure in office, he had consistently advocated the cause of the common man. Nevertheless, he and the Allens were anxious to reestablish good relations with Great Britain in the hope that the British would build a canal on the Richelieu River to open up the St. Lawrence River as a trade route and increase the value of their own land holdings. Thus, at a meeting in Williston on January 12, 1794, Chittenden entered into a private agreement with William Jarvis, who was the secretary to John Graves Simcoe, the first lieutenant-governor of Upper Canada. At this meeting Chittenden, in the presence of Joseph

Fay, "criticized the excesses of the French Revolution, declared Vermont was opposed to the United States' joining France in war against Great Britain, and asked Jarvis to give his compliments to Simcoe." [41]

The situation was inflamed further in February 1794, when the governor, Lord Dorchester, suggested in a speech to the Iroquois that the British-American impasse might lead to war. The Vermonters who lived in Royalton and other areas that suffered from previous raids were alarmed and outraged. During the spring of 1794 relations along the border became very tense. The British still maintained military forts in the western territories and a twelve-man British detachment was still located at Dutchman's Point in North Hero. On May 9 Congress authorized President Washington to detach eighty thousand troops from the militia for service in any emergency. On May 16 the *Vermont Gazette* reported the Democratic Society of Chittenden County had condemned Dorchester and threatened an invasion of Lower Canada. [42]

Governor Chittenden was not about to support any invasion of British territory. On June 21, however, in response to the congressional mandate of May 9, he did order "the detachment of three regiments of Vermont militia, numbering 2,129 men in all, to be held in readiness as minute men. Of these Major General Ira Allen's division was to furnish one regiment . . . [and] . . . Allen ordered the militia of Alburgh and the neighboring islands . . . to be organized as a regiment which surrounded the small British outpost on North Hero." [43]

During the spring and summer of 1794, Vermont's political societies used the state's newspapers to conduct open warfare on their opponents. These opponents were quick to fire back. On August 1, 1794, the *Gazette* printed a letter from Nathaniel Chipman asserting that Democratic-Republican societies were not merely useless, they were mischievous and a very dangerous imposition. Thus, the lines hardened as the Democratic societies evolved into proto-political parties in support of Thomas Jefferson's policies. As historian H. Nicholas Muller observed, "Vermont politics divided along national lines defined by the disciples of Alexander Hamilton and Thomas Jefferson. The constitutions of the Democratic-Republican Societies launched in Rutland, Addison and Chittenden Counties in 1794 claimed the cause of the 'purest principles of republicanism' which they freely translated into support for the popular version of Jeffersonian policies." [44]

Despite this political turmoil, Governor Chittenden still hoped to persuade the British to build the Richelieu Canal. To aid the negotiations, Chittenden and his colleagues, according to historian Chilton Williamson, "hoped to persuade the Vermont Assembly to grant lands to the S.P.G." [45]

The S.P.G. issue originally arose from the fact that, whenever Benning Wentworth had made a land grant, he set aside one share in each township for the use of the Society for the Propagation of the Gospel in foreign parts (S.P.G.), and also another share as glebe land to support the Anglican Church. In October 1787 the Vermont General Assembly passed an act "authorizing the selectmen of the towns to take care of and improve both the S.P.G. and the glebe lands, for the space of seven years, and to apply any incomes to the improvement of these lands. The act made an exception for glebe rights in the possession of Episcopal ministers." [46]

By 1794 the seven-year provisions of the 1787 act were about to expire, and the assembly began to reconsider the issue of what to do with the S.P.G. and glebe lands. Although both Governor Chittenden and Ira Allen were anxious to court favor with the British, they disagreed about the S.P.G. lands. Instead of supporting any plans to have them revert to the Church of England, on October 14 Allen submitted a petition to the Vermont General Assembly proposing that all of the S.P.G. lands in Vermont be appropriated to the University of Vermont. He later indicated in another petition that he would be willing to provide further funds of his own to help finance UVM with the proviso that its name should be changed to Allen's University. [47]

In the end, neither proposal gained much support, and on October 29, 1794, the assembly, by a vote of 100 to 15, approved an act granting the glebe lands to the towns for the "purpose of appropriating the rents and profits of such lands, to and for the support of religious worship in such towns forever." In a companion bill the S.P.G. lands were "distributed to the several school districts in such towns" [48]

Actually this was not the end of the story. In November 1799 the assembly voted to repeal the 1794 act, and the glebe lands issue led to a lengthy legal squabble before the issue was finally resolved.[49]

On November 19, 1794, war with the British was avoided when Jay's Treaty between Great Britain and the United States was signed in London. The treaty provided for British evacuation of their northwestern forts and unrestricted navigation on the Mississippi River. It did not remove all British trade restrictions, however, nor did it guarantee the protection of American seamen from seizure and impression. In addition, many Vermonters were bitterly disappointed when the treaty failed to open up the St. Lawrence River to free navigation.

Once the threat of war ended, the political societies gradually began to disappear in favor of a more structured party system, and Vermont's leadership gravitated toward the two emerging national political parties. Thomas Chittenden, Matthew Lyon, and other oldtimers were sympathetic with the Jeffersonian Democratic-Republicans, while Nathaniel Chipman, Isaac Tichenor, Moses Robinson, and their colleagues became Federalists. By 1795 Thomas Chittenden was sixty-five years old, and his lengthy service as governor had begun to sap his energy. In December 1795 Ira Allen removed himself from the Vermont political scene entirely when he sailed on a disastrous mission to England and France. Forty-nine-year-old firebrand Matthew Lyon was taking over as the spokesman for the more progressive forces in Vermont politics and was actively campaigning for a seat as one of Vermont's representatives in the federal Congress.[50]

Chittenden's Last Term

On October 13, 1796, Thomas Chittenden was elected to serve his nineteenth term as governor. Since no one received enough votes for lieutenant governor, the assembly met the following day and selected Paul Brigham of Norwich for that office.

Governor Chittenden's final assembly session in Rutland reflected the stability of the times, a sharp contrast from the strife that characterized his early years of leadership. During Chittenden's last years in office, the assembly continued to consider a variety of internal improvements. The legislators granted the exclusive privilege to run a stagecoach from Windsor through Montpelier to Burlington Bay. It had also amended the Bellows Falls locks contract to provide for a toll of fifteen cents a ton for all lumber that passed through the locks.[51]

The assembly also approved a number of important acts during Chittenden's final years. The first act replaced pounds, shillings, and pence with dollars, cents, and mills as the money account of the state. The second act authorized the printing and distribution of Vermont's first authoritative map "from actual surveys by Surveyor General James Whitelaw Esq." The third act adopted "so much of the common law of England as is not repugnant to the constitution, or any Acts of the legislature of this State." Finally, to remove any doubt, the assembly passed an act ratifying the 1793 amendments and "adopted the Constitution of Vermont as the Supreme Law of the State." [52]

By the time the 1796 assembly convened, Governor Chittenden and many of the other early state leaders were aging rapidly, a reality that was captured poignantly in a letter of resignation the assembly received from former Lieutenant Governor Joseph Marsh of Hartford, dated October 15: "Age, infirmity, and a wish not to stand in the way of the usefulness of one better qualified, forbid my any longer exercising the office of Chief Justice of the Windsor County Court." [53]

Only three days later, on October 18, 1796, Thomas Chittenden gave what turned out to be his last speech to the legislature on the same day it was making a number of public appointments. He began by observing that it was only "a few years since we were without constitution, law, or government, in a state of anarchy & confusion, at war with a potent foreign power, opposed by a powerful neighboring state, discountenanced by the Congress, distressed by internal dissentions, all our landed property in imminent danger & without means of defence."

He then went on to thank God for this "happy day when we are in full and uninterrupted enjoyment of a well regulated government, suited to the situation & genius of the people, acknowledged by all the powers on the earth, supported by the Congress, at peace with our sister states, among ourselves and all the world."

He called upon the people of Vermont to be "faithful, virtuous, moral, and industrious," and the legislature "to encourage virtue, industry, morality, religion and learning." He concluded his address, which sounded like a valedictory, by instructing the legislators, "in all your appointments, have regard to none but those who maintain a good moral character, men of integrity, distinguished for wisdom and abilities. In doing this, you will encourage virtue, which is the glory of a people."[54]

It was somewhat ironic that as soon as Governor Chittenden withdrew from the assembly, the house resumed its business, and "comfortable to the order of the day," it elected his old adversary, Isaac Tichenor, Esq., to replace Moses Robinson as a United States Senator.[55] The old order was changing—within a year Isaac Tichenor would replace Thomas Chittenden as Vermont's governor.

After the assembly adjourned on November 8 Governor Chittenden fell ill and was unable to attend the follow-up assembly session in February 1797, which was presided over by Lieutenant Governor Paul Brigham. Chittenden continued to serve as governor, however, and he remained true to his old wartime friends to the very end. His final official actions involved Ira Allen. After sailing to England in December 1795, Allen failed to gain British support to build the Richelieu Canal. He then left for France, where he proposed an audacious scheme to arm American troops with French weapons and overthrow the British government in Canada. The French approved the plan, and in November 1796 Ira slipped out to sea with 20,000 French muskets and twenty-four cannon on an American ship, the *Olive Branch*.[56]

Unfortunately for Allen, a British warship captured the *Olive Branch* eight days later and confiscated its cargo. Allen attempted to convince the British that he had bought the arsenal for the Vermont state militia, and he called on Governor Chittenden for help. Before Allen had left for Europe, Governor Chittenden had written an open letter of introduction for him. Now Chittenden asked the Vermont congressional delegation to assure the British ambassador that the arms were intended for the Vermont militia. On May 4, 1797, Chittenden even swore a deposition to Samuel Hitchcock, United States district judge for Vermont, asserting that "I had requested Gen. Ira Allen to purchase arms and other implements of war in Europe, for the use of the Militia of this State." [57] The British ignored Chittenden's entreaties, but they allowed Allen to return to France. There, it was his misfortune to be arrested as a suspected British spy, and he spent a year in a Paris prison before he finally came back to Vermont in 1801.

After Thomas Chittenden returned to his Williston home in the fall of 1796, he continued to engage in the purchase and sale of land. He was not well, but land was in his blood. His last recorded sale of fifty acres to John Jones was made in May 1797, three months before his death, and the deed of sale for this land was not recorded by the Williston town clerk until December 20, 1797, almost four months after his death.[58]

In July 1797 Governor Chittenden advised the people of Vermont that "impaired as I am as to my health . . . I decline being considered as a candidate at the ensuing election." [59] A month later, on August 24, 1797, Thomas Chittenden died in Williston, where he is buried, and where, a century later, the state erected a Vermont granite monument to mark his grave. The obituaries reporting his death were overflowing in their praise. Fittingly, one the most eloquent of all appeared in the *Vermont Gazette:*

> That Governor Chittenden was possest of great talents and a keen discernment, in affairs relative to men, no one can deny. . . . His many and useful services to his country, to the state of Vermont, and the vicinity wherein he dwelt will long be remembered by a grateful public. . . . Nor were his private virtues less conspicuous: In times of scarcity and distress . . . his granary was open to all the needy. Such was the man, and such the citizen Vermont has lost. Superior to a PRINCE, A GREAT MAN here has fallen.[60]

CHAPTER IX

Thomas Chittenden's Legacy

~X|X~

During his long service as Vermont's first governor, Thomas Chittenden proved himself able to meet the extraordinarily challenging and sometimes contradictory demands of his office. A tough, decisive leader, astute politician, and savvy and wealthy entrepreneur, he was also known for his personal compassion and concern for the plight of the common settlers. His skills, his ability to relate to others, and his deep commitment to Vermont enabled him to lead the state through its chaotic and perilous early years and to ensure its stability and prosperity after the war.

Leadership Style

Vermont's 1777 Constitution was hastily approved in Windsor at the same time British forces swept south along Lake Champlain and recaptured Fort Ticonderoga. In an effort to deal with this emergency, the members of the Constitutional Convention delegated all the sovereign authority of the newly founded State of Vermont to one group, the Council of Safety, which was empowered to take any actions its members deemed to be necessary to govern the state during its massive military and political crisis.

At its first meeting in Manchester, a quorum of the members of the council elected Thomas Chittenden as president, Joseph Fay as vice president, and Ira Allen as secretary. "The most energetic labors of the Council were demanded immediately." [1] The most pressing of these demands was to provide protection for the settlers in the western towns by organizing the state's defenses as rapidly as possible.

In order to raise money for the militia, Ira Allen proposed a program of sequestration of Tory (Loyalist) property. In addition, the council wrote to New Hampshire and Massachusetts to request military aid. On July 15, 1777, Chittenden commissioned Samuel Herrick to command a regiment of rangers to supplement Colonel Seth Warner's Green Mountain militia, who were later joined by General Stark's New Hampshire troops. The situation was so dangerous the council sent an ominous dispatch to all militia officers: "This is perhaps the last express we may be able to send you from this post. Your immediate assistance is absolutely necessary. . . . Pray send all the Troops you can possibly raise; we can Repulse them if we have assistance." [2]

The measure the council initially approved to raise revenues— sequestration—involved the seizure and sale of Loyalist property. This policy was implemented very rapidly under Chittenden's leadership. On July 28 the council issued orders "to seize all lands, goods, tenements, and chattels of any person or person in this State who . . . have repaired to the enemy." [3] "The Council of Safety quickly appointed at least thirteen men to act as commissioners of sequestration, and sales of Tory properties began as early as August. During the balance of the Council of Safety's tenure as the acting government of Vermont, the continuing sales of Loyalist properties produced funds not only for military purposes, but also for the day-to-day expenses of civil government." [4]

In addition to relying on sequestration to raise money, Chittenden and his colleagues on the council used this practice to intimidate their opponents and strengthen the authority of the new Vermont government. Many of the Loyalists in the state were prominent citizens, particularly those from the southwestern towns such as Arlington. Another group of dissenters from southeastern Vermont were not pro-British. Instead, "Yorkers," as they were called, remained loyal to the state of New York. In July 1776 the delegates to the Dorset convention had voted to require all residents to subscribe to a convenant declaring their allegiance to Vermont, with the stipulation that every male over the age of sixteen who refused to sign was an "enemy." The Council of Safety used the policy of sequestration to remove Yorker "enemies" who failed to sign the Dorset convenant.

As soon as the Vermont state government was organized on March 26, 1778, the assembly moved a step further by voting to grant the Governor and Council judicial powers of confiscation to seize and sell Tory homes and real estate. The council divided itself into both western and an eastern courts of confiscation. The western court under Governor Chittenden was much more aggressive than its east-side counterpart, and it continued to sell confiscated estates until the early 1780s. Thomas Chittenden, Matthew Lyon, and other wartime leaders bought confiscated estates for themselves in Arlington and other towns in Bennington County. The revenues from these sales paid for most of the costs of state government, which helped to maintain the popularity of Thomas Chittenden and his associates.

On the surface, it certainly appears that some of the actions Chittenden and the Council of Safety took against their opponents were quite harsh. Yet, in fairness, it must be noted that conditions in Vermont during the early years of the Revolutionary War were chaotic and desperate. In addition, it is important to emphasize that the delegates to the Constitutional Convention in Windsor had granted the Council of Safety unlimited authority. The council was, quite simply, the government of Vermont, and there was no system of checks and balances to control any of its actions. In retrospect, Chittenden and his colleagues acted very forcefully, but they did show self-restraint in their use of the unrestricted powers that had been delegated to them. Chittenden did not hesitate to use his authority, but he did so only when he judged it necessary to protect and enhance the interests of the State of Vermont.

A later example of the tough, decisive approach advocated by Chittenden during his tenure as governor is seen in his actions dealing with the Yorker dissidents in the southeastern towns of Cumberland County. Once again, his actions were forceful and vigorous when dealing with individuals who challenged the authority of the State of Vermont. During both the first "Cow War" in 1779 and the second Guilford uprising in 1782, Chittenden ordered Ethan Allen to assemble military forces to quell the rebellions. Ethan Allen's famous threat that he would lay Guilford "as desolate as Sodom and Gomorrah" was fully backed by Chittenden, who authorized Allen to use whatever force was necessary to crush the Yorkers. Allen succeeded in his mission, but the suffering in and around Guilford during the 1782 uprising was substantial, with many farms laid waste and much property despoiled. Chittenden never harbored any doubt that this use of force was fully justified.

Although Chittenden could be tough, even brutal, in his governing, there are many indications that he displayed a much more compassionate demeanor in his personal relationships with others. First, there is the example of his family of ten children. By all accounts, he and his wife, Elizabeth, were caring parents. Their four sons were active in public service, and each of them served in the Vermont General Assembly as representatives from Williston or Jericho. Noah, the oldest, was a farmer from Jericho who served as the first sheriff of Chittenden County, a judge, and a member of the Governor and Council. Martin, who also farmed in Jericho, graduated from Dartmouth College and later became a Vermont governor and congressman. Giles, a Williston farmer, was a colonel in the militia. Truman, the youngest son, also farmed in Williston, and he served as a judge, a member of the Governor and Council, and a trustee of the University of Vermont for twenty-six years.[5] All six of the Chittendens' daughters married well, including Hannah, the wife of General Isaac Clark; Beulah, the wife of Vermont Congressman Matthew Lyon; and Mary, the wife of Vermont Governor Jonas Galusha.[6] Interestingly, Jonas Galusha, an early Jeffersonian, was a political rival of Mary's Federalist brother, Martin, and the two men engaged in numerous political battles.

Many of the stories about the Chittendens involve their generosity to those who were in need. According to an account by the Reverend F. A. Wadleigh, Governor Chittenden's concern for others was clearly shown during the bitterly cold winter of 1777–78, when he was first serving as president of the Council of Safety. In Wadleigh's words, "so great had been the disorders of the times and so many men had left the county that fields were unharvested, and there was imminent danger of famine. The Governor took upon himself the task of visiting, from time to time, every family and taking account of the provisions on hand. Under his oversight and by his impartial and disinterested counsel, distribution was so made that, although all were pinched, none perished." [7]

Chittenden demonstrated this same sense of concern in letters he signed as president of the council to the wives of Loyalists whose property had been seized by the state. On February 28, 1778, for example, Chittenden directed the commissioner of sequestration in Clarendon to lease Mrs. Walker the farm taken from her husband, Daniel Walker, not exceeding one year, in order to procure a sufficient surety for the maintenance of her family. In March he signed another letter permitting the wife of Samuel Adams, a Tory from Arlington, to carry off furniture, bedding, kitchenware, and apparel from her home for the use of her and her family.[8]

The most astonishing incident involved two of Thomas Chittenden's nephews, Timothy and Eli Evarts. They were the sons of his sister, Elisheba, and his brother-in-law, Sylvanus Evarts, the man who had joined him in Salisbury, Connecticut, and later moved his family to Castleton. "On February 20, 1779, the General Assembly of the State of Vermont joined the Governor and Council in granting to Timothy and Eli Evarts 120 acres of land in Castleton, in recompense for a debt owed by the state to their father. Six days later, their father, Sylvanus Evarts, was proscribed as a Tory, and all his property ordered seized for the benefit of the state." [9] According to Thomas Chittenden's code of conduct, the acts of the father were not to be visited on the sons, at least not within his own extended family.

The Evarts story illustrates another personal trait Thomas Chittenden demonstrated very frequently. Throughout his career he displayed a powerful sense of loyalty to his family, his friends, and other associates who worked closely with him. Nowhere is this seen more clearly than in his defense of his wayward friend Ira Allen on numerous occasions, particularly during the last months of Chittenden's life. Ira was captured at sea by the British fleet during the audacious *Olive Branch* affair and, when he claimed he had bought 20,000 muskets and twenty-four cannon from the French to supply the Vermont state militia, he called on Governor Chittenden to back him up. Although he was very ill at the time, the governor tried to provide help. On April 29, 1797, Chittenden wrote to the Vermont congressional delegation advising them that the loss of the arms "will not only ruin General Allen, but would be severely felt by the militia. This was almost the last service Chittenden could render to his friend; he died in August of this year." [10] Critics might argue that, at times, Chittenden's sense of loyalty was a drawback. It did end up getting him into trouble on occasion, but he placed a very high value on standing by his friends and family, even when it made his political life more difficult.

Certainly Chittenden cared deeply about the common set-tlers. In the years following the Revolutionary War this con-cern could be seen in his willingness to sponsor the Betterment Act and debtor relief measures. Although he served as governor of Vermont for a longer time than any other person, Thomas Chittenden never acted pretentiously or divorced himself from his constituents. Instead, he remained a man of the people, a leader who had an extraordinary bond with the ordinary citizen.

Chittenden portrayed himself as a simple frontier farmer. Dorothy Canfield Fisher compiled some Vermont folklore that captures this portrayal. Her first story involved a well-dressed traveler from the south who found the road was blocked by a big hay wagon as he approached Arlington. An old fellow driv-ing two horses sat high up on the wagon in plain farmer's clothes. The traveler, who wore a three-cornered hat and a bright blue coat with lace ruffles and gold buttons, called up: "Can you tell me where His Excellency Governor Thomas Chittenden lives?" The farmer called back: "I'm going there. Follow me." The wagon crawled slowly along a narrow road until the farmer fi-nally turned and came to a halt in a barnyard. He slid to the ground, turned to the man in the fine clothes, dusted off his hands, and said in a pleasant voice, "I'm Governor Chittenden. What can I do for you?"

The second story involves Mrs. Chittenden. Some business-men from Boston had journeyed up to Vermont to see her hus-band. After preparing the dinner, Mrs. Chittenden came into her dining room, where a long table was set, and she rang a big bell to signal the men working in a hayfield. Seeing the busi-nessmen look surprised, she said, "I know it may seem odd to you that we eat at the same table with the haymakers. By rights, they should eat first, and we should wait our turn. However, I thought since you were company, they wouldn't mind having us all eat together at the same time this evening." [11]

Some authors have argued that Governor Chittenden delib-erately perpetuated this image to enhance his popularity with the common settlers. Frederick Van de Water, for example, comments that Chittenden concealed his virtues "under a pretext of ignorance. His pose was intensely rural. . . . He had chosen for himself the role of farmer—a particularly artless pioneer farmer—and he stuck to it." [12]

There are other accounts of Thomas Chittenden's lack of vanity and his sense of hospitality. In the fall of 1791 John Lincklaen, a Dutch agent for the Holland Land Company of western New York, visited the governor at his farm in Williston. According to this account, "He received us without ceremony in the country fashion. . . . Born in Connecticut, he still retains the inquisitive character of his compatriots, & overwhelms one with questions to which one can scarcely reply. He is one of the largest & best farmers of the state, & is believed to own 40,000 acres beside a considerable number of horned cattle. His house & way of living have nothing to distinguish them from those of any private individual, but he offers heartily a glass of grog, potatoes & bacon to anyone who wishes to come and see him." [13]

Two years earlier, the Reverend Nathan Perkins of Hartford, Connecticut, who had also visited with Chittenden, offered a less flattering portrait, although he expressed admiration for the governor's hospitality and his agrarian skills. Reverend Perkins, who seems to have been a rather priggish city type, describes his visit as follows: "Thursday 20 of May, 1789, set out for Williston where governor Chittenden lives. . . . A low poor house—a plain family—low, vulgar man, clownish, excessively parsimonious,—made me welcome—hard fare, a very great farm—1000 acres—hundred acres of wheat on ye onion river—200 acres of extraordinary interval land. A shrewd cunning man—skilled in human nature & in agriculture—he understands extremely well ye mysteries of Vermont." [14]

Chittenden's instinctive understanding of "ye mysteries of Vermont" and his uncanny ability to relate to common frontier settlers were certainly factors that help explain his political success. He was a perfect fit in terms of the leadership needs of the state at the time he arrived in Vermont. He was a mature man in his mid-forties who had a variety of military and governmental experiences in Connecticut. In addition, his religious views were acceptable to eastern leaders such as Jacob Bayley, who was a deacon in the Newbury church, and Congregational minister Reverend Eleazar Wheelock of Dartmouth College, as well as the "New Light" and separatist members of the Green Mountain Boys on the western side of the state. The Chittendens owned three pews in the Williston meeting house, and even Reverend Perkins later expressed a more favorable view of the governor and his family. When he returned to their Williston farm for a second visit, he commented that Mrs. Chittenden and her sixteen-year-old daughter Leita (Electa), "seem to love me as a brother, and ye Governor as a son. I struck them upon ye right key. . . . His Excellency picked me out to understand human nature, at first sight." [15]

In terms of social activities, Thomas Chittenden, like many of the leaders of his day, was a member of the Ancient Order of Freemasonry, which first came to Vermont in 1781. "Masonry exerted a strong appeal to men high in the affairs of the state. The lists of early lodge members resembled a roll call of the Legislature and the bar. The Allen brothers, Ethan and Ira, and Governor Thomas Chittenden were members of old North Star Lodge of Manchester." [16]

On a somewhat lighter note, one report indicates that Governor Chittenden even operated a tavern in his home for the travelers who passed his farm on the Winooski River. "Mr. Pennoyer, one of His Majesty's Justices of the Peace at Missiskoui [*sic*] Bay, states in a letter to a friend the dire effects he feels tavern-keeping may have had on Governor Chittenden. 'A few days before he died, he was fined One Hundred and Eighty Dollars for selling Liquors by small measure without license. . . . Whether the fine killed him or not, I can't say.'" [17]

Governor Chittenden's relationships with his family, and with the many people he met during his lengthy service as the state's chief executive, were characterized by a mixture of toughness and kindness. Some of his actions were self-serving, and he could be particularly aggressive in defending the interests of the State of Vermont, but he consistently showed deep concern for others who were less fortunate than himself. In the final analysis, it was this latter group that constituted the core of his political base and helped him to retain his position as the governor of Vermont for such a long time.

Political Acumen

Thomas Chittenden was a natural politician and an intuitively astute decision-maker. Ethan Allen is said to have described Chittenden as "the only man he ever knew who was sure to be right in all, even the most difficult and complex, cases and yet could not tell or seem to know why it was so." [18] Another version quotes Ethan Allen's description of Chittenden as "a man without words (who) formed accurate judgments, but was unable to tell how he arrived at them." [19] Both of these statements indicate that Chittenden relied heavily on his intuition when making decisions.

Many examples can be cited to illustrate that Chittenden was an exceptionally shrewd leader who was capable of protecting the authority of Vermont while at the same time enhancing his own interests. Chittenden and the other western leaders of the state faced a very early challenge in June 1778, when the newly organized Vermont General Assembly annexed sixteen New Hampshire towns to form the first eastern union. In addition to stirring up trouble with New Hampshire and the Continental Congress, this action threatened the power base of the western leaders by significantly increasing the number of assembly delegates from the eastern towns.

In October 1778, at the next Vermont General Assembly meeting in Windsor, Ethan Allen, a newly elected delegate from the town of Arlington, gave a speech spelling out the dangers of the new union. He advised his fellow delegates that congressional leaders had warned him that unless Vermont disbanded the union, "the whole power of the confederacy of the United States of America will join to annihilate the state of Vermont, and vindicate the right of New Hampshire." [20] Governor Chittenden then notified the assembly about a letter of protest he had received from Meshech Weare, the leader of the New Hampshire Council.

A bitter and lengthy debate broke out in the assembly, but the eastern union proponents still had the edge before Governor Chittenden and his colleagues brought all their political muscle and powers of persuasion to bear on the problem. In what must have been a tremendous lobbying effort, they managed to persuade a majority of assembly members to vote against providing county government for the sixteen New Hampshire towns. The easterners who supported the union left the assembly in protest, but the assembly's remaining members continued to conduct important business, despite the fact that they lacked a quorum. In fact, in a blatant display of political expediency, they approved a gigantic land grant for the town of the Two-Heroes in the Lake Champlain Islands, and the members of the assembly who had voted against the union were rewarded by being named proprietors in this new town. The easterners who had walked out of the assembly chastised Governor Chittenden and the remaining assembly members for violating the quorum provisions of the state constitution. Governor Chittenden, however, reasoned that the constitution would be worthless unless Vermont survived as a state. Once he and Ethan Allen became convinced that the eastern union posed a threat to the viability of Vermont—as well as to their power base—they felt justified in orchestrating their hard-line attack.

The destruction of the first eastern union gives clear indication that the Chittenden faction took a very flexible view of the law if they felt this served the state's interest. Daniel Chipman notes in his memoir, "Governor Chittenden . . . had remarkable tact in adapting his measures to the existing state of things and he was but very little deterred by any constitutional restrictions." He then goes on to make a remarkable comment about his older brother, Judge Nathaniel Chipman, who had consistently opposed Chittenden. "Judge Chipman, a young lawyer, and of course somewhat technical, did not in all cases approve of the course pursued by Governor Chittenden but I have often heard Judge Chipman remark that he did not believe the government would have been sustained, had any man but Governor Chittenden been at the head of it." [21]

A second example of Governor Chittenden's political acumen can be observed in the controversial Haldimand negotiations with the British in Canada, which began in the spring of 1780 and continued until the American victory at Yorktown in October 1781. These negotiations involved a small group of Vermont leaders—Governor Chittenden, Ethan and Ira Allen, Joseph Fay, Isaac Clark, and others—who communicated with the British leaders in Canada. The initial subject under consideration was an exchange of prisoners, but this was later expanded to encompass the issue of whether Vermont would rejoin the British empire.

H. Nicholas Muller noted that there have been three distinct interpretations of these negotiations. The first is that they were "a cunning, if extremely dangerous, form of Vermont and American patriotism. . . . By seizing the opportunity to tantalize the British . . . [the Vermont leaders] . . . cleverly neutralized the military threat to Vermont's unprotected frontiers and at the same time attempted to pressure the Congress for recognition of independence and a grant of statehood." A second revisionist group of scholars has pointed to "the sizable financial stake the leaders held in protecting their vast land holdings," and argued that the negotiations were deadly serious, with their fundamental motive being the Vermont leaders' deep-seated concern to protect their own economic interests. Finally, a third group has concluded that the Vermont leaders were "guilty but justified." Although this group found the affair to be "an ugly and sordid bit of business, the conspirators were motivated by a genuine concern for the future of Vermont."[22]

No single interpretation of the negotiations has been fully accepted. The situation can only be assessed accurately in terms of the existing conditions. In an address to the Vermont Historical Society, Henry Steele Wardner observed:

> Let us orient for ourselves the military situation in Vermont in 1780. . . . Except for a few hundred Vermonters in Seth Warner's Continental Regiment, and possibly, a handful of other regiments of the Continental forces, Vermont had under arms but two hundred and thirty men. At that time no Continental troops were assigned for Vermont's protection. Ira Allen . . . repeatedly averred that General Haldimand had in his command not less than 10,000 troops. Governor Chittenden put Haldimand's force at 7,000. In addition, Vermont's political situation . . . had become critical in 1780 [since] Vermont had never been one of the united colonies and had been refused representation in Congress.[23]

As Wardner makes clear, conditions in Vermont in 1780 were very precarious. Outmanned by the British to the north, under political attack from New York on the west, facing potential land claims from both New Hampshire and Massachusetts to the east and south, and ignored by the Continental Congress, Vermont confronted dangerous threats on all sides. Under such circumstances it certainly made sense for Vermont's leaders to stall any British invasion from Canada. Even beyond this, a very strong argument can be made that Vermont actually had legitimate reasons to consider a union with the British. To quote from Wardner's address:

> If the welfare of the State required reunion with Great Britain then, according to law, a citizen must be doing right in working for such an end as long as the State was unbound to the Federal

Union. There was, in my opinion, pretty solid ground on which Allen and Chittenden could, in good faith, seek affiliation with Great Britain if they were convinced that Congress intended to victimize Vermont in the interest of New York.[24]

Although some critics accused Chittenden, the Allens, and their close associates of being traitors for negotiating with the British, it is difficult to understand the rationale for this charge. They certainly were not traitors to the Continental Congress, which refused to admit them into the Union. In addition, they did not hide information about their meetings. In his letter of November 14, 1781, to George Washington, Governor Chittenden made it clear that he and his associates had negotiated a truce with the British in order to work out a prisoner exchange, and that "the plan succeeded, the frontiers of this state were not invaded." [25] In the end the Haldimand negotiations not only helped to avoid a British invasion, but they also enabled Vermont to survive and eventually become the fourteenth state.

A third example of Chittenden's political sagacity was his strategy to work with the small frontier towns at the 1786 Vermont Constitutional Convention. He was fully aware of the fact that his lawyer reformer opponents had the academic background and the legal expertise to challenge him in the legislature. He was able to strengthen his position, however, by insuring that each of the smaller towns retained independent representation, and, as a result, he secured their allegiance as the base of his political support.

Although Thomas Chittenden was usually persistent and steady, he could become emotional. Such was the case when he leveled his outburst against the lawyers in his 1786 address, which called for new taxes on lawsuits. Another example is seen in his correspondence regarding the Alburgh incident in 1792, when he expressed his sense of outrage over perceived British violations of Vermont's sovereignty. On a number of occasions, he punctuated his customary steady leadership with brief lapses into a more personal and emotional style.

Finally, Governor Chittenden possessed a political leadership quality that was uniquely important. This was what Reverend Nathan Perkins had referred to as Chittenden's instinctive understanding of "ye mysteries of Vermont"—his uncanny ability to relate to the average frontier settler.[26] As the *Vermont Gazette* noted, "He was . . . possest of a keen discernment in affairs of men. . . . His conversation was easy, simple and instructive." [27] By all accounts he was a good listener, and he instinctively seemed to know how to motivate others to do his bidding. Roland Robinson sums it up beautifully when he states, "he was a masterful man, yet carried his points without appearing to force them, and seemed to fall into the ways of others while, in fact, he led them imperceptibly into his own." [28]

This was perhaps Chittenden's greatest asset—his ability to relate to the people he governed in a manner that gained their confidence and support. They trusted him, and they were willing to follow him. Vermont historian Charles A. Jellison provided a very perceptive assessment of Thomas Chittenden when he stated, "Although close to illiterate and somewhat rough around the edges, 'One eye Tom' was a person of rare quality. Possessed of no special talents of his own, he had, nevertheless, the ability to marshal the talents of others and direct them toward a common purpose. By all accounts he was the great cohesive factor of Vermont's most critical years. Men trusted him. They rallied behind him. Without him it is unlikely that the Republic of Vermont would have survived its infancy." [29]

Entrepreneurial Skills

When Thomas and Elizabeth Chittenden left Salisbury for the New Hampshire Grants in 1774, they had a family of four sons and six daughters. Although it is difficult to determine the precise wealth of the Chittendens at that time, the available evidence indicates they were very well off. Thomas Chittenden's original land holding in Salisbury was the farm his father, Ebenezer, gave to him in 1751. Thomas began farming as soon as he moved to Salisbury. In February 1754 he bought ten additional acres of excellent land, and in December of that year he acquired another 210 acres.[30]

By 1760 Thomas Chittenden was already a wealthy landowner. According to the 1760 Salisbury records, his tax payment in that year of 130 pounds was the seventh largest in town.[31] At the time Chittenden was buying Salisbury land, "a major agricultural change began (in Connecticut) involving a gradual shift away from soil tillage to grazing. Growing markets in other mainland colonies and the West Indies stimulated farmers to put heavy emphasis upon cattle, horses, mules, sheep, and hogs. . . . The important by-products of these efforts—butter and cheese—were exported, especially from Windham and Litchfield counties, to the south and to the West Indies." [32] Since Chittenden's sizable Salisbury farm was located on gently rising Prospect Hill just north of town, it is logical to assume that he made a great deal of his money by exporting cattle.

During the 1760s and early 1770s Thomas Chittenden received more than 1,000 pounds from various tracts of land he sold in Salisbury. In May 1773 he and Jonathan Spafford paid the Allen's Onion River Land Company 500 pounds for 1,236 acres in Williston, and the two men later acquired an additional one-half interest in 4,017 acres of Williston intervale land from Heman Allen.[33] Thomas Chittenden later received 700 pounds when he sold Jonathan Spafford all the land he still owned in Salisbury, so Chittenden retained large holdings of both land and capital to speculate in further land transactions after he had arrived in Vermont.[34]

In 1776 British military actions on the northern frontier forced the Chittendens to desert their farm in Williston and flee south. According to David Chipman's memoir, they resided briefly in Danby, Manchester, Pownal, and Williamstown, Massachusetts, before they finally settled in the town of Arlington, Vermont. On June 10, 1779, Thomas Chittenden signed a deed with John Fassett, the Bennington County Commissioner of Confiscated Lands, and he paid the State of Vermont 3,000 pounds for a confiscated house plus 617 acres of land in Arlington, previously owned by Loyalist Jehiel Hawley.

Although his duties as a wartime governor kept Thomas Chittenden very busy, he never received an enormous salary. In 1781 the assembly voted to fix his compensation at 150 pounds per year (495 Spanish milled dollars), and it was still the same in 1795.[35] As a result, he supplemented his income through farming and land speculation. Beginning in 1779 the Vermont General Assembly began to grant land for new frontier towns in the unoccupied central and north-central areas of the state. The state granted these lands to raise revenue and to gain allies who would support Vermont's independence movement.

Normally sixty-four to seventy-two initial proprietors would purchase one or more charter rights in each town while the assembly reserved five rights for public uses. The proprietors paid the costs to survey the towns and take steps to encourage settlement. There were exceptions, however, on both the high and the low sides. As was already noted, one of the first Vermont land grants on the Champlain Islands, made in October 1779, was the Two-Heroes, known today as South Hero, Grand Isle, and North Hero. This gigantic town had a huge number of proprietors, including Governor Chittenden, virtually all of the members of the Governor and Council, and forty-one members of the assembly. In other cases, land petitions did not have a large enough group of proprietors to cover the costs, and the assembly would add names to these grants. Many of these proprietary shares went to members of the militia, judges, council members, legislators, and also to Governor Chittenden.

During the period from 1779 to 1791 the state issued a total of 128 charters for new towns.[36] Thomas Chittenden is listed as one of the original proprietors in forty-five of these charters. Although he didn't match the record of New Hampshire Governor Benning Wentworth (who had reserved a proprietary share for himself in every one of the 129 towns he chartered), Chittenden did manage to have his name as a proprietor on one-third of the towns chartered by Vermont. Other members of his family also appeared on some of these town charters—Noah was listed on fourteen, Martin on six, Elizabeth on two, and all four sons were proprietors of the town of Starksboro. Many other early Vermont leaders were also listed as proprietors on various town charters.

The fact that these names were listed does not mean that all of these individuals permanently owned shares of land in each of these towns. Some failed to pay fees and taxes, and they forfeited their claims. Others sold off their claims to other buyers, who settled and farmed the land. Actually, the only proprietary land grant that appeared in the final probate inventory of Chittenden's

After Thomas Chittenden returned from Arlington to Williston in 1787, he built a large brick house with a ballroom on the third floor. In 1835 the Chittenden farm was purchased by the Wright Clark family, who lived in this house until it was destroyed by fire in 1926. The Clarks still operate the Chittenden farm today. (Clark family photo)

estate after he died in 1797 was his share of the town of Carthage (later named Jay), which the assembly had awarded to him in partial payment of his wartime salary. Carthage was located next to the Canadian border, where land was worth considerably less than acreage in the southern part of the state. The 7,010 acres of land Chittenden owned in the town of Jay was valued at $6,362 in his estate inventory, or just over ninety cents an acre. Although he profited from the sale of his proprietary rights, Chittenden's major gains from land came from his private speculation.

Specifically, Thomas Chittenden made his largest amount of money buying and selling parcels of land in the towns of Arlington and Williston. During the eight years from 1779 to 1787, when he lived in Arlington, he purchased a home and 617 acres of land from the confiscated estate of Jehiel Hawley for 3,000 pounds. Three years later, in July 1782, he bought an additional 418 acres of undivided land at a tax sale for only six pounds and eighteen shillings, or about five cents per acre in Spanish milled dollars. One of his purchases on this occasion was a thirty-nine-and-a-half acre lot originally owned by Ben-ning Wentworth.[37] In 1782 Chittenden was classified as the sixth largest taxpayer in town with a listing of sixty-seven pounds, ten shillings.[38]

After spending eight years in Arlington the Chittenden family moved back to Williston in March 1787. At this time Thomas began to build a fine brick mansion near the location of his old log cabin. He started a very large farm operation, which he managed for the rest of his life. In addition, he had obtained so much land in Williston from the Allen family in 1773–74 that he sold off lots to twenty-two different buyers between 1787 and 1797.[39]

At the same time Chittenden was selling land, he, his wife, and his sons were also buying more land in Williston. Eventually Noah, Giles, and Truman Chittenden bought so much land they were each listed in the Williston Book of Proprietors that was issued in 1804. At that time Noah was listed as the owner of five lots containing 67.75 acres while Giles had three lots totaling 803.75 acres and Truman had seven lots at 1,268.5

acres. The only son without major Williston holdings was Martin, who owned land in neighboring Jericho.[40]

It is difficult to keep track of all the land transactions, but their magnitude demonstrates that Thomas Chittenden, his wife, and his sons were very well off by the time Chittenden died in 1797. The extent of Thomas Chittenden's wealth is summarized very clearly in the probate inventory of his estate, which was filed on October 7, 1797. This estate inventory provides a host of facts and insights about Governor Chittenden and his family.[41]

Thomas Chittenden's estate inventory totaled 12,435 pounds, two shillings, and five pence, which was equivalent to $41,450.40 Spanish milled dollars. According to Michael Bellesiles' analysis of 300 Vermont probate records for the years 1774–88, only two percent of Vermonters left personal property in their estates in excess of 2,000 pounds ($6,600).[42] Thomas Chittenden's estate is well beyond this, and it seems fair to state that he was one of the wealthiest men in Vermont when he died. The $41,450.40 in Chittenden's estate in 1797 would be worth more than $370,000 in 1995 dollars adjusted for inflation and without anything being added for interest.[43]

The estate inventory reveals a number of other interesting facts about Thomas Chittenden and his lifestyle. When broken down into its components, Chittenden's estate tracks relatively closely to the 185 Vermont probate averages from Rutland, Bennington, and Windham counties that are listed in Bellesiles' book.[44]

Percentages of Total Probated Wealth

	Vermont Averages	Chittenden's Estate
Landholdings	65.0%	64.9%
Notes of Credit	14.9%	23.9%
Livestock	8.5%	6.5%
Household Goods	5.1%	3.4%
Cash	0.6%	0.2%
Other	5.9%	1.1%

The breakdown of Governor Chittenden's estate reveals almost two-thirds of his assets (65%) were in real estate and land holdings. These holdings included one-half of the home farm in Williston, containing 900 acres and the buildings, valued at $6,600. The other half of the home farm was left to Chittenden's wife, Elizabeth. An additional 2,652 acres of land were listed in Williston valued at $7,884. Finally, four major parcels of land were located outside of Williston. None of these lands, except those in Jay, were in any of the towns where Chittenden was listed as a proprietor. This indicates he either sold, gave away, or was delinquent in maintaining his proprietors' rights in these towns. The four parcels listed outside of the town of Williston were 7,010 acres in Jay (valued at $6,362); 700 acres in Essex ($690); 150 acres in Castleton ($1,848); and a gristmill and sawmill, plus 637 acres of land, in Jericho ($3,250). Thus, the total probate value of Chittenden's landholdings was $26,634.

The second largest portion of Governor Chittenden's estate (23.9%) appeared as notes due on outstanding debts. In this category his estate was well above the probate averages. Although Governor Chittenden was not able to create an official state bank in Vermont, he served as his own private bank. A total of 178 people owed Chittenden more than $9,000 at the time of his death. His two largest debtors were Matthew Lyon, who owed him $1,430, and Ira Allen, who owed him $668. The first two pages of his estate inventory list the names of everyone who had borrowed money from him, no matter how small the amount. For example, Nathan Murrey and D. Bates are each listed as owing one shilling, eight pence (about seventeen cents) apiece. Even his four sons are listed as debtors—Noah owed $55.25, Martin $39.00, Truman $29.50, and Giles $18.50. Chittenden was such a large creditor that it must have placed him under considerable pressure as the state's political leader. In terms of his ideology, he was sympathetic with the needs of the common man, especially to those who were in debt. Yet, as a capitalist and a creditor, he must also have harbored an interest in assuring that his own money was safe and not subject to inflationary depreciation.

A third item in Chittenden's estate inventory reveals that Chittenden's Williston farm operated on a scale well beyond the subsistence level. Instead, he owned a very large farm, and he was heavily involved in raising cattle. One of the most profitable means of farming in Vermont during the 1790s was to raise meat in order to make "grain walk to market." A summary of Chittenden's livestock reveals that he owned four pairs of large oxen, a two-year-old bull, nine heifers, eighty-five cows, sixteen horses and colts, thirty sheep, three hog(g)s, and sixteen steer. The large herd of cows provided milk, cheese, and butter, while the sheep provided both meat and wool for nearby markets. The steer were being fattened for trips to markets farther away, such as Montreal to the north or Albany, Hartford, or Boston to the south. A farm operation of this size required a very high degree of managerial skill and proficiency. Chittenden was an incredibly meticulous businessman whose records were extraordinarily detailed. As the Reverend Nathan Perkins of Hartford noted during his visit in 1789, this was "a very great farm" and Chittenden was indeed "skilled in human nature and agriculture." [45]

A final insight gained from the estate inventory grows out of its description of the more intimate details of the Chittendens' everyday life. There are pages listing furniture, clothing, silverware, and china. The family owned pews in the Williston Congregational meeting house valued at one hundred pounds. There is even a record of five books. The first is *The Great Bible*, followed by two Psalm books. The fourth is described as the *History of Redemption*. This is undoubtedly *The History of the Work of Redemption*, a collection of a series of sermons that Jonathan Edwards, the great Calvinist theologian, delivered in 1739 during the "Great Awakening" religious revival that swept New England. The final book is most intriguing. It is

Thomas Paine's *The Rights of Man*, published in 1791, which defends the French Revolution on the grounds that there are natural rights that are common to all men and only democratic institutions are able to guarantee these rights.

A review of Thomas Chittenden's career as governor, farmer, land speculator, businessman, and creditor reveals that he backed up his political success with superior administrative skills. It also confirms that he mixed hard-headed pragmatism with a caring nature. While he was able to amass a very sizable estate, there is no indication that Chittenden was vindictive or miserly in his treatment of others. He was willing to lend money to many people, but he kept very careful accounts of his debts. There are also examples that he was generous in sharing his wealth. According to one popular (albeit unverified) legend, during the darkest days of the war, when the Council of Safety was first meeting in July 1777, Thomas Chittenden pleaded with his colleagues to raise enough money to finance a Vermont regiment. "The men must be raised," he said, "poor as we are. I have ten head of cattle and my wife has a gold necklace. It is an heirloom, but we will begin with the cattle and the necklace! Then the Lord will show us what to do." [46]

Is this fact or fiction? It is hard to say. Official state records reveal, however, that Thomas Chittenden did provide loans to the new state during the war. On October 1786 the State of Vermont reimbursed him in the amount of 2,064 pounds, five shillings, and eight pence for money he had lent the state to pay for "Arms and ammunition Expended for the Defence of the State in the late War." [47]

Chittenden's estate inventory makes it obvious that he was a prudent, capable, and sensible man who had a keen awareness of his own assets and limitations. He had an easy way with people, but he also possessed a disciplined, orderly mind. Above all, he maintained a sense of perspective and rarely overextended himself. In this respect he was quite different from some of his

old wartime colleagues. In 1801 Levi Allen died while impris-
oned for debt in a Burlington jail. In 1814 Ira Allen died destitute in Philadelphia and was buried in a pauper's grave. When
Thomas Chittenden died in Williston in 1797, and he left a
rich legacy to his family and to the state he had served for so
many years.

Chittenden's Legacy

In a brief biographical sketch of Governor Chittenden, Walter
H. Crockett describes a series of political challenges facing the
early Vermont leaders. These challenges involved "setting up a
system of government in a region where nearly all the partici-
pants were ignorant of legislative, executive, and judicial duties; extending the jurisdiction of the new state in areas where
not a few of the people were indifferent or hostile; guarding
against the intrigues of hostile neighbors and attacks from British troops in Canada; impressing Congress with Vermont's
claims for admission as a state of the Union; securing the en-
actment and the execution of wise laws, and raising revenues to
carry on the functions of government." [48]

During his long service as governor, Thomas Chittenden
played a vital role in dealing with all of these challenges, but
his importance as a leader transcends any one of the many specific tasks he performed. Thomas Chittenden's most lasting
legacy is, quite simply, the State of Vermont. Many other leaders played important roles in establishing Vermont as an independent state, but Chittenden made critical contributions while
leading Vermont's through its darkest and most difficult time.
The existing evidence indicates that Vermont could not have
survived without Thomas Chittenden's leadership during 1777–
1782, its most trying years of challenge.

In a seminal article that questions some of the myths surrounding Vermont's early government, historian H. Nicholas
Muller III concludes that even "a cursory look at the evidence

suggests the traditional view of the early development of Vermont government and the platitudes about pristine republican virtue uttered by Ira Allen and a host of subsequent observers need drastic revision. Multiple office holding, the longevity of terms and the small number of men who served in the office of Governor and on the Council are no statistical accident and leave the impression of a political oligarchy." [49]

The fact that Vermont's twelve-member Council of Safety was granted unlimited power to meet the state's wartime challenges provides clear evidence that this early government was, indeed, an oligarchy. During the eight months from July 1777 to March 1778, when Thomas Chittenden served as the President of the Council of Safety, he and his eleven colleagues completely dominated Vermont's government. They occasionally cut corners to achieve their objectives, and some of their actions were self-serving. Yet, although the members of the Council of Safety were granted dictatorial powers, they never became dictators. As James Madison warned in Federalist Paper No. 51, "in framing a government which is to be administered by men over men, the great difficulty lies in this: You must first enable to government to control the governed; and in the next place oblige it to control itself." [50]

Thomas Chittenden and the other early leaders of Vermont met this test. At times they relied on some artful maneuvers to maintain their control of the state, but they never succumbed to the temptations of absolute power. The fact that Thomas Chittenden offered to resign as governor in the fall of 1780 indicates that he was not power hungry or consumed by ambition. Instead, it appears that he possessed one of the most unappreciated of all political traits—a strong sense of perspective and self-control.

By the mid-1780s, when the state began its difficult transition to a more professional government, competition for public offices grew to a point where no single group was able to dominate Vermont's politics. Chittenden exercised his greatest degree of authority during the first half of his governorship from 1777 to 1786. The second half of Chittenden's tenure was quite different. As was the case in other American states, many of the first settlers who moved into Vermont were adventurous entrepreneurs who possessed only minimal common school educations and limited financial resources. They moved to Vermont precisely because it offered new opportunities for themselves and their children. Their style of governance was relatively crude, not only because they lacked knowledge, but also because they relied upon an informal network of personal and fraternal relationships to get things done.

These first settlers established the independence of the New Hampshire Grants and organized its original government. They were followed by a more highly educated, professional, and urban-oriented gentry, who were anxious to bring the amenities of civilized life to the frontier. In addition to appreciating art, music, and literature, the members of this gentry valued a sophisticated and refined system of government based on the rule of law. It was inevitable that the leaders of this new gentry would eventually challenge the oldtime settlers for political control of the territory.

When viewed in this context, Thomas Chittenden's political career was unique in that he was able to bridge the gap between the original settlers and the more sophisticated reformers. He certainly personified the ideal of the frontier entrepreneur, and, like many other American frontiersmen, he did not have a finished education. He was hardly "a backwoodsman who lacked polish," however, as his conservative lawyer opponents labeled him.[51]

In his Pulitzer Prize-winning book on William Cooper, an early frontier entrepreneur in New York, Professor Alan Taylor observes, "as Cooper achieved wealth, celebrity, and influence, he tried to reinvent himself as a gentleman. . . . His ambitions were those of an eighteenth-century gentleman to acquire wealth and to spend it in ways that built influence and reputation." In the end, Cooper's pretensions led to his downfall.[52] Thomas Chittenden, on the other hand, followed a different route. Although he enjoyed considerable social status as a result of his military and public service in both Connecticut and Vermont, he presented himself as a simple farmer, and he never tried to be a member of the gentry. Instead, he was a tenacious survivor who possessed the personal qualities and the self-confidence needed to govern through two decades of crisis and change.

It is no exaggeration to observe that many aspects of Chittenden's role in Vermont were analogous to the role of George Washington on the larger national stage. The parallels between the two men are striking. In private life, both of them were extremely successful and wealthy land speculators. In their direction of military affairs, they both demonstrated tremendous tenacity and perseverance under the most trying conditions. Finally, both men presided over new postwar governments in a "patriarchal" manner, to use the phrase Daniel Chipman applied to Thomas Chittenden.[53]

Chittenden provided a sense of continuity and stability to the state during the postwar years until his death in 1797. Like President Washington, Chittenden played a critical role in maintaining public confidence in a new governmental experiment during a period of transition, when it was being refined by a more professional and knowledgeable group of leaders. The fact that he occupied the governor's office for such a long time provided the older frontier settlers with time to adjust to the changes and reforms that were taking place.

Thomas Chittenden's struggle for political power with the younger reformers ended up shaping the character of the state's governmental system for more than 150 years after his death. Way back in 1786, the Council of Censors had recommended that Vermont's constitution should be amended to limit the assembly to only fifty members, to be selected by districts rather than by towns.[54] This proposal represented a fundamental change in Vermont's governmental philosophy. Up to this point the state had been created by conventions of towns, and the constitution had been legitimated by the representatives from the towns who met and acted in the assembly. The censors' proposal threatened Chittenden's base of political support, which rested in the small towns.

It was no coincidence that the proposal would have shifted Vermont's political balance of power away from the small northern frontier towns that supported Chittenden to the more populous southern towns, where many of the reformers lived. After the delegates to the 1786 Constitutional Convention rejected the censors' proposal to limit the size of the assembly, the basic concept of "one town, one vote" prevailed in Vermont until the 1960s. As a result of Thomas Chittenden's successful defense of town-based government, Vermonters, throughout most of their history, have looked to their towns, and to their town meetings, as their primary governmental components. The state's role in the delivery of public services was relatively limited until recently.

All of this has changed dramatically, of course, during the last three decades. Today Vermonters have come to rely on a much more centralized state government to provide a growing array of services. We have entered a new era, and this newly evolving system of state services is fundamentally different from the system that was in place when Chittenden served as governor.

In the final analysis, one of the reasons Governor Chittenden's contributions to Vermont have been underestimated is that he was less theatrical and less exciting than his contemporaries. He was a wise and pragmatic leader who guided the actions of his colleagues to achieve his goals, but he often worked behind the scenes. As a result, history celebrates Ethan Allen's flamboyance, Ira Allen's cleverness, and Seth Warner's military glory, while virtually ignoring the man who directed much of their effort and achievement.

In 1839 Daniel Pierce Thompson's saga, *The Green Mountain Boys*, solidified Ethan Allen's reputation as the heroic personality of early Vermont. In 1942 Daniel Thompson's grandson, Charles Thompson, wrote a much more informative and balanced history of independent Vermont. As the following excerpt indicates, however, Charles Thompson remained captivated by the legend his grandfather had helped to create:

> Ethan Allen always gave a vivid splash of scarlet to any scene on any stage. . . . No one else in the state had anything like so true an instinct for drama as he. Ira, active, persevering, and clever as he was, seems drab beside Ethan; the inarticulate Chittenden, though you sense his rocklike figure in the background, is—like a rock—undramatic. . . . If this work were not a narrative, but a play, the stage direction would be, 'Enter Ethan Allen with a Flourish of Trumpets.' [55]

As Peter S. Onuf has noted, "Vermont was the only true American republic, for it alone had truly created itself." [56] There is no question that both Ethan and Ira Allen played important roles in the earliest formative years of the New Hampshire Grants. It was Governor Thomas Chittenden who was both present and active at the time when the new Republic of Vermont was actually created, however, and it was Governor Chittenden who guided Vermont during the first two decades of its existence. In many respects Charles Thompson's characterization of Chittenden is uniquely accurate. He was a rock—an undramatic but critically important foundation stone for the State of Vermont.

Before Thomas Chittenden died in Williston on August 24, 1797, he could take great pride in the role he had played in making Vermont the nation's fourteenth state. Hopefully the narrative on these pages will bring this fascinating man back to life, perhaps even with a "flourish of trumpets" of his own, so that he will become better known to those who still benefit from his achievements more than two hundred years later.

Thomas Chittenden Genealogy

William CHITTENDEN b. 1594, Marden, Kent, England	m.(1630)	Joanna Sheaffe b. 1606?, Cranbrook, Kent, England
Thomas CHITTENDEN b. 1637, Cranbrook, Kent, England	m.(1663)	Joanna Jordan b. 1642, Guilford, CT
William CHITTENDEN b. 1666, Guilford, CT	m.(1798)	Hannah _____
Ebenezer CHITTENDEN b. 1699, Guilford, CT	m.(1723)	Mary Johnson b. 1699, Guilford, CT
Gov. Thomas CHITTENDEN b. 1730, East Guilford, CT	m.(1749)	Elizabeth Meigs b. 1731, Guilford, CT

CHITTENDEN Children
(All born in Salisbury, Connecticut)

Mabel b. 1750; married Thomas Barney
Noah b. 1753; married Sally Fassett
Hannah b. 1756; married Isaac Clark
Mary b. 1758; married Jonas Galusha
Elizabeth b. 1761; married James Hill
Beulah b. 1763; married Matthew Lyon
Martin b. 1766; married Anna Bentley
Giles b. 1768; married Polly Hawley
Truman b. 1770; married Lucy Jones
Electa b. 1773; married Jonathan Spafford

Chittenden-Spafford-Pratt Original Williston Land Deed
May 17, 1773

To all People to whom these presents Shall Come Greeting Know that we Thomas Chittenden, Jonathan Spafford and Abijah Pratt are Holden and Stand firmly Bound Unto Allens & Baker in Company Otherwise Called the Onion River Company in the Final Sum of Five Hundred Pounds Current Money of the Province of New York to which Payment well and Truly to be Made and Done we jointly and severally Bind ourselves our Heirs Executors and administrators firmly by these presents sealed with our Seals & Signed with our Hand May 17, 1773. The Condition of the Above Obligation is such that if the above bounden Thomas Chittenden, Jonathan Spafford and Abijah Pratt or Either of them shall repair to the Township of Williston situate on the Onion River the fifteenth day of April (and) from that Time forward Except in Winter season Constantly employ (three) Men in Clearing Land they Purchased from Allens & Baker in Company Till they Have Done and performed the same Duty and Settlement Both as to Clearing and Building Improvement & Agriculture as is required of three New Hampshire grantees by the Conditions of the Charter Under the Great Seal of that Province require reference thereunto being had then the

Foregoing Obligation is to be Null and Void but otherwise to remain in full Fource and Virtue Signed Seald and Delivered in presents of Proper Signators the 17th Day of May 1773 and the Thir-
teenth Year of His Majesty's Reign

/s/ Thomas Chittenden
Jonathan Spafford
Abijah Pratt

Writing sample from the original deed.

APPENDIX C

Heman Allen's Williston Land Agreement with Thomas Chittenden and Jonathan Spafford
March 29, 1774

⫷⫸

Whereas Heman Allen has on the 29th Day of March 1774 Sold to Thomas Chittenden & Jonathan Spafford in Company Thirteen Rights or Shares and One Third part of One Right or Share of Land in the Township of Williston on Onion River the S'd Heman Allen had on the or about the 24th Day of this Instant March Liberty Granted to him in the Name of the Onion River Land Company to pitch & lay out Twenty Hundred acre Lots first in S'd Town Except One, and whereas S'd Heman Allen still owns about the same Quantity of Land Exclusive of Fourteen Hundred Acres that he in Company sold Before to the S'd Thomas Chittenden & Jonathan Spafford & Alijah Pratt It is agreed between the S'd Heman Allen & the S'd Thomas Chittenden & Jonathan Spafford in Company that the S'd Chittenden & Spafford are by Virtue of their S'd Deed of sail from the S'd Heman Intitled to their Equal Share of the Priviledge of Pitching & Laying out their equal proportion of the S'd 20 Lots Except the S'd 14 hundred acres sold to the S'd Chittenden Spafford and Pratt made to the Onion River Company, And Also it is further agreed that the whole of S'd Rights or Shares of Land that was owned by the S'd Heman in Company as well that he Now owns as well as that that was sold to the S'd Chittenden & Spafford in Company on the 29th of March 1774 Exclusive of the 14 Hundred shall still remain in Company Between the S'd Thomas Chittenden & Jonathan Spafford in Company & the S'd Heman Allen and Company, and it is further agreed that the S'd Chittenden & Spafford have full Liberty to make Sail of any part of the S'd Lands in Company as afores'd or all at their Discretion they paying to the S'd Heman & Company the One half of the Money Arising on S'd Sailes & it further agreed that the S'd Thomas Chittenden & Spafford Shall be at their Equal proportion of the Cost of Laying out S'd. Land & the S'd Heman Allen & Company shall be at the Equal part of the Cost & Trouble of Selling the Land now to be sold in Company & that the S'd Heman Allen & Company shall give Deeds of the one half of the Land sold by the S'd Chittenden & Spafford as afores'd to the Persons they sell to - In witness whereof we have here unto Set our Hands this 29th Day of March 1774

(A True Copy of the Bond Left at Esq. Hutchinson & Test. Original (is now) in Secretary of State's office, Heman Allen Papers, The Stevens Collection, Vermont State Archives, Montpelier, Vermont.)

Vermont Town Charters That List Thomas Chittenden as One of the Proprietors

Town	Chief Proprietor	Charter Date
1. Benson	James Meachum	May 5, 1780
2. Berkshire	William Goodrich	June 22, 1781
3. Braintree	Jacob Spear	August 1, 1781
4. Brookfield	Phineas Lyman	August 5, 1781
5. Cabot	Jesse Levenworth	August 17, 1781
6. Cambridge	Col. Samuel Robinson & John & Jonathan Fassett	August 30, 1781
7. Canaan	John Wheeler	February 25, 1782
8. Chittenden	Gershom Beach	March 16, 1780
9. Concord	Reuben Jones	September 15, 1781
10. Danville	Jacob Bayley	October 31, 1786
11. Eden	Col. Seth Warner	August 28, 1781
12. Enosburg	Roger Enos	May 15, 1780
13. Fair Haven	Capt. Ebenezer Allen	October 27, 1779
14. Greensboro	Harris Colt	August 20, 1781
15. Groton	Lt. Thos. Butterfield	October 20, 1789
16. Hardwick	Col. Danforth Keyes	August 19, 1781
17. Hyde Park	Jedediah Hyde Esq.	August 27, 1781
18. Isle of Motte	Major Benjamin Wait	October 27, 1779
19. Jamaica	Col. Samuel Fletcher	November 7, 1780

20. Jay (South) (7,600 acres)	Hon. Thomas Chittenden	November 7, 1792
21. Landgrove	William Utley	November 9, 1780
22. Lincoln	Col. Benjamin Simonds	November 9, 1780
23. Littleton	Benjamin Whipple Esq.	November 8, 1780
24. Lyndon	Hon. Jonathan Arnold	November 20, 1780
25. Montgomery	Stephen Rowe Bradley	March 15, 1780
26. Montpelier	Col. Timothy Bigelow	August 14, 1781
27. Northfield	Major Joel Matthews	August 10, 1781
28. Orange	Amos Robinson Esq.	August 11, 1781
29. Roxbury	Benjamin Emmons Esq.	August 6, 1781
30. St. Johnsbury	Jonathan Arnold Esq.	November 1, 1786
31. Sheffield	Stephen Kingbury	October 25, 1793
32. Starksboro	David Bridia & Gen. John Stark	November 9, 1780
33. Sterling	Hon. Samuel Safford Esq.	February 25, 1782
34. Turnersburgh (Chelsea)	Bela Turner Esq.	August 4, 1781
35. Two-Heroes	Col. Ethan Allen & Col. Samuel Herrick	October 27, 1779
36. Vershire	Capt. Abner Seelye	August 3, 1781
37. Victory	Capt. Ebenezer Fisk	September 6, 1781
38. Walden	Hon. Moses Robinson	August 18, 1781
39. Wardsborough	William Ward	November 7, 1780
40. Westfield	Daniel Owen	May 15, 1780
41. Westford	Capt. Uriah Seymour	August 17, 1781
42. Wildersburgh (Barre)	Col. William Williams	August 12, 1781
43. Williamstown	Samuel Clark & Absalom Baker	August 9, 1781
44. Woodbury	William Lyman Esq. & Col. Ebenezer Wood	August 16, 1781

Franklin H. Dewart, *Charters Granted By the State of Vermont* (State Papers of Vermont, II, 1922), 19–230. The above list covers town charters issued under the authority of Vermont. It does not include any of the earlier New Hampshire (Wentworth) town grants in which Thomas Chittenden may have been a proprietor.

Thomas Chittenden
Estate Inventory

NOW ALL MEN by these Presents, That we Noah Chittenden & Martin Chittenden of Jericho in the County of Chittenden and the State of VERMONT, as Principal, and I Truman Chittenden of Williston in the County of Chittenden - and State aforesaid, as Surety, are holden and bound unto Soloman Miller Esq. Judge of the Court of Probates within and for the Probate District of Chittenden or his Successors in said Office, in the full and just Sum of forty thousand Dollars; for which payment well and truly to be made and done, we bind Ourselves, our Heirs, Executors, and Adminstrators, jointly and severally, by these Presents—Signed with our Hands, and sealed with our Seals, in Probate-Office, this Seventh Day of Oct.r in the Year of our LORD, One thousand seven hundred and ninety-Seven.

THE Condition of this Obligation is such, That if the above-bounden Noah & Martin Chittenden Administrators of all and singular the Goods, Chattels, Credits, and Estate of Thomas Chittenden Esq. late of Williston in the County of Chittenden deceased, do make, or cause to be made, a true and perfect Inventory of all and singular the

Goods, Chattels, Credits, and Estate of the said deceased, which have or shall come into the Hands, Possession, or Knowledge of the said Noah & Martin Chittenden or into the Hands or Possession of any Person or Persons for him; and the samedo made, do exhibit, or cause to be exhibited into the Registry of the said Court of Probates in the District of Chittenden at or before the Seventh Day of June next ensuing; and the same Goods, Chattels, Credits, and Estate, and all others of the Goods, Chattels, Credits, and Estate of the said deceased, at the Time of his Death, which at any Time after shall come into the Hands or Possession of the said Noah & Martin - or into the Hands or Possession of any Person or Persons for them, do well and truly administer according to Law: And further, do make, or cause to be made, a true and just Account of their said Administration, at or before the Seventh Day of Oct.r 1799 [sic 1797], and all the Rest and Residue of said Goods, Chattels, Credits, and Estate, which shall be found remaining upon the said Administrator's Account (the same first examined and allowed by the said Court of Probate) shall deliver or pay unto such Person or Persons respectively, as the said Court of Probates, by their Decree or Sentence, pursuant to the true Intent and Meaning of the Law, shall limit and appoint: And if it shall hereafter appear that any last Will and Testament was made by the said deceased, and the Executor or the Executors therein named exhibit the same into the said Court, making Request to have it allowed and approved accordingly: If the said Noah & Martin being thereunto required, do render and deliver the said Letters of Administration, (Approbation of such Testament being first had and made) in the said Court, then this Obligation to be void and of no Effect, or otherwise to remain in full Force and Virtue.

[s] Noah Chittenden
[s] Martin Chittenden
[s] Truman Chittenden

Inventory

of the estate of his Excellency Thos. Chittenden Esq. Late of Williston deceased Sh(e)wn to us by the Administrators.

I - OUTSTANDING LOANS (All in pounds, shillings, pence):

	P | s | d		|P | s | d
John Hall Note	19 - 14 - 4	Ichabod Bartlit	21 - 16 - 9
Samuel Chamberlin	15 - 9 - 8	Samuel Lane Jr.	3 - 4 - 0
Robert Whitcome	6 - 12 - 0	Jonas Galusha	3 - 11 - 2
Timothy Parther	9 - 10 - 6	John Pumroy	15 - 12 - 0
Robert Parther	2 - 4 - 10	Leonard Hodges	30 - 10 - 4
John Cooper	3 - 17 - 6	Jonathan Spafford	46 - 13 - 3
John Deuveruse	15 - 19 - 2	Jonathan Spafford Jr.	11 - 6 - 7
James Blodget	40 - 12 - 0	Smally Spafford	4 - 14 - 7
Robert Stinson	13 - 17 - 9	John Chamberlin	21 - 13 - 9
Joseph McFarson	23 -19 - 2	John Morse	2 - 0 - 0
Benj. Bartlit	7 - 3 - 0	Daniel Morse	0 - 18 - 10
Isaac Hitchcock	7 - 6 - 0	Benj. Morse	1 - 11 - 10
Eliet Colby	75 - 4 - 0	Peter & James Crane	4 - 2 - 4
Elias Bewel	19 - 0 - 8	Timothy Betts	1 - 7 - 0
Henry Jones	7 - 12 - 7	Daniel Hutchinson	2 - 7 - 7
Stephen Nobles	4 - 5 - 8	Ebenezer Bartlit	2 - 17 - 0
James Whitcom	17 - 10 - 7	Hugh McCutchin	0 - 10 - 0
Asa Poland	1 - 5 - 2	John Lee	18 - 0 - 0
Solomon Miller	3 - 2 - 0	Martin Bartlit	1 - 9 - 8
John Kelly	54 - 4 - 0	Francis Jinos	1 - 1 - 7
Aaron Stone	2 - 11 - 0	Daniel Lee	0 - 1 - 8
David Whitmarsh	1 - 12 - 0	Abraham Smith	2 - 19 - 10
Gamaliel Painter	8 - 0 - 0	Matthew Cole	14 - 5 - 6
Elijah Nye	19 - 13 - 0	John Kenady	0 - 13 - 0
John Matthews	47 - 5 - 1	James Blair	3 - 0 - 1
Jef.y Cole	1 - 5 - 8	Benj. Farnsworth	1 - 8 - 6
David Nye	46 - 7 - 6	Richard Corning	4 - 13 - 0
David Hubbard	0 - 13 - 0	Ira Barney	4 - 6 - 4

Jacob Fairfield	26 - 13 - 2	Thos. Barney	16 - 6 - 8
Jesse Evarts Jr.	0 - 19 - 0	James Whitcome	0 - 15 - 0
Daniel Marsh	23 - 19 - 5	Noah Chittenden	16 - 15 - 6
Waid Catling	36 - 5 - 7	Barnabas Evens	0 - 6 - 0
Noah Chittenden	32 - 11 - 0	Walter Avery	49 - 12 - 9
Abraham Smith	59 - 3 - 6	Jacob Spafford	67 - 0 - 0
Peter Crane	49 - 13 - 5	Jas. Broadley	0 - 6 - 1
James Crane	49 - 13 - 5	David Hatch	0 - 12 - 0
Thomas Moore	1 - 4 - 0	Amos More	1 - 12 - 0
James Fairman	15 - 18 - 4	Jas. Nichols	1 - 14 - 7
John Cowe	30 - 13 - 11	John Tailor	0 - 5 - 4
Timothy Tuttle	43 - 4 - 2	Duon Bates	0 - 1 - 8
John Holmbeck	0 - 15 - 0	Allen Carpenter	0 - 12 - 5
Martin Chittenden	11 - 16 - 1	Peter McCarthur	0 - 17 - 6
Daniel Bills	2 - 11 - 3	Duon Butler	0 - 4 - 8
Samuel Hinkson	0 - 3 - 6	Jonathan Page	1 - 6 - 1
Samuel Hicks	3 - 2 - 6	John Raymond	0 - 7 - 7
Moses Billings	0 - 9 - 3	Dart of Richmond	0 - 3 - 0
Deodat Morton	70 - 1 - 1	David Warren	0 - 13 - 0
Nathan Allen	0 - 3 - 4	Nathaniel Alger	1 - 14 - 8
Thos. Palmer	4 - 3 - 10	Chauncy Smith	0 - 19 - 8
Nathan Smith	0 - 8 - 4	Archalus Page	0 - 7 - 4
Daniel Allis	1 - 0 - 7	Henry Fay	3 - 5 - 4
Daniel O'Brion	1 - 14 - 5	Wm. Douglass	2 - 0 - 0
Ephraim More	1 - 8 - 7	Martin Barber	2 - 19 - 9
— Edgerly	0 - 18 - 5	Jas. Hall	5 - 10 - 2
David Fields	1 - 11 - 0	John Bushiel	8 - 9 - 0
Caleb Nash	0 - 10 - 6	Seth Cole	3 - 5 - 6
Roderick Messinger	1 - 19 - 4	Abijah Hall	2 - 6 - 6
Josiah Jones	13 - 13 - 7	Ira Allen	202 - 10 - 8
Matthew Coxlin	1 - 4 - 0	Samuel Martin	1 - 16 - 0
John Heaton Jr.	0 - 15 - 0	Eli Barnard	3 - 6 - 5
Ezra Mead	3 - 16 - 0	Israel Williams	1 - 4 - 0
Kasiah Murey	0 - 10 - 6	Amos Brownson	0 - 8 - 8
Abraham Bethrong	3 - 3 - 3	Silas Hitchcock	5 - 10 - 0
Jehial Johns	0 - 3 - 1	Thos. Barney	34 - 15 - 6

Belah Dudley	0 - 10 - 0	Caleb Hull	7 - 17 - 0
Gaius Peers	0 - 6 - 0	John Jones	45 - 18 - 3
Asa Alger	1 - 12 - 4	Giles Chittenden	5 - 10 - 9
Notes in Buckley's		Stephens & Skinner	26 - 10 - 0
Hands	21 - 4 - 8	Safford Stephens	1 - 15 - 8
Timothy Morgan	2 - 9 - 6	John Hallock	0 - 7 - 4
Stinson & More	7 - 0 - 6	Stephen Nobles	70 - 0 - 0
Joseph McNall	9 - 13 - 5	Matthew Lyon	433 - 11 - 6
Aaron Warren	5 - 18 - 0	Joseph Hall	6 - 8 - 1
Nathaniel Winslow	0 - 10 - 6	Consider Shattuck	7 - 16 - 0
Edmund Evens	0 - 12 - 0	Joseph Bullin	1 - 0 - 0
James Smith	1 - 6 - 6	Ismead Cannon	7 - 16 - 0
Thos. Montgomery	1 - 14 - 6	James Hill	29 - 17 - 0
Orange Stephens	0 - 10 - 9	Peter Martin	6 - 12 - 0
Kesiah Tolcott	0 - 3 - 4	Nathan Wheeler	13 - 13 - 0
Nathan Murry	0 - 1 - 8	Peter Neal	7 - 16 - 0
Aaron Curtis	0 - 13 - 0	Noah Spencer	1 - 10 - 0
David Bates	0 - 10 - 5	Jonathan Shepherd	8 - 10 - 0
Abraham Smith	0 - 10 - 0	Dan J. Alis	3 - 0 - 0
Winthrop Hill	14 - 6 - 9	Samuel Scribner	1 - 10 - 0
Joel Brownson	0 - 11 - 0	Mathew Miller	1 - 10 - 0
Taylor Smith	1 - 6 - 3	Truman Barney	7 - 16 - 0
Ebenezer Kingsbury	0 - 6 - 0	Brayman & Nye	22 - 10 - 0
Elisha Bentley	0 - 12 - 3	Shutliff & Nye	42 - 10 - 0

Loan Total: 2,561 - 10 - 12

II - LIVESTOCK (Accounts II–IX are consolidated)

4 pair of Oxen	78 - 0 - 0	5 Mares	86 - 10 - 0
1 Bull	6 - 10 - 0	10 Colts	131 - 10 - 0
2 Hoggs	10 - 6 - 0	30 Sheep	13 - 10 - 0
18 Steer	78 - 5 - 0	1 Sorrel Horse	25 - 0 - 0
8 Heifers	34 - 17 - 0	1/2 Stud Horse	37 - 0 - 0
82 Cows	317 - 14 - 0		

Livestock Total: 819 - 2 - 0

III - TOOLS

1 Old Cart	4 - 15 - 0	3 Handsaws	12 - 0 - 0
1 Wagon	1 - 10 - 0	2 pair Plow Irons	2 - 2 - 0
1 Sleigh	3 - 6 - 0	1 Grindstone	0 - 6 - 0
5 Axheads	0 - 6 - 0	2 Cranes	2 - 4 - 4
2 pair Yoke Irons	0 - 9 - 0	1 Log Chain	0 - 17 - 6
3 Pitchforks	0 - 6 - 0	18 Drag Teeth	3 - 0 - 0
3 Draft Chains	0 - 18 - 0	Other	6 - 3 - 0

Tools Total: 38 - 2 - 10

IV - CLOTHES

1 Black Coat	3 - 8 - 6	6 pair cotton hose	2 - 5 - 0
1 Blue Suit	4 - 10 - 0	3 pair strip hose	1 - 10 - 0
1 Summer Suit	2 - 8 - 0	2 pair silk hose	1 - 2 - 0
1 Red Coat	1 - 16 - 0	6 pair lime hose	1 - 7 - 0
1 Silk Vest &		1 pair silver spurs	1 - 0 - 8
Breeches	3 - 10 - 0	2 silver watches	12 - 0 - 0
1 Blue vest	0 - 15 - 0	20 yds. black cashmir	15 - 7 - 6
6 Shirts	3 - 3 - 0	21 yds. buff cashmir	7 - 0 - 10
6 Cravats	1 - 15 - 0	11 yds. cotton denim	2 - 8 - 9
2 yds. black		14 doz. coat	
broadcloth	4 - 5 - 0	buttons	0 - 14 - 0
3/4 yd. red		14 pair buckles	4 - 8 - 0
broadcloth	1 - 14 - 0	3 yards lawn	1 - 6 - 0
11 yds. blue		Other	3 - 0 - 2
broadcloth	22 - 3 - 6		

CLOTHES TOTAL: 103 - 1 - 11

V - FURNITURE

6 Bedsteads w/ Cords	3 - 12 - 2	1 Small Leaf Table	2 - 0 - 0
1 Warming Pan	0 - 12 - 0	1 Large Leaf Table	2 - 2 - 0
10 Winsor Chairs	4 - 10 - 0	1 Round Table	0 - 12 - 0

6 Dining Chairs	2 - 8 - 0	3 Old Tables	1 - 8 - 8
6 Common Chairs	0 - 15 - 0	3 Stands	1 - 7 - 0
3 Looking Glass		1 Trunk	1 - 4 - 0
Mirrors	4 - 2 - 0	1 Tall Clock	26 - 2 - 0
1 Desk	5 - 5 - 0	1 Chest	0 - 6 - 0

Furniture Total: 56 - 5 - 10

VI - HOUSEHOLD

1 large Brass Kettle	3 - 0 - 0	1 T. Paine,	
20 Earthen Plates	8 - 4 - 0	Rights of Man	0 - 7 - 0
1 large Iron Pail	1 - 4 - 0	12 Pewter Plates	0 - 15 - 1
1 set China Teacups	1 - 0 - 0	110 pounds of Flax	4 - 2 - 6
6 Silver Tablespoons	7 - 10 - 0	93 bushels of Corn	18 - 14 - 0
6 Teaspoons	1 - 8 - 0	1425 lbs. Fresh Pork	25 - 10 - 0
1 Great Bible	0 - 15 - 0	10 bushels Wheat	11 - 17 - 0
2 Psalm Books	0 - 4 - 0	20 panes of glass	0 - 11 - 0
1 History of		5 dozen cakes soap	1 - 5 - 0
Redemption	0 - 3 - 0	Other	23 - 3 - 0

Household Total: 109 - 12 - 7

VII - Linens

2 Sets Curtains/		6 pair Woolen Sheets	8 - 8 - 0
spreads	9 - 0 - 0	4 Rose Blankets	3 - 0 - 0
4 Bed Spreads	5 - 14 - 0	52 New Linen Sheets	24 - 0 - 0
6 Bed Quilts	7 - 10 - 0	1 set Holland Sheets	1 - 15 - 0
2 Birdseye Coverlets	2 - 5 - 0	2 Holland Pillow Cases	0 - 8 - 0
7 Blankets	7 - 4 - 0	37 Linen Pillow Cases	3 - 14 - 0
5 Underblankets	2 - 14 - 0	20 Towels	2 - 6 - 0
6 Dutch Blankets	2 - 0 - 0	3 Tablecloths	2 - 4 - 0

LINENS TOTAL: 82 - 2 - 0

VIII - FINANCIAL ASSETS

Cash On Hand	138 - 4 - 0	Capt. Bonney Balance	90 - 17 - 2
Nye & Hubbard		Truman Chittenden	
Note	28 - 0 - 0	Due	8 - 19 - 0
State's Notes	132 - 0 - 0	4 Meeting House	
Due from Williston	92 - 5 - 0	Pews	100 - 0 - 0

Assets Total: 590 - 05 - 2

IX - LAND

Half of Home Farm	
(Bldgs,+ 900 acres in Williston)	2,000 - 0 - 0
The Lower Bow (98 acres)	480 - 0 - 0
One acre by Talbotts	15 - 0 - 0
40 acres Improved Land	140 - 0 - 0
298 acres Lower Gore	520 - 4 - 0
482 acres Williston Land	361 - 10 - 0
650 acres Williston Land	585 - 0 - 0
118 acres Williston Land	88 - 10 - 0
150 acres Castleton Land	560 - 0 - 0
700 acres of Essex Land	210 - 0 - 0
Grist Mill & Saw Mill in Jericho	375 - 0 - 0
Land in Underhill	612 - 0 - 0
7010 acres in Township of Jay	1,927 - 15 - 0
150 acres Williston Land	200 - 0 - 0

Land Total: 8,074 - 19 - 0

Sum total twelve thousand four hundred and
thirty five Pounds, two Shillings & four Pence   12,435 - 2 - 4

Equal to forty-one thousand four hundred fifty
    dollars & forty cents   **$41,450.40**

(Chittenden County Courthouse, Burlington, Vermont, Probate Records: Wills
and Estate Inventories.).

Endnotes

Introduction

1. Daniel Chipman, *A Memoir of Thomas Chittenden* (Middlebury: D. Chipman, 1849).

2. Hon. David Read, "Thomas Chittenden: His Life and Times," ed. Abby M. Hemenway in *Vermont Historical Gazetteer,* volume I (Burlington: A.M. Hemenway, 1867), 905-29.

3. Marshall True, "Why Are There No Biographers of Thomas Chittenden?" ed. Jennie G. Versteeg in *Lake Champlain: Reflections on Our Past* (Burlington: UVM Center for Research on Vermont, 1987), 210-15.

4. J. Kevin Graffagnino, "The Vermont Story: Continuity and Change in Vermont Historio-graphy," *Vermont History*, vol. 46, no. 2 (Spring 1978): 77-81.

5. *Vermont State Papers*, volume XVII, 1969.

6. Robert E. Shalhope, *Bennington and the Green Mountain Boys* (Baltimore: The Johns Hopkins University Press, 1996); Charles A. Jellison, *Ethan Allen: Frontier Rebel* (Syracuse: Syracuse University Press, 1969); J. Kevin Graffagnino (ed.) *Ethan and Ira Allen: Collected Works* (Benson: Chalidze Publications, 1992); and Michael A. Bellesiles, *Revolutionary Outlaws* (Charlottesville: University Press of Virginia, 1993).

7. Chilton Williamson, "A New Deal for Vermont History," *Vermont History,* vol. XXII, no. 1 (January 1954): 33.

CHAPTER 1

The Early Chittendens

1. Nicholas Canny, *Europeans on the Move* (Oxford, England: Clarendon Press, 1994), 49.

2. Virginia D. Anderson, *New England's Generation* (Cambridge, England: Cambridge University Press, 1991), 42-4.

3. Ibid., 16.

4. C.C.R. Pile, *Cranbrook: A Wealden Town* (Cranbrook, England: Cranbrook and District Local Historical Society, 1990), 21; Ephaim Lipson, *A Short History of Wool and Its Manufacture* (Cambridge: Harvard University Press, 1953), 52.

5. C.C.R. Pile, *Cranbrook: Broadcloth and Clothiers* (Cranbrook, England: Cranbrook and District Local Historical Society, 1981), 4.

6. Elsdon C. Smith, *New Dictionary of American Family Names* (New York: Gramercy Publishing Company, 1988), 84; Eilart Ekwall, *The Concise Oxford Dictionary of English Place Names* (Oxford, England: Clarendon Press, 1991), 106, 141.

7. C.C.R. Pile, *Watermills and Windmills of Cranbrook* (Cranbrook, England: Cranbrook and District Local Historical Society, 1992), 5.

8. Pile, *Cranbrook Broadcloth*, 10-11.

9. Genealogical data on the Chittenden and Sheafe families came from a variety of different sources. The birthdate of William Chittenden appears to be relatively certain. He is listed in the *Mormon International Genealogical Index* (IGI A0783, 5594) for the British Isles as being christened in March 1594 in Marden (Cranbrook, Kent), the son of Robert Chittenden. This same information also appears in typewritten notes in the archives of the Cranbrook History Society as follows: "In the record of the Baptisms of the Parish of Marden, near Cranbrook, appears this entry - March, 1594, William, son of Robert Chittenden, signed, Salmon Boxer, Vicar of Marden." This same information is provided in Alvan Talcott, *Families of Early Guilford, Connecticut* (Baltimore: Genealogical Publishing Company, Inc., 1984), 167.

10. The birth date of Joanna Sheafe is more uncertain. Four entries appear in the *Mormon International Genealogical Index* (IGI A0824, 24,733). All of them list her parents as Edmund Sheaf(f)e and Joan (or Joanna) Jordan. However, her birth dates vary as follows: "about 1598 (Cranbrook); 1606 (Kent); abt. 1613 (Cranbrook.); and 1614 (Kent)."

11. Bernard C. Steiner, *History of Guilford and Madison, Connecticut* (Guilford: Guilford Free Library, 1975), 12-29.

12. Ibid., 24-5.

13. Andrew C. McLaughlin, *Foundations of American Constitutionalism* (New York: New York University Press, 1932), 12.

14. Albert E. Van Dusen, *Connecticut* (New York: Random House, 1964), 19, 41-50.

15. David Horowitz, *The First Frontier* (New York: Simon and Schuster, 1978), 39.

16. Neal Salisbury, *Manitou and Providence* (New York: Oxford University Press, 1982), 221-22.

17. Benjamin Trumbull, *A Complete History of Connecticut*, volume I (New London, CT: H.D. Utley, 1898), 82.

18. Steiner, *History of Guilford*, 29. The deed records that Shaumpishuh received payments as follows for this land: "the said sachem squaw . . . received 12 coates, 12 fathom of wompom, 12 glasses, 12 payer of shoes, 12 Hatchets, 12 paire of stockings, 12 Hooes, 4 kettles, 12 knives, 12 hatts, 12 poringers, 12 spoons, and 2 English coates."

19. Douglas E. Leach, *The Northern Colonial Frontier: 1607-1763* (New York: Holt, Rinehart and Winston, 1966), 44.

20. Isabel M. Calder, *The New Haven Colony* (New Haven, CT: Yale University Press, 1934), 147-49.

21. Alvan Talcott, *William Chittenden of Guilford, Connecticut, and His Descendents* (New Haven, CT: Tuttle, Morehouse, and Taylor, 1882), 8.

22. W.R. Dudley, *Proceedings at the Celebration of the 250th Anniversary of Guilford, Connecticut* (New Haven, CT: Stafford Printing Company, 1889), 224; Talcott, *William Chittenden*, 10.

23. Dorothy Deming, *The Settlement of Connecticut Towns* (New Haven: Yale University Press, Tercentenary Paper no. VI, 1933), 21.

24. Talcott, *William Chittenden*, 8; Edward E. Atwater, *History of the Colony of New Haven*, volume II (Meridan, CT: The Journal Publishing Company, 1902), 629. According to one account William Chittenden "had been a soldier in the Netherlands in the Thirty Years War and had reached the rank of Major" before he left England. James Savage, *A Genealogical Dictionary of the First Settlers of New England*, volume I (Baltimore: Genealogical Publishing Company, 1981), 382.

25. Steiner, *Guilford History*, 24-5; Charles J. Hoadly, *Records of the Colony & Plantation of New Haven from 1638 to 1649* (Hartford, CT: Case, Tiffany & Company, 1857), 303, 511.

26. Calder, *New Haven Colony*, 152.

27. J.L. Rockey, *History of New Haven County, Connecticut*, volume II (New York: W. W. Preston & Company, 1892), 126.

28. Christopher Rand, *The Changing Landscape* (New York: Oxford University Press, 1968), 131.

29. Van Dusen, *Connecticut*, 50-52.

30. James Truslow Adams, *The Founding of New England*, volume I (Boston: Little Brown & Company, 1927), 206-7.

31. Charles M. Andrews, *The Rise and Fall of the New Haven Colony* (New Haven, CT: Yale University Press, Tercentenary Paper no. XLVIII, 1936), 20.

32. *New Haven Colonial Records* (1660-61), 417; cited in Talcott, *William Chittenden*, 11.

33. Van Dusen, *Connecticut*, 53. According to Van Dusen's breakdown, estates of 1,000 pounds or more were classified as wealthy; 500 to 900 pounds as substantial; 100 to 499 pounds as medium; and 10 to 50 pounds as the poorer class.

34. Alvan Talcott, *Families of Early Guilford, Connecticut* (Baltimore: Genealogical Publishing Company, 1984), 167.

35. Talcott, *Guilford Families*, 168.

36. Ibid., 169.

37. Ibid., 21.

38. Ibid., 170-71.

39. Letter, A.M. Chard, Madison Historical Society, to Frank Smallwood (September 28, 1995).

40. Hiram Carlton, *Genealogical and Family History of the State of Vermont* (New York: Lewis Publishing Company, 1908), 1.

41. Steiner, *Guilford History*, 209.

42. Roland M. Hooker, *The Colonial Trade of Connecticut* (New Haven, CT: Yale University Press, Tercentenary Paper no. L, 1936), 1.

43. Milna E. Rindge, *Shipbuilding in Madison, Connecticut* (Madison, CT: Madison Historical Society, 1993), 1.

44. Mary S. Evarts, "Madison Shipping," ed. Philip S. Platt in *Madison's Heritage* (Madison, CT: Madison Historical Society, 1964), 200.

45. Hooker, *Colonial Trade*, 29; Rockey, *New Haven County*, 109.

46. Hon. David Read, "Thomas Chittenden: His Life and Times," ed. Abby M. Hemenway in *Vermont Historical Gazetteer*, volume I (Burlington: A.M. Hemenway, 1867), 906.

47. Esther M. Swift, *Vermont Place-Names* (Camden Maine: Picton Press, 1996), 157.

48. Paul S. Gillies, "Adjusting to Union: An Assessment of Statehood," ed. Michael Sherman in *A More Perfect Union* (Montpelier: Vermont Historical Society, 1991), 130.

49. Chilton Williamson, "A New Deal for Vermont History," *Vermont History*, vol. XXII, no. 1 (January 1954): 33.

50. Ignatius Thomson, *The Patriot's Monitor for Vermont* (Randolph: S. Wright, 1810), 199-201.

51. *The Vermont Gazette* (September 12, 1797).

52. John Lincklaen,"The Beginnings of Ease," ed. T.D. Seymour Bassett in *Outsiders Inside Vermont* (Brattleboro: The Stephen Greene Press, 1967), 48-49.

53. Ibid., 49.

54. Daniel Chipman, *A Memoir of Thomas Chittenden* (Middlebury: D. Chipman, 1849), 20.

55. Mary S. Evarts, "Early Schools in East Guilford," ed. Platt in *Madison*, 31.

56. Edward E. Atwater, *History of the Colony of New Haven* (Meridan, CT: Journal Publishing Company, 1902), 261.

57. Orwin B. Griffin, *The Evolution of the Connecticut State School System* (New York: Columbia University Teachers College, 1928), 4.

58. Florence S.M. Crofut, *Guide to the History and Historic Sites of Connecticut* (New Haven, CT: Yale University Press, 1937), 181; *Documentary History of the Protestant Episcopal Church in the Diocese of Vermont* (New York: Pott & Amery - Cooper Union, 1870), 110; Kenneth S. Rothwell, *A Goodly Heritage* (Burlington: Cathedral Church of St. Paul), 1-3; Lori F. Wilson, *God With Us* (Shelburne: The Trinity Episcopal Church, 1990); and Edward Mayo Green, *The Episcopal Church in Vermont* (Woodstock: Elm Tree Press, 1959), 1-4.

59. Jackson Turner Main, *Society and Economy in Colonial Connecticut* (Princeton, NJ: Princeton University Press, 1985).

60. Hon. Lucius E. Chittenden, *Address at the Dedication of the Thomas Chittenden Monument* (Williston: Printed by order of the Vermont legislature, August 19, 1896.)

61. Marshall True, "Why Are There No Biographers of Thomas Chittenden?" ed. Jennie G. Versteeg in *Lake Champlain: Reflections on Our Past* (Burlington: UVM Center for Research on Vermont, 1987), 214.

62. Marcus A. McCorison, *Vermont Imprints 1778-1920* (Worcester, MA: American Antiquarian Society, 1963), 6.

63. Frederick Wells, "How Important Was It to Be a Good Speller in Early Vermont?" *Vermont History*, vol. 43, no. 1 (Winter 1975): 74; Kenneth A. Lockridge, *Literacy in Colonial New England* (New York: W.W. Norton and Company, 1974); William J. Gilmore, "Elementary Literacy on the Eve of the Industrial Revolution: Trends in Rural New England 1760-1830," *Proceedings of the American Antiquarian Society*, vol. 92, part I (1982).

64. True, *Chittenden*, 214.

65. Thompson, *Independent Vermont*, 533-4

CHAPTER 2

The Education of Thomas Chittenden

1. Richard Hofstadter, *America at 1750: A Social Portrait* (New York: Random House, 1973), 148-9.

2. Rising L. Morrow, *Connecticut Influences in Western Massachusetts and Vermont* (New Haven: Yale University Press, Tercentenary Paper no. LVIII, 1936), 3.

3. Hofstadter, *America 1750*, 149.

4. Geoffrey Rossano, *Salisbury Town Meeting Minutes: 1741-1784* (Salisbury, CT: The Salisbury Association, 1988), 130.

5. Florence S.M. Crofut, *Guide to the History and the Historic Sites of Connecticut*, volume I (New Haven, CT: Yale University Press, 1937), 426.
6. Ibid., 79.
7. Rossano, *Salisbury Minutes*, xv.
8. Ibid., 157-60.
9. Donna V. Russell, *Deeds & Taxpayers 1739-1763*, Salisbury, Connecticut, Records, volume II (Middletown, MD: Catoctin Press, 1983), 60.
10. Salisbury, Connecticut, Scoville Memorial Library, Original Land Deed Maps, 4th Div., 22nd Lot.
11. Rossano, *Salisbury Minutes*, 34.
12. Gwilym R. Roberts, "An Unknown Vermonter," *Vermont History*, vol. XXIX, no. 2 (April 1961): 92.
13. Russell, *Salisbury Records*, 67; Julia Pettee, *The Early History of the Town of Salisbury, Connecticut* (Salisbury, CT: The Salisbury Association, 1957), 206.
14. *Town of Salisbury Historical Collections*, volume I (Salisbury, CT: The Salisbury Association, 1913), 40.
15. Russell, *Salisbury Records*, 124-5.
16. Jay Mack Holbrook, *Vermont 1771 Census* (Oxford, MA: Holbrook Research Institute, 1982), 18.
17. Rossano, *Salisbury Minutes*, 47, 164.
18. Ibid., 47, 49-57, 59-60, 63-64, 69, 71-75, 79, 83, 87.
19. Charles J. Hoadly, *Public Records of the Colony of Connecticut*, volumes 11-13 (Hartford: Case, Lockwood & Brainard C., 1880).
20. Robert E. Shalhope, *Bennington and the Green Mountain Boys* (Baltimore: The Johns Hopkins Press, 1996), 143.
21. Hoadly, *Public Records*, vol. 12, 607-9; vol. 13, 290.
22. Shalhope, *Bennington*, 143-4.
23. Town of Salisbury Historical Collections, 40.
24. Pettee, *Early History*, 150.
25. Ibid., 127-9.
26. Ibid., 131.
27. David L. DeWolfe, *The Chittendens of Salisbury, Connecticut*, Address at the Thomas Chittenden memorial dedication (Madison, CT, July 27, 1968), 3.
28. Morrow, *Connecticut Influences*, 11.
29. Rossano, *Salisbury Minutes*, 153.
30. Ibid., 153.
31. W. Storrs Lee, *Town Father* (New York: Hastings House, 1952), 5.
32. Esther M. Swift, *Vermont Place-Names* (Camden, ME: Picton Press, 1996), 48.
33. Albert S. Batchellor, *The New Hampshire Grants, Charters of Townships*, volume XXVI (Concord, NH: New Hampshire State Papers, 1895), 281-82, 318, 397.
34. Roberts, *Unknown Vermonter*, 93.
35. J. Kevin Graffagnino, "The Country My Soul Delighted In: The Onion River Land Company and the Northern Frontier," *The New England Quarterly*, vol. LXV, no. 1 (March 1992): 32-3.

36. Walter H. Crockett, ed., *Vermonters: A Book of Biographies* (Brattleboro: Stephen Daye Press, 1931), 45.
37. Rossano, *Salisbury Minutes*, 139.
38. Michael A. Bellesiles, *Revolutionary Outlaws* (Charlottesville, VA: University Press of Virginia, 1993), 36.
39. Allen Family Papers, University of Vermont, Bailey-Howe Library, Special Collections, box III, nos. 14 & 15; James B. Wilbur, *Ira Allen*, volume I (Boston: Houghton Mifflin, 1928), 44.
40. Russell S. Taft Esq., "Williston," ed. Abby M. Hemenway in *Vermont Historical Gazetteer*, volume I (Burlington: A.M. Hemenway, 1867), 902.
41. Deed from Heman Allen to Thomas Chittenden and Jonathan Spafford, dated March 29, 1774. Montpelier, Vermont, Secretary of State's office. A complete listing of all the acreage Chittenden and Spafford obtained in Williston from the Allens is contained in Wilbur, *Ira Allen*, volume II, 523.
42. Ruth Wright, *The History of the Town of Colchester* (Burlington: Queen City Printers, 1963), 20.

CHAPTER III
The Arrival of Thomas Chittenden

1. Ira Allen, in James B. Wilbur, *Ira Allen*, volume I (Boston: Houghton Mifflin, 1928), 43.

2. Julia Pettee, *The Early History of Salisbury, Connecticut* (Salisbury, CT: The Salisbury Association, 1957), 209.
3. Thomas H. Canfield, "Lake Champlain," ed. Abby M. Hemenway in *Vermont Historical Gazetteer*, volume I (Burlington: A.M. Hemenway, 1867), 661.
4. Hon. David Read, "Thomas Chittenden, His Life and Times," in Ibid., 456, 908-10
5. Esther M. Swift, *Vermont Place-Names* (Camden, ME: Picton Press, 1996), 14-16. It is estimated that Benning Wentworth's land grants west of the Connecticut River amounted to as many as 3,000,000 acres. Matt Bushnell Jones, *Vermont in the Making* (Cambridge: Harvard University Press, 1939), 278.
6. *Governor and Council*, I, 6.
7. Donald A. Smith, "Green Mountain Insurgency: Transformation of New York's Forty-Year Land War," *Vermont History*, vol. 64, no. 4 (Fall 1996): 198, 206, 227; Robert E. Shalhope, *Bennington and the Green Mountain Boys* (Baltimore: Johns Hopkins Press, 1996), 164.
8. *Governor and Council*, I, 110-11.
9. Henry Steele Wardner, *The Birthplace of Vermont* (New York: Charles Scribner's Sons, 1927), 191; Edwin A. Bayley Esq., *An Address Commemorative of the Life and Public Services of Brig. Gen. Jacob Bayley* (Montpelier: Vermont Historical Society, 1919).
10. Bayley, *Life and Services*, 11.

11. Wardner, *Birthplace*, 226.
12. Bayley, *Life and Services*, 13.
13. John M. Comstock, *Principal Officers of Vermont, 1777 to 1918* (St. Albans: Messenger Company Publishers, 1918), 268-9.
14. Marshall True and William Doyle, *Vermont and the New Nation* (Hyde Park: Vermont Council on the Humanities, 1984), 33.
15. Jones, *Vermont in the Making*, 365-6; Walter H. Crockett, *Vermont: The Green Mountain State*, volume II (New York: Century History Company, 1921), 179-81.
16. Jones, *Vermont in the Making*, 366.
17. Crockett, *Vermont*, I, 179-82
18. *Governor and Council*, I, 27-36.
19. Jay Mack Holbrook, *Vermont 1771 Census* (Oxford, MA: Holbrook Research Institute, 1982), *xii*.
20. *Governor and Council*, I, 30.
21. Wardner, *Birthplace*, 304.
22. Crockett, *Vermont*, II, 32.
23. Earle Newton, *The Vermont Story 1749-1949* (Montpelier: Vermont Historical Society, 1949), 74. There are different accounts of when the Chittendens left Williston, and where they lived in the south. Evidence indicates they first moved to Danby, because Thomas Chittenden was listed as a delegate from Danby at the July 1777 Constitutional Convention in Windsor. According to Daniel Chipman's *Memoir*, the family then moved to Pownal and Williamstown, Massachusetts. They later ended up in Arlington, where Chittenden bought

a deed, dated June 10, 1779, for Jehiel Hawley's confiscated land and house.
24. *Governor and Council*, I, 39.
25. Ibid., 41.
26. John A. Williams, ed., *The Public Papers of Governor Thomas Chittenden* (Montpelier: Vermont State Papers, vol. XVII, 1969), *iii*; Newton, *Vermont Story*, 79
27. *Governor and Council*, I, 403.
28. Charles M. Thompson, *Independent Vermont* (Boston: Houghton Mifflin, 1942), 271.
29. Michael A. Bellesiles, *Revolutionary Outlaws* (Charlottesville, VA: University Press of Virginia, 1993), 160.
30. Ibid., 161; Bayley, *Life and Services*, 21.
31. Ira Allen, *History of the State of Vermont* (Rutland: Charles E. Tuttle Co., 1969), 63.
32. *Governor and Council*, I, 83-4, 393-6.
33. John N. Shaeffer, "A Comparison of the First Constitutions of Vermont and Pennsylvania," *Vermont History*, vol. 43, no.1 (Winter 1975): 56.
34. Paul S. Gillies and D. Gregory Sanford, *Records of the Council of Censors of the State of Vermont* (Montpelier: Vermont Secretary of State, 1991), 11.
35. *Governor and Council*, I, 108.
36. Ibid., 109-129.
37. Aleine Austin, *Matthew Lyon* (University Park, PA: Pennsylvania State University Press, 1981), 21.

38. Sarah V. Kalinoski, "Sequestration, Confiscation, and the 'Tory' in the Vermont Revolution," *Vermont History*, vol. 45, no. 4 (Fall 1977): 244-5.

39. Craig L. Symonds, *Battlefield Atlas of the American Revolution* (Baltimore: N & A Publishing Company, 1991), 45, 51.

40. Williams, *Public Papers*, 178, 193-5, 215.

41. Roland Robinson, *Vermont: A Study in Independence* (Boston: Houghton Mifflin & Co., 1899), 184.

42. Benjamin H. Hall, *History of Eastern Vermont* (New York: Appleton & Co., 1858), 309-10.

43. Williams, *Public Papers*, 252.

44. Hall, *Eastern Vermont*, 311.

45. John Krueger, *Address at Ethan Allen Homestead*, Burlington, Vermont (June 29, 1997).

46. Michael A. Bellesiles, *Revolutionary Outlaws*, 105.

47. Ira Allen expressed doubts very early in his *History of Vermont* whether ratification would have been possible in light of the political divisions within the Grants. (Allen, *History*, 72) Recent scholars such as Bellesiles, however, have noted "the preamble, written by Ira Allen and Thomas Chittenden, asserts the people's right to establish their own form of government." He concludes "every state's constitution was an experiment on some level--Vermont's system of government bore the same legitimacy as the rest." Bellesiles, *Revolutionary Outlaws*, 137, 162.

48. Charles A. Jellison, *Ethan Allen: Frontier Rebel* (Syracuse, NY: Syracuse University Press, 1969), 209.

CHAPTER IV
Defending the Republic

1. Technically, Vermont was an independent government until Congress admitted it as the fourteenth state in 1791. As a result, it was often called a republic during its early years, even though its constitution referred to it as "the Commonwealth or State of Vermont." In this book, the author has used the word "state" to describe Vermont during its earliest years of existence. For more information, see Daniel A. Metraux, "Was Vermont Ever a Republic?" *Vermont History*, vol. 55, no. 3 (Summer 1987): 167-73.

2. Benjamin Hall, *History of Eastern Vermont* (New York: Appleton & Co., 1858), 244-5, 252.

3. *Assembly Journal*, I, 3-5.

4. Mary Greene Nye, ed., *Sequestration, Confiscation and Sale of Estates* (Montpelier: Vermont State Papers, volume VI, 1939), 20.

5. Sarah V. Kalinoski, "Sequestration, Confiscation, and the 'Tory' in the Vermont Revolution," *Vermont History*, vol. 45, no. 4 (Fall 1977): 242-3.

6. Jere Daniell, *Experiment in Republicanism* (Cambridge, MA: Harvard University Press, 1970), 145-6.

7. *Assembly Journal*, I, 24-29; *Governor and Council*, I, 273.
8. *Governor and Council*, I, 415-6.
9. *Assembly Journal*, I, 41-4.
10. Ibid., I, 48.
11. *Governor and Council*, I, 424-6.
12. Allen Soule, ed., *Laws of Vermont 1777-1780* (Montpelier: Vermont State Papers, volume XII, 1964), 36-7.
13. E. P. Walton, "The First Legislature of Vermont," in *Essays in the Early History of Vermont* (Montpelier: Vermont Historical Society Collections, volume VI, 1943), 245.
14. Ibid., 245.
15. *Assembly Journal*, I, 54-6.
16. Soule, *Laws*, 40-154.
17. Ibid., 175.
18. *Assembly Journal*, I, 53, 62.
19. *Governor and Council*, I, 289.
20. *Official History of Guilford, Vermont* (Brattleboro: Broad Brook Grange #151, 1961), 46.
21. *Governor and Council*, I, 518-19.
22. *Assembly Journal*, I, 71; Charles A. Jellison, *Ethan Allen: Frontier Rebel* (Syracuse, NY: Syracuse University Press, 1969), 225.
23. *Land Records of the Town of Arlington, Vermont*, volume I (1761-1785), 29-30.
24. *Governor and Council*, I, 521.
25. *Governor and Council*, II, 188.
26. *Governor and Council*, I, 524.
27. *Governor and Council*, II, 187.
28. J. Kevin Graffagnino, ed., *Ethan and Ira Allen: Collected Works*, volume I (Benson: Chalidze Publications, 1992), 181-232.
29. *Governor and Council*, II, 184.
30. Ibid., 185.

CHAPTER V
Vermont on the Offensive

1. John A. Williams, ed., *The Public Papers of Governor Thomas Chittenden* (Montpelier: Vermont State Papers, volume XVII, 1969), 474.
2. Ira Allen, *History of the State of Vermont* (Rutland: Charles E. Tuttle Co., 1969), 85.
3. Williams, *Public Papers*, 476.
4. *Assembly Journal*, I, 83.
5. Ibid., 90, 94-5.
6. *Governor and Council*, II, 248-9; Walter Hill Crockett, Vermont: *The Green Mountain State*, volume II (New York: Century History Company, 1921), 301-2.
7. Williams, *Public Papers*, 326-30.
8. *Assembly Journal*, I, 106.
9. Franklin H. Dewart, ed., *Charters Granted by the State of Vermont* (Montpelier: Vermont State Papers, volume II, 1922), introduction.
10. Matt Bushnell Jones, *Vermont in the Making* (Cambridge, MA: Harvard University Press, 1939), 278.
11. Dewart, *Charters*, 19-230. In contrast, according to one account, Ira Allen "either owned or controlled at the lowest and most reasonable estimate 75,000 acres, and at the highest 300,000 acres." Charles M. Thompson, *Independent Vermont* (Boston: Houghton Mifflin, 1942), 135.

12. *Governor and Council,* II, 63.
13. Ibid., 64; Florence M. Woodward, *The Town Proprietors in Vermont* (New York: New York University Press, 1936).
14. *Governor and Council,* II, 261.
15. Ibid., 264-66.
16. *Assembly Journal,* I, 127.
17. *Governor and Council,* 326-35.
18. Ira Allen, *History,* 92.
19. *Governor and Council,* II, 277-308.
20. *Assembly Journal,* I, 147.
21. *Governor and Council,* II, 270.
22. *Assembly Journal,* I, 221-3.
23. *Governor and Council,* II, 397.
24. Charles A. Jellison, *Ethan Allen: Frontier Rebel* (Syracuse, NY: Syracuse University Press, 1969), 247.
25. *Governor and Council,* II, 400.
26. Jellison, *Ethan Allen,* 259.
27. *Governor and Council,* II, 406-7.
28. Ibid., 428.
29. Ira Allen, *History,* 108.
30. *Governor and Council,* II, 315.
31. Ibid., 320.
32. Ibid., 439.
33. Ibid., 442-3.
34. Ibid., 334.
35. Ira Allen, *History,* 124.
36. *Governor and Council,* II, 350-3.
37. Ibid., 354.
38. *Assembly Journal,* II, 61.
39. Dewart, *Charters,* 148-9.
40. Peter S. Onuf, "State-Making in Revolutionary America: Independent Vermont as a Case Study," *Journal of American History,* vol. 67, no. 4 (March 1981): 815.

CHAPTER VI
Reform and the Rise of Rival Leaders

1. John A. Williams, ed., *Laws of Vermont 1781-84* (Montpelier: Vermont State Papers, volume XIII, 1965), 98.
2. *Official History of Guilford, Vermont* (Brattleboro: Broad Brook Grange #151, 1961), 66. This fascinating bicentennial town history portrays these events from a Yorker's perspective, referring to the "invasions" and suffering in Guilford. It is particularly critical of Allen, noting that "Ethan Allen, immensely elated by his shallow victory . . . was unable to restrain the blatant boasting and vulgar oaths so characteristic of him." (68).
3. *Governor and Council,* III, 253.
4. Benjamin H. Hall, *History of Eastern Vermont* (New York: Appleton & Co., 1858), 541-47.
5. *Guilford History,* 70.
6. Walter H. Crockett, *Vermont: The Green Mountain State,* volume II (New York: The Century History Company, 1921), 377-8.
7. Williams, *Public Papers,* 593, 604.
8. Ibid., 608-10.
9. *Governor and Council,* III, 291.
10. Williams, *Laws,* XIII, 30.
11. Sarah V. Kalinoski, *Property Confiscation in Vermont during the American Revolution,* University of Vermont graduate thesis, 1975.
12. Franklin H. Dewart, *Index to the Papers of the Surveyors-General*

(Montpelier: Vermont State Papers, volume I, 1918), 6-7.

13. Williams, *Laws*, XIII, 67-8.

14. Daniel Chipman, *A Memoir of Thomas Chittenden* (Middlebury: D. Chipman, 1849), preface, *v.*

15. Charles M. Thompson, *Independent Vermont* (Boston: Houghton Mifflin, 1942), 479.

16. Walter H. Crockett, *Vermonters: A Book of Biographies* (Brattleboro: Stephen Daye Press, 1931), 37.

17. Samuel B. Hand and P. Jeffrey Potash, "Nathaniel Chipman: Vermont's Forgotten Founder," ed. Michael Sherman in *A More Perfect Union* (Montpelier: Vermont Historical Society, 1991), 54.

18. Biographies from Hiland Hall, *The History of Vermont* (Albany: Joel Munsell, 1868), 451-76.

19. Williams, *Laws*, XIII. 231-2.

20. Williams, *Laws*, XIV, 64-7.

21. Aleine Austin, "Vermont Politics in the 1780's: The Emergence of Rival Leadership," *Vermont History*, vol. 42, no. 2 (Spring 1974), 147.

22. *Governor and Council*, III, 398-9.

23. Hand and Potash, *Nathaniel Chipman*, 57.

24. Cato quotes from *The Vermont Journal and Universal Advertiser*, nos. 81, 82, and 85 (February 8 to March 25, 1785).

25. Paul S. Gillies and D. Gregory Sanford, eds., *Records of the Council of Censors of the State of Vermont* (Montpelier: Secretary of State, 1991), 769-70.

26. James B. Wilbur, *Ira Allen*, volume I (Boston: Houghton Mifflin, 1928), 471.

27. Crockett, *Vermont*, volume II, 404.

28. Gillies and Sanford, *Records*, 30-31.

29. Ibid., 58.

30. *Vermont Gazette*, vol. III, no. 138 (January 23, 1786): 3.

31. *Vermont Gazette*, vol. III, nos. 137-8 (January 17 and 23, 1786): 1-3.

32. *Governor and Council*, III, 359.

33. Charlotte C. Brown, *The Vermont Council of Censors 1777-1870*, University of Vermont Ph.D. dissertation, microfilm M595 (1946), 40

34. Crockett, *Vermont*, II, 406.

35. *Governor and Council*, III, 110.

36. John M. Comstock, ed., *Principal Civil Officers of Vermont, 1777 to 1918* (St. Albans: Messenger Company Publishers, 1918), 278-98. The five convention delegates who were serving in the 1785-86 assembly were Peletiah Bliss of Bradford, Asahel Smith of Benson, John Coffeen of Cavendish, Gideon Ormsby of Manchester, and Stephen R. Bradley of Westminster.

37. *Arlington, Vermont, Town Records* (1761-1850), 42.

38. Gillies and Sanford, *Records*, 89.

39. Ibid., 95.

40. Ibid., 94.

41. Crockett, *Vermont*, volume II, 397-98.
42. F. Kennon Moody and Floyd D. Putnam, *The Williston Story* (Essex Junction: Roscoe Printing House, 1961), 14-19.
43. Gillies and Sanford, *Records*, 11.
44. Ibid., 47.
45. *Baker v. Carr, 369 U. S. 186* (1962); *Reynolds v. Sims, 377 U. S. 533* (1964). Technically, during the early years, some of the small Vermont towns had shared a representative until the state supreme court ruled otherwise in 1824.
46. Gillies and Sanford, *Records*, 48, 91.
47. *Governor and Council*, III, 357.
48. Paul S. Gillies, "The Evolution of the Vermont Tax System," *Vermont History*, vol. 65, nos. 1 and 2 (Winter/Spring 1997): 28. In an earlier article Gillies indicates the 1780 Revolutionary War levy "ordered the towns to raise 72,700 pounds of beef; 36,389 pounds of salt pork; 218,309 pounds of wheat flour; 3,068 bushels of rye; and 6,125 pounds of Indian corn; all for the support of Vermont troops in the Revolutionary War." See: Paul S. Gillies, "Adjusting to Union," in Michael Sherman, ed., *More Perfect Union*, 117.
49. Williams, *Laws*, XIII, 207.
50. *Governor and Council*, III, 359-61.
51. Austin, *Vermont Politics*, 150.
52. Williams, *Laws*, XIV, 83, 116.
53. Samuel B. Hand, "Lay Judges and the Vermont Judiciary to 1825," *Vermont History*, vol. 46, no. 4 (Fall 1978): 206-7.

CHAPTER VII
The Shift of Power

1. *Governor and Council*, III, 371-2.
2. Earle Newton, *The Vermont Story* (Montpelier: Vermont Historical Society, 1949), 90.
3. Ibid., 92.
4. *Vermont Journal and Universal Advertiser*, vol. IV, nos. 160-68 (1786).
5. *Governor and Council*, III, 370-71.
6. *Vermont Gazette*, vol. IV, no. 196 (March 5, 1787): 1.
7. John A. Williams, ed., *The Public Papers of Thomas Chittenden* (Montpelier: Vermont State Papers, volume XVII, 1969), 681; Chilton Williamson, *Vermont in Quandary 1763-1825* (Montpelier: Vermont Historical Society, 1949), 171.
8. John A. Williams, ed., *Laws of Vermont* (Montpelier: Secretary of State, volume XIV, 1966), 229-30.
9. Ibid., 281-4.
10. Ibid., 337-9.
11. Ibid., 245-7.
12. Williams, *Public Papers*, 689.
13. James B. Wilbur, *Ira Allen*, volume I (Boston: Houghton Mifflin, 1928), 506.
14. Esther M. Swift, *Vermont Place-Names* (Camden, ME: Picton Press, 1996), 157-61, 386-9.

15. *Assembly Journal*, II, 212; Williams, *Laws*, XIII, 220-1.
16. *Governor and Council*, III, 509-10.
17. Williams, *Public Papers*, 667-71.
18. *Governor and Council*, III, 510.
19. Williams, *Laws*, XIV, 389-90.
20. *Assembly Journal*, IV, 104-5.
21. Williams, *Public Papers*, 708.
22. *Governor and Council*, III, 187.
23. *Town of Williston Land Records*, volume I, 21, 24, 25, 40, 42, 44, 51, 62, 64, 96.
24. Crockett, *Vermont*, volume II, 429.
25. Michael A. Bellesiles, "Anticipating America," ed. Michael Sherman in *A More Perfect Union* (Montpelier: Vermont Historical Society, 1991), 94.
26. *Assembly Journal*, IV, 104.
27. *Governor and Council*, III, 422-4, 438.
28. Ibid., 444.
29. Williamson, *Quandary*, 154-5. It should be noted that Michael Bellesiles takes strong issue with Williamson for giving the impression that the Chittenden/Allen group opposed statehood. Bellesiles, "Anticipating America," 109.
30. *Governor and Council*, III, 441.
31. Ibid., 442-3.
32. Ibid., 447.
33. *Assembly Journal*, IV, 135.
34. Ibid., 220; Williams, *Laws*, XIV, 532-4.
35. Williams, *Public Papers*, 720-21.
36. Ibid., 752.
37. Aleine Austin, *Matthew Lyon* (University Park, PA: Pennsylvania State University Press, 1981).

CHAPTER VIII
The Final Years

1. *Governor and Council*, IV, 3.
2. John M. Comstock, *Principal Civil Officers of Vermont, 1777 to 1918* (St. Albans: Messenger Company Publishers, 1918), 348-9.
3. Marlene B. Wallace, *Assembly Journal*, volume III, part VI (1972), introduction, xv, 103; John A. Williams, ed., *Laws of Vermont* (Montpelier: Secretary of State, volume XIV, 1966), 211.
4. Marlene Wallace, "A Vermont Bookshelf," *Vermont History*, vol. 38, no. 4 (Fall 1970): 328.
5. Earle Newton, *The Vermont Story* (Montpelier: Vermont Historical Society, 1949), 93.
6. *Governor and Council*, IV, 7.
7. Ibid., 11-12
8. Chilton Williamson, *Vermont in Quandary 1763-1825* (Montpelier: Vermont Historical Society, 1949), 192.
9. Perry Merrill, *Vermont Under Four Flags* (Montpelier: P. Merrill, 1975), 263.
10. *Assembly Journal*, III, part V, 38.
11. *Governor and Council*, III, 222. The area that became the town of Alburgh had numerous names over the years. The French called it Point Algonquin, Point du Detour, and Point Detouror. Other local names were Missisco Tongue, Missisco Leg, and Turn-about (from the shape of the land). The English name was Caldwell's Upper Manor. After Ira Allen ob-

tained a grant for the town on February 23, 1781, it was called Allenburgh, later shortened to Alburgh and more recently to Alburg.

12. *Governor and Council*, IV, 455.

13. John A. Williams, ed., *The Public Papers of Thomas Chittenden* (Montpelier: Vermont State Papers, volume XVII, 1969), 770.

14. Ibid., 772-3

15. Ibid., 774.

16. Ibid., 775.

17. Ibid., 776.

18. Ibid., 778.

19. Ibid., 812.

20. *Assembly Journal*, III, part V, 134.

21. Ibid., 112. The dispute was finally settled when Allen gave the university some property he owned in Plainfield in 1804 and paid UVM $10,000 in cash in 1807. James B. Wilbur, *Ira Allen*, volume II (Boston: Houghton Mifflin, 1928), 399.

22. *Assembly Journal*, III, part V, 112-4.

23. *Governor and Council*, IV, 39; *Assembly Journal*, III, part V, 209.

24. Williamson, *Quandary*, 186.

25. Williams, *Laws*, XV, 100-102.

26. Paul S. Gillies and D. Gregory Sanford, eds., *Records of the Council of Censors of the State of Vermont* (Montpelier: Secretary of State, 1991), 770-72.

27. Ibid., 131-2.

28. *Journal of the Vermont Constitutional Convention held at Windsor July 3 to 9, 1793*, University of Vermont, Bailey/Howe (Microfiche no. 170), 194.

29. Ibid., 194.

30. Gillies and Sanford, *Records*, 135.

31. *Assembly Journal*, III, part VI, 5-7.

32. Willard Sterne Randall, "Thomas Jefferson Takes a Vacation," *American Heritage* vol. 47, no. 4 (July/August 1996): 76. The summary of Jefferson's trip is abridged from Randall's article.

33. Judah Adelson, "The Vermont Newspapers and the French Revolution," *Vermont History*, vol. 33, no. 3 (July 1965): 376-7.

34. Tyler Resch, *The Rutland Herald History* (Rutland: The Rutland Herald Association, 1995), 17-27.

35. Robert E. Shalhope, *Bennington and the Green Mountain Boys* (Baltimore: The Johns Hopkins University Press, 1996), 199.

36. Eugene Perry Link, *Democratic-Republican Societies, 1790-1800* (New York: Octogon Books, 1965), 13-15.

37. Judah Adelson, "The Vermont Democratic-Republican Societies and the French Revolution," *Vermont History*, vol. 32, no. 1 (January 1964): 7-8.

38. Aleine Austin, *Matthew Lyon* (University Park, PA: The Pennsylvania State University Press, 1981), 82.

39. Williamson, *Quandary*, 200-203.

40. Ibid., 204.

41. Ibid., 212.

42. Ibid., 210.

43. *Governor and Council*, IV, 472.

44. H.N. Muller III, "The United States Includes the Republic of Vermont," *Vermont History*, vol. 45, no. 3 (Summer 1977): 188.

45. Williamson, *Quandary*, 210.

46. C.R. Batchelder, *Documentary History of the Protestant Episcopal Church of the Diocese of Vermont* (Claremont, NH: Claremont Publishing Company, 1870), 11.

47. *Assembly Journal*, III, part VI, 157; Allen Soule, ed., *General Petitions* (Montpelier: Vermont State Papers, volume X, 1958), 249.

48. Williams, *Laws*, XV, 332-4.

49. Walter T. Bogart, *The Vermont Lease Lands* (Montpelier: Vermont Historical Society, 1950) provides an exhaustive study of the glebe and S.P.G., plus other lease lands in Vermont.

50. Austin, *Matthew Lyon*, 64-75.

51. *Assembly Journal*, III, part VII, introduction, *xiii-xvi*.

52. Ibid., 341.

53. *Governor and Council*, IV, 441.

54. Ibid., 530.

55. *Assembly Journal*, III, part VII, 201.

56. J. Kevin Graffagnino, "Twenty Thousand Muskets! Ira Allen and the Olive Branch Affair, 1796-1800," *The William and Mary Quarterly*, 3d Series, vol. XLVIII (July 1991): 417-22.

57. Williams, *Public Papers*, 821.

58. Town of Williston, *Land Records*, vol. I, 295.

59. Williams, *Public Papers*, 845-6.

60. Ibid., 849-51.

CHAPTER IX
Thomas Chittenden's Legacy

1. *Governor and Council*, I, 130.

2. Williams, *Public Papers*, 68-76.

3. Ibid., 77.

4. Sarah V. Kalinoski, "Sequestration, Confiscation, and the 'Tory' in the Vermont Revolution," *Vermont History*, vol. 45, no. 4 (Fall 1977): 239.

5. John M. Comstock, *Principal Civil Officers of Vermont, 1777-1918* (St. Albans: Messenger Company Publishers, 1918), 367.

6. Walter H. Crockett, *Vermont: The Green Mountain State*, volume II (New York: The Century History Company, 1921), 551-2.

7. Rev. F.A. Wadleigh in Abby Hemenway, ed., *Vermont Historical Gazetteer*, volume I (Burlington: A.M. Hemenway, 1867), 130.

8. Williams, *Public Papers*, 244-5.

9. Gwilym R. Roberts, "An Unknown Vermonter," Vermont History, vol. XXIX, no. 2, (Spring 1961): 92.

10. James B. Wilbur, *Ira Allen*, volume II (Boston: Houghton Mifflin, 1928), 120.

11. Dorothy Canfield Fisher, "The Chittenden Way of Life," in *Memories of Arlington, Vermont* (New York: Duell, Sloan and Pearce, 1955), 43-5.

12. Frederick Van de Water, *The Reluctant Republic: Vermont 1724-1791* (New York: John Day Co., 1941), 173.

13. T.D. Seymour Bassett, ed., *Outsiders Inside Vermont* (Brattleboro: Stephen Greene Press, 1967), 48-9.

14. Rev. Nathan Perkins, *A Narrative of a Tour through the State of Vermont, April 27 to June 12, 1789* (Woodstock: Elm Street Press, 1920), 17.

15. Ibid., 22.

16. David M. Ludlum, *Social Ferment in Vermont* (New York: AMS Press, 1966), 89-90.

17. John C. Wriston Jr., *Vermont Inns and Taverns* (Rutland: Academy Books, 1991), 597; Wilbur, *Ira Allen*, volume II, 147.

18. Hon. David Read, "Thomas Chittenden, His Life and Times," ed. Abby M. Hemenway in *Vermont Historical Gazetteer*, volume I (Burlington: A.M. Hemenway, 1867), 929.

19. Charles M. Thompson, *Independent Vermont* (Boston: Houghton Mifflin, 1942), 532.

20. *Governor and Council*, I, 415-6.

21. Daniel Chipman, *A Memoir of Thomas Chittenden* (Middlebury: D. Chipman, 1849), 142-3.

22. H.N. Muller, III, "Diplomacy of the Republic: The Haldimand Negotiations," in Muller and Samuel B. Hand, *In a State of Nature* (Montpelier: Vermont Historical Society, 1982), 63-5.

23. Henry Steele Wardner, "The Haldimand Negotiations," *Proceedings of the Vermont Historical Society*, vol. II, no. I (March 1931): 5-6.

24. Ibid., 28.

25. *Governor and Council*, II, 353.

26. Perkins, *Narrative Tour*, 17.

27. *Vermont Gazette* (September 12, 1797).

28. Roland Robinson, *Vermont: A Study in Independence* (Boston: Houghton Mifflin, 1890), 190.

29. Charles A. Jellison, *Ethan Allen: Frontier Rebel* (Syracuse, NY: Syracuse University Press, 1969), 78-9.

30. Robert E. Shalhope, *Bennington and the Green Mountain Boys* (Baltimore: Johns Hopkins University Press, 1996), 138-9.

31. Donna V. Russell, *Deeds and Taxpayers 1739-63*, Salisbury, Connecticut, Records, volume II (Middletown, MD: Catoctin Press, 1983), 124-5.

32. Albert E. VanDuren, *Connecticut* (New York: Random House, 1961), 111-12.

33. Wilbur, *Ira Allen*, volume I, 44; volume II, 523.

34. *Land Records, Town of Salisbury, Connecticut* (March 14, 1777).

35. *Governor and Council*, IV, 99, 531. In 1801 the governor's salary was raised to $750 per annum, and in 1857 it was set at $1,000.

36. Esther M. Swift, *Vermont Place-Names* (Camden, ME: Picton Press, 1996), 601.

37. *Land Records of the Town of Arlington, Vermont*, volume I (1761-1785), 66-7.

38. *Arlington, Vermont, Town Records* (1761-1850), 23.
39. *Town of Williston, Vermont, Land Records*, volume I, 4-123; volume II, 53-295.
40. *Record of Proprietors and Land Owners in Williston, 1804* (Giles 53-79; Truman 80-125; Noah, 82-170).
41. *Chittenden Estate Inventory* (October 7, 1797).
42. Bellesiles, *Revolutionary Outlaws*, 269.
43. Letter from Professor Arthur G. Woolf, the University of Vermont, Department of Economics, to Frank Smallwood (June 24, 1996).
44. Bellesiles, *Revolutionary Outlaws*, 270-1.
45. Perkins, *Narrative Tour*, 17.
46. Lucius E. Chittenden, *Address at the Dedication of the Thomas Chittenden Monument*, Williston, Vermont (August 19, 1896), 49.
47. Mary Greene Nye, ed., *Sequestration, Confiscation and Sale of Estates* (Montpelier: Vermont State Papers, volume VI, 1941), 371.

48. Walter H. Crockett, ed., *Vermonters: A Book of Biographies* (Brattleboro: Stephen Daye Press, 1931), 46.
49. H.N. Muller, III, "Early Vermont State Government: Oligarchy or Democracy? 1778-1815," ed. Reginald L. Cook in *Growth and Development of Government in Vermont* (Middlebury: Academy of Arts and Sciences, 1970), 9.
50. Clinton Rossiter, *The Federalist Papers* (New York: The New American Library, 1961), 322.
51. Williamson, *Quandary*, 186.
52. Alan Taylor, *William Cooper's Town* (New York: Random House, 1995), 141-3.
53. Daniel Chipman, *Memoir*, preface.
54. Paul S. Gillies and D. Gregory Sanford, eds., *Records of the Council of Censors* (Montpelier: Vermont Secretary of State, 1991), 47.
55. Thompson, *Independent Vermont*, 347-8.
56. Peter S. Onuf, *The Origins of the Federal Republic* (Philadelphia: University of Pennsylvania Press, 1983), 145.

Bibliography

Books and Pamphlets

Adams, James T. *The Founding of New England.* Boston: Little Brown, 1927.

Allen, Ira. *The Natural and Political History of the State of Vermont.* Rutland: Charles S. Tuttle Co., 1969.

Anderson, Virginia C. *New England's Generation.* Cambridge: Cambridge University Press, 1991.

Andrews, Charles M. *The Rise and Fall of the New Haven Colony.* Tercentenary XLVII. New Haven: Yale University Press, 1936.

Atwater, Edward E. *History of the Colony of New Haven.* 2 volumes. Meridan, CT: Journal Publishing Company, 1902.

Austin, Aleine. *Matthew Lyon: "New Man" of the Democratic Revolution.* University Park: Pennsylvania State University Press, 1981.

Badamo, Michael A. *The Republic of Vermont 1777–1791: A Short History.* Montpelier: Woodchuck Press, 1992.

Bartley, Scott A. *Vermont Families in 1791,* volume I. Camden, ME: Picton Press, 1992.

Bassett, T.D. Seymour. *Outsiders Inside Vermont.* Brattleboro: Stephen Greene Press, 1967.

Bassett, T.D. Seymour. *Vermont: A Bibliography of Its History.* Hanover: University Press of New England, 1983.

Batchelder, Calvin, ed. *Documentary History of the Protestant Episcopal Church in Vermont.* Claremont, NH: 1876.

Bayley, Edwin A. *The Life and Public Service of Brig. Gen. Jacob Bayley.* Montpelier: Vermont Historical Society, 1919.

Beckley, Hosea. *The History of Vermont: With Descriptions, Physical and Topographical.* Brattleboro: G. H. Salisbury, 1832.

Bellesiles, Michael A. *Revolutionary Outlaws.* Charlottesville: University Press of Virginia, 1993.

Bogart, Walter T. *The Vermont Lease Lands.* Montpelier: Vermont Historical Society, 1950.

Broad Brook Grange #151. *Official History of Guilford, Vermont.* Brattleboro: 1961.

Brown, Charlotte C. *The Vermont Council of Censors 1777–1870.* Ph.D. diss., University of Vermont microfiche M 595, 1946.

Calder, Isabel M. *The New Haven Colony.* New Haven: Yale University Press, 1934.

Canny, Nicholas. *Europeans on the Move.* Oxford: Clarendon Press, 1994.

Carlisle, Lilian Baker, ed. *Look Around Essex and Williston, Vermont.* Burlington: George Little Press, 1973.

Carlton, Hiram. *Genealogical and Family History of Vermont,* volume I. New York: Lewis Publishing Company, 1908.

Chipman, Daniel. *Life of Honorable Nathaniel Chipman.* Boston: C.C. Little & Brown, 1846.

Chipman, Daniel. *A Memoir of Thomas Chittenden.* Middlebury: D. Chipman, 1849.

Chipman, Nathaniel. *Principles of Government: A Treatise on Free Institutions.* Burlington: Edward Smith, 1833.

Collins, Edward. A *History of Vermont.* Boston: Ginn & Co., 1903.

Comstock, John M. *Principal Civil Officers of Vermont from 1777 to 1918.* St. Albans: Messenger Company Publishers, 1918.

Comstock, John M. *The Congregational Churches of Vermont.* St. Johnsbury: The Cowles Press, 1942.

Coolidge, A.J. & Mansfield, J.B. *History and Description of New England: Vermont.* Boston: A.J. Coolidge, 1860.

Countryman, Edward. *The American Revolution.* New York: Hill & Wang, 1985.

Crockett, Walter H. *Vermont: The Green Mountain State.* 4 volumes. New York: The Century History Company, 1921.

Crockett, Walter H., ed. *Vermonters: A Book of Biographies.* Brattleboro: Stephen Daye Press, 1931.

Crofut, Florence S. Marcy. *Guide to the History and Historic Sites of Connecticut.* New Haven: Yale University Press, 1937.

Daniell, Jere R. *Experiment in Republicanism.* Cambridge: Harvard University Press, 1970.

Daniell, Jere R. *Colonial New Hampshire: A History.* Millwood, NY: KTO Press, 1981.

Deming, Dorothy. *The Settlement of Connecticut Towns.* Tercentenary VI. New Haven: Yale University Press, 1933.

Deming, Leonard. *The Principal Officers of Vermont 1777 to 1851.* Middlebury: L. Deming, 1851.

Dodge, Bertha S. *Vermonters By Choice: The Earliest Years.* Shelburne: New England Press, 1987.

Doyle, William. *The Vermont Political Tradition*. Barre: Northlight Studio Press, 1994.

Duffy, John. *Vermont: An Illustrated History*. Northridge, Calif: Windsor Publications, 1985.

Ekwall, Eilert. *Concise Oxford Dictionary of English Place Names*. Oxford: Clarendon Press, 1991.

Elliott, Stephen P., ed. *Madison: Three Hundred Years By the Sea*. Madison, CT: Madison Historical Society, 1991.

Ferm, Vergilus. *Puritan Sage: Collected Writings of Jonathan Edwards*. New York: Library Publishers, 1953.

Fisher, Dorothy C. *Memories of Arlington, Vermont*. New York: Duell, Sloan & Pearce, 1955.

Fox, Dixon R. *Yankees and Yorkers*. New York: New York University Press, 1940.

Gillies, Paul S. *Confronting Statehood*. Burlington: UVM Center for Research on Vermont, 1992.

Gilman, M.D. *The Bibliography of Vermont*. Burlington: The Free Press Association, 1897.

Graffagnino, J. Kevin. *The Shaping of Vermont*. Rutland: Vermont Heritage Press, 1983.

Graffagnino, J. Kevin. *Ethan and Ira Allen, Collected Works*. 3 volumes. Benson: Chalidze Publications, 1992.

Greene, Edwin M. *The Episcopal Church in Vermont*. Woodstock: Elm Tree Press, 1959.

Griffin, Orwin B. *The Evolution of the Connecticut School System*. New York: Columbia University Teachers College, 1928.

Hall, Benjamin H. *History of Eastern Vermont*. New York: D. Appleton & Company, 1858.

Hall, Hiland. *The History of Vermont, From Its Discovery to Its Admission into the Union in 1791*. Albany: J. Munsell, 1868.

Hayden, Chauncey T., ed. *History of Jericho, Vermont*. Burlington: Free Press Publishing Company, 1916.

Heimert, Alan and Miller, Perry., eds. *The Great Awakening*. Indianapolis:Bobbs-Merrill, 1967.

Hemenway, Abby M. *Vermont Historical Gazetteer*, volume 1. Burlington: A. M. Hemenway, 1867.

Hill, Ralph N. *Yankee Kingdom: Vermont and New Hampshire*. New York: Harper and Brothers, 1960.

Hofstadter, Richard. *America at 1750: A Social Portrait*. New York: Random House, 1973.

Holbrook, Jay M. *Vermont 1771 Census*. Oxford, MA: Holbrook Research Institute, 1982.

Holbrook, Stewart H. *Ethan Allen*. New York: The Macmillan Company, 1940.

Hooker, Roland M. *Colonial Trade of Connecticut*. Tercentenary L. New Haven: Yale University Press. 1936.

Horowitz, David, *The First Frontier: The Indian Wars and America's Origins 1607–1776*. New York: Simon & Schuster, 1978.

Hoskins, Nathan. *History of the State of Vermont*. Vergennes: J. Shedd, 1831.

Jellison, Charles A. *Ethan Allen: Frontier Rebel*. Syracuse: Syracuse University Press, 1969.

Jones, Matt B. *Vermont in the Making 1750–1777*. Cambridge: Harvard University Press, 1939.

Leach, Douglas E. *The Northern Colonial Frontier*. New York: Holt Rinehart & Winston, 1964.

Lee, W. Storrs. *Town Father: A Biography of Gamaliel Painter*. New York: Hastings House, 1952.

Link, Eugene P. *Democratic–Republican Societies 1790–1800*. New York: Octagon Books, 1965.

Lockridge, Kenneth A. *Literacy in Colonial New England*. New York: W. W. Norton and Company, Inc., 1974.

Ludlum, David M. *Social Ferment in Vermont 1791–1850*. New York: AMS Press, 1966.

Maguire, J. Robert., ed. *The Tour to the Northern Lakes of James Madison and Thomas Jefferson*. Ticonder-oga: Fort Ticonderoga, MCMXCV.

Main, Jackson T. *Society and Economy in Colonial Connecticut*. Princeton: Princeton University Press, 1985.

Merrill, Perry. *Vermont Under Four Flags*. Montpelier: P. Merrill, 1975.

Moody, F. Kennon & Putnam, Floyd D. *The Williston Story*. Essex Junction: Roscoe Printing House, 1961.

Morel, Joseph R. *Governing a Republic: Vermont State Government 1777–1791*. Hanover: Dartmouth History Honors Thesis, 1995.

Morrissey, Brenda., ed. *Abby Hemenway's Vermont*. Brattleboro: Stephen Greene Press, 1972.

Morrissey, Charles T. *Vermont: A History*. New York: W. W. Norton and Company, 1984.

Morrow, Rising. *Connecticut Influences in Western Massachusetts and Vermont*. Tercentenary LVIII. New Haven: Yale University Press, 1936.

Muller, H. Nicholas III and Hand, Samuel B. *In a State of Nature*. Montpelier: Vermont Historical Society, 1982.

McCorison, Marcus A. *Vermont Imprints 1778–1924*. Worcester: American Antiquarian Society, 1963.

McLaughlin, Andrew C. *Foundations of American Constitutionalism*. New York: New York University Press, 1932.

Newton, Earle. *The Vermont Story 1749–1949*. Montpelier: Vermont Historical Society, 1949.

Onuf, Peter S. *The Origins of the Federal Republic*. Philadelphia: University of Pennsylvania Press, 1983.

Pell, John. *Ethan Allen*. Boston: Houghton Mifflin, 1929.

Perkins, Rev. Nathan. *A Narrative of a Tour through the State of Vermont in 1789*. Woodstock: Elm Tree Press, 1920.

Peterson, James E. *Otter Creek*. Salisbury: Dunmore House, 1990.

Pettee, Julia. *The Early History of the Town of Salisbury, Connecticut*. Salisbury, CT: Salisbury Association, Inc., 1957.

Pile, C.C.R. *Cranbrook: A Wealden Town*. Cranbrook, England: Cranbrook & District Local Historical Society, 1990.

Pile, C.C.R. *Broadcloth and Weavers*. Cranbrook, England: Cranbrook & District Local Historical Society, 1981.

Pile, C.C.R. *Watermills and Windmills of Cranbrook*. Cranbrook, England: Cranbrook & District Local Historical Society, 1992.

Platt, Philip S. *Madison's Heritage*. Madison, CT: Madison Historical Society, 1964.

Potash, P. Jeffrey. *Vermont's Burned-over District: Patterns of Community Development and Religious Activity, 1761–1850*. Brooklyn: Carlson Publishers, 1991.

Rand, Christopher. *The Changing Landscape*. New York: Oxford University Press, 1968.

Resch, Tyler. *The Rutland Herald History*. Rutland: Rutland Herald Association, 1995.

Robinson, Roland E. *Vermont: A Study in Independence*. Boston: Houghton Mifflin and Company, 1892.

Rockey, J.L., ed. *History of the New Haven Colony*. New York: W.W. Preston and Company, 1892.

Rossiter, Clinton. *The Federalist Papers*. New York: New American Library, 1951.

Roth, Randolph A. *The Democratic Dilemma: Religion, Reform and the Social Order in the Connecticut River Valley of Vermont, 1791–1850*. New York: Cambridge University Press, 1987.

Rothwell, Kenneth S. *A Goodly Heritage*. Burlington: Cathedral Church of St. Paul, 1973.

Rudd, Malcolm D. *Men of Worth of Salisbury Birth*. Salisbury, CT: The Salisbury Association, Inc., 1991.

Salisbury, Neal. *Manitou and Providence: Indians, Europeans, and the Making of New England, 1500–1643*. New York: Oxford University Press, 1982.

Savage, James. *Genealogical Dictionary of First New England Settlers*. Baltimore: Genealogical Publishing Company, 1981.

Shalhope, Robert E. *Bennington and the Green Mountain Boys*. Baltimore: Johns Hopkins University Press, 1996.

Sherman, Michael A., ed. *A More Perfect Union: Vermont Becomes a State, 1777–1816*. Montpelier: Vermont Historical Society, 1991.

Smith, Chard P. *The Housantonic*. New York: Rinehard and Company, 1946.

Smith, Elsdon C. *New Dictionary of American Family Names*. New York: Gramercy Pubishing Company, 1988.

Smith, Ralph D. *History of Guilford, Connecticut*. Albany: J. Munsell, 1877.

Steiner, Bernard C. *History of Guilford and Madison, Connecticut*. Guilford, CT: Guilford Free Library, 1975.

Stone, Mason. *History of Education in the State of Vermont*. Montpelier: Capital City Press, 1937.

Swift, Esther M. *Vermont Place-Names*. Camden, Maine: Picton Press, 1996.

Symonds, Craig L. *A Battlefield Atlas of the American Revolution*. Baltimore: N & A Publishing Company, 1986.

Talcott, Alvan. *William Chittenden of Guilford, Connecticut, and His Descendents*. New Haven: Tuttle, Morehouse and Taylor, 1882.

Talcott, Alvan. *Families of Early Guilford, Connecticut.* Baltimore: Genealogical Publishing Company, 1984.

Taplin, Winn L., *The Vermont Problem in the Continental Congress and in Interstate Relations, 1776–1786.* Ph.D. diss. Montpelier: Vermont Historical Society Manuscript Collection, 1966.

Taylor, Alan, *William Cooper's Town.* New York: Random House, 1995.

Thompson, Charles M. *Independent Vermont.* Boston: Houghton, Mifflin, 1942.

Thompson, Daniel P. *The Green Mountain Boys.* New York: A.L. Burt and Co. Publishers, 1839.

Thompson, Zadock. *History of the State of Vermont.* Burlington: Edward Smith, 1833.

True, Marshall and Doyle, William. *Vermont and the New Nation.* Hyde Park: Vermont Council on Humanities and Public Issues, 1984.

Van Dusen, Albert E. *Connecticut.* New York: Random House, 1964.

Van de Water, Frederick F. *The Reluctant Republic: Vermont 1724–91.* New York: John Day, 1941.

Versteeg, Jennie, ed. *Lake Champlain: Reflections on Our Past.* Burlington: UVM Center for Research on Vermont, 1987.

Wardner, Henry S. *The Birthplace of Vermont: A History of Windsor to 1781.* New York: Charles Scribner's Sons, 1927.

Weeks, John M. *History of Salisbury, Vermont.* Middlebury: A.H. Copeland, 1860.

Wells, Fredric P. *History of Newbury, Vermont.* St. Johnsbury: Caledonian, 1902.

Williams, Samuel. *The Natural and Civil History of Vermont.* Walpole: Isiah Thomas & David Carlisle Jr., 1794.

Williamson, Chilton. *Vermont in Quandary 1763–1825.* Montpelier: Vermont Historical Society, 1949.

Williston Historical Committee. *History of the Town of Williston 1763–1913.* (1991 edition).

Wilson, Lori F. *God With Us.* Shelburne: Trinity Episcopal Church, 1990.

Wood, Gordon S. *The Creation of the American Republic 1776–1787.* Charlotte: University of North Carolina Press, 1969.

Woodward, Florence M. *The Town Proprietors in Vermont.* New York: Columbia University Press, 1936.

Wright, Ruth. *History of the Town of Colchester.* Burlington: Queen City Printers, 1963.

Journals and Newspapers

Achille, Gary J. "Making the Vermont Constitution 1777–1824," in Sherman, ed. *A More Perfect Union: Vermont Becomes a State 1777–1816.* Montpelier: Vermont Historical Society (1991): 2–34.

Adelson, Judah. "The Vermont Democratic–Republican Societies and the French Revolution." *Vermont History* 32 (1964): 3–23.

Adelson, Judah. "The Vermont Newspapers and the French Revolution," *Vermont History* 33 (1965): 375–94.

Austin, Aleine. "Vermont Politics in the 1780's: Emergence of Rival Leadership." *Vermont History* 42 (1974): 140–54.

Bandel, Betty. "The 1798 Census in Vermont." *New England Historical and Genealogical Register* 137 (1983): 4–17

Batchelder, J.K. "History of the Town of Arlington." Burlington: UVM, Bailey-Howe Library, Special Collections (1919).

Bellesiles, Michael A. "The Establishment of Legal Structures on the Frontier: The Case of Revolutionary Vermont." *Journal of American History* 73 (1987): 895–915.

Bellesiles, Michael A., "Anticipating America: Levi Allen and the Case for an Independent Vermont," in Sherman, ed. *Perfect Union*: 79–111.

Chittenden, Lucius E. "Commemorative Address at the Dedication of the Thomas Chittenden Memorial in Williston." (1896): 45–53.

Conant, J.H. "Imprisonment for Debt in Vermont." *Vermont History* XIX (1951): 67–80.

DeWolfe, David. "The Chittendens of Salisbury, Connecticut." Salisbury: Scoville Memorial Library Collections (July 27, 1968).

Dudley, W.R. "Proceedings at Guilford, Connecticut, Two Hundred Fiftieth Anniversary." New Haven: Stafford Printing Co. (1889).

Edwards, Jonathan. "A History of the Work of Redemption," in V. Ferm, ed. *Puritan Sage*. New York: Library Publishers (1953): 602–13.

Freeman, Stephen A. "Puritans in Rutland 1770–1818." *Vermont History* 33 (1965): 342–8.

Fussell, Clyde G. "The Emergence of Public Education in Vermont." *Vermont History* XXVIII (1960): 268–81.

Gerlach, Larry R. "Connecticut, The Continental Congress, and the Independence of Vermont." *Vermont History* 34 (1966): 188–93.

Gillies, Paul S. "Adjusting to Union," in Sherman, ed. *Perfect Union* 114–49.

Gillies, Paul S. "The Evolution of the Vermont State Tax System." *Vermont History* 65 (1997): 26–44.

Gilmore, William J. "Elementary Literacy on the Eve of the Industrial Revolution: Trends in Rural New England, 1760–1830." *Proceedings of the American Antiquarian Society* 92 (1982): 87–178.

Graffagnino, J. Kevin. "The Vermont Story: Continuity and Change in Vermont Historiography." *Vermont History* 46 (1978): 77–99.

Graffagnino, J. Kevin. "'Vermonters Unmasked': Charles Phelps and the Patterns of Dissent in Revolutionary Vermont." *Vermont History* 57 (1989): 133–61.

Graffagnino, J. Kevin. "Twenty Thousand Muskets!! Ira Allen and the Olive Branch Affair." *William and Mary Quarterly* 3d series, XLVII (July 1991).

Graffagnino, J. Kevin. "'The Country My Soul Delighted In': The Onion River Land Company and the

Vermont Frontier." *The New England Quarterly* LXV (1992): 24–60.

Hand, Samuel B. "Lay Judges and the Vermont Judiciary to 1825." *Vermont History* 46 (1978): 205–20.

Hand, Samuel B. and Potash, P. Jeffrey. "Nathaniel Chipman: Vermont's Forgotten Founder," in Sherman, ed. *Perfect Union* 52–78.

Hendricks Nathaniel. "The Experiment in Vermont Constitutional Government." *Vermont History* XXXIV (1966): 63–5.

Hendricks, Nathaniel. "A New Look at the Ratification of the Vermont Constitution of 1777." *Vermont History* XXXIV (1966): 136–40.

Kalinoski, Sarah V. "Sequestration, Confiscation and the 'Tory' in the Vermont Revolution." *Vermont History* 45 (1977): 236–46.

Maguire, J. Robert. "The British Secret Service and the Attempt to Kidnap General Jacob Bayley of Newbury, Vermont." *Vermont History* 44 (1976): 141–51.

Maguire, J. Robert. "The Public Papers of Thomas Chittenden." Review. *Vermont History* 38 (1970): 70–7.

Meeks, Harold A. "An Isochronic Map of Vermont Settlement." *Vermont History* XXXVIII (1970): 95–102.

Metraux, Daniel A. "Was Vermont Ever a Republic?" *Vermont History* 55 (1987): 167–73.

Muller, H. Nicholas III. "Early Vermont State Government, 1778–1815: Oligarchy or Democracy?" in Reginald Cook, ed. *Growth and Development of Government in Vermont*. Waitsfield: Vermont Academy of Arts and Sciences. Occasional Paper 5 (1970): 5–10.

Muller, H. Nicholas III. "The United States Includes the Republic of Vermont." *Vermont History* 45 (1977): 187–91.

Muller, H. Nicholas III. "Diplomacy of the Republic: The Haldimand Negotiations," in Muller and Hand, eds. *In a State of Nature*. Montpelier: Vermont Historical Society (1982): 63–5.

Nye, Mary Greene. "Vermont State Papers: Rich Sources for the Study of Vermont History." *Vermont History* 38 (1970): 214–22.

Onuf, Peter S. "State Making in Revolutionary America: Independent Vermont as a Case Study." *Journal of American History* 67 (1981): 797–815.

Page, John. "The Economic Structure of Society in Revolutionary Bennington." *Vermont History* 49 (1981): 69–84.

Pemberton, Ian C. "The British Secret Service in the Champlain Valley during the Haldimand Negotiations." *Vermont History* 44 (1976): 129–40.

Potash, P. Jeffrey. "State Government and Education." *Vermont History* 65 (1997): 45–64.

Randall, Willard S. "Thomas Jefferson Takes a Vacation." *American Heritage* 47 (1996): 74–85.

Raymond, Alan R. "Benning Wentworth's Claims in the New Hampshire-New York Border Controversy: A Case of Twenty-Twenty Hindsight." *Vermont History* 43 (1975): 20–32.

Read, Hon. David. "Thomas Chittenden: His Life and Times," in Abby Hemenway, ed. *Vermont Historical Gazetteer*, volume I (1867): 905–29.

Rindge, Milna E. "Shipbuilding in Madison, Connecticut." Madison Historical Society (1993): 1–9.

Roberts, Gwilym R. "An Unknown Vermonter: Sylvanus Evarts, Governor Chittenden's Tory Brother-in-Law." *Vermont History* XXIX (1961): 92–102.

Shaeffer, John N. "A Comparison of the First Constitutions of Vermont and Pennsylvania." *Vermont History* 43 (1975): 33–43. .

Smith, Donald A. "Green Mountain Insurgency: Transformation of New York's Forty-Year Land War." *Vermont History* 64 (1996): 197–231.

Taft, Russell S. "Town of Williston," in Hemenway, ed. *Gazetteer:* 901–5.

Thompson, Ignatius. *The Patriot's Monitor*. Randolph: S. Wright (1810).

True, Marshall. "Why Are There No Biographies of Thomas Chittenden" in Jennie Versteeg, ed. *Lake Champlain* (1987): 210–15.

Vermont Journal and Universal Advertiser (Windsor). 1785–1786 (Vermont State Library, Montpelier, Microfiche M568–570).

Vermont Gazette (Bennington). 1786–87, 1797 (Vermont State Library, Montpelier, Microfiche M595).

Vermont Historical Society, *Collections of the Vermont Historical Society*, 12 volumes (1870–1946).

Wallace, Marlene B. "A Vermont Bookshelf." *Vermont History* 38 (1970): 326–34

Wardner, Henry S. "The Haldimand Negotiations." *Proceedings of the Vermont Historical Society*, volume II (1931): 3–29.

Wadleigh, Rev. F.A. "History of the Town of Arlington," in Hemenway, ed. *Gazetteer* (1867): 123–35.

Wells, Frederic P. "Could Anyone Spell in Early Vermont?" *Vermont History* 43 (1975): 74.

Williamson, Chilton. "A New Deal for Vermont History." *Vermont History* XXII (1954): 29–34.

Public Records

Allen Family Papers. Burlington: University of Vermont Bailey-Howe Library, Special Collections.

Batchellor, Albert S., ed. *The New Hampshire Grants: The Charters of Townships 1749 to 1764*. Concord: New Hampshire State Papers, volume XXVI, III (1895).

Church of Jesus Christ of Latter-Day Saints. Salt Lake City, Utah: *International Genealogical Index* Kent County, England; Connecticut and Vermont (microfiche).

Crockett, Walter H., ed. *Journals and Proceedings of the General Assembly of the State of Vermont, 1778–1791*. State Papers of Vermont, III, Parts I–IV (1924–29).

Crockett, Walter H., ed. *Reports of*

Committees to the General Assembly of the State of Vermont 1778–1801. State Papers of Vermont, volume IV (1932).

Dewart, Franklin H. *Index to the Papers of the Surveyors-General.* State Papers of Vermont, I (1918).

Dewart, Franklin H., ed. *Charters Granted by the State of Vermont.* State Papers of Vermont, II (1922).

Gillies, Paul S. and Sanford, H. Gregory. *Records of the Council of Censors of the State of Vermont.* Montpelier: Secretary of State, 1991.

Hoadley, Charles J. *Records of the Colony and Plantation of New Haven 1638–1649.* Hartford: Case & Tiffany, 1857.

Hoadley, Charles J. *Public Records of the Colony of Connecticut.* vols.11–13. Hartford: Case, Lockward & Brainard, 1880.

Hoyt, Edward A. *General Petitions 1778–1787.* State Papers of Vermont, VIII (1952).

Hoyt, Edward A. *General Petitions 1788–1792.* State Papers of Vermont, IX (1955).

Journal of the Vermont Constitutional Convention of 1793. Burlington: UVM Bailey–Howe Library (microfiche 170).

Nye, Mary G., ed. *Petitions for Grants of Land 1778–1811.* State Papers of Vermont, V, (1939).

Nye, Mary G., ed. *Sequestration, Confiscation and Sale of Estates.* State Papers of Vermont, VI (1941).

Nye, Mary G., ed. *New York Land Patents 1688–1786.* State Papers of Vermont, III (1947).

Papers of the New Haven Colony Historical Society, volume I. New Haven (1865).

Probate Estate Inventory of Thomas Chittenden. Burlington: Chittenden County Courthouse (1797).

Rossano, Geoffrey, ed. *Salisbury Town Meeting Minutes 1741–1784 .* Salisbury, CT: The Salisbury Association (1988).

Russell, Donna V., ed. *Salisbury, Connecticut, Records: Deeds and Taxpayers 1739–1763,* volume II. Middletown, MD: Catoctin Press (1983).

Slade, William, ed. *Vermont State Papers.* Middlebury: J. W. Copland, (1823).

Soule, Allen, ed. *General Petitions 1793–1796.* State Papers of Vermont, XI (1958).

Soule, Allen, ed. *General Petitions 1797–1799.* State Papers of Vermont, X (1962).

Soule, Allen, ed. *Laws of Vermont, Constitution of 1777, Laws of 1778–1780.* State Papers of Vermont, XII (1964).

Town of Arlington, Vermont. *Deeds and Town Records 1761–1785.*

Town of Salisbury, Connecticut. *Deeds and Historical Collections, Vital Records,* volume I. Salisbury, CT: The Salisbury Association, (1913).

Town of Williston, Vermont. *Land Records,* volumes I and II (1763–1805).

Walton, E.P. *Records of the Council of Safety and Governor and Council of the State of Vermont 1775–1804.* Volumes I to IV. Montpelier: Steam Press of J. & J. M. Poland (1873–76).

Williams, John A., ed. *Journals and Proceedings of the General Assembly of the State of Vermont, 1791–1796.* State Papers of Vermont, III, Parts V through VII (1970–1973).

Williams, John A., ed. *Laws of Vermont 1781–1799.* State Papers of Vermont, XIII to XVI (1965–1968).

Williams, John A., ed. *The Public Papers of Governor Thomas Chittenden 1778–1789, 1790–1797.* State Papers of Vermont XVII (1969).

Index